CONTEMPORARY ESSAYS

EDITED BY

WILLIAM THOMSON HASTINGS, A.M.

Associate Professor of English, Brown University

HOUGHTON MIFFLIN COMPANY

BOSTON · NEW YORK · CHICAGO · DALLAS · SAN FRANCISCO

The Riverside Press Cambridge

The Riverside Press

CAMBRIDGE · MASSACHUSETTS

PRINTED IN THE U.S.A.

BY WAY OF PREFACE

AMONG the bronzes in the Fine Arts Museum at Brussels one particularly arrests the eye. Three youthful figures side by side are stepping forward vigorously hand in hand. Their heads are raised and their eyes fixed ardently on the distance. The energy of the modelling, the eagerness, courage, and confidence imparted to the figures, are happily gathered up in the phrase cut in the base, *Vers la Vie*. It is toward life, indeed, that youth instinctively turns, for experience, for knowledge, for understanding; it is the yearning for fullness in the experience or comprehension of life that distinguished the more vital ages of the past; it is, by contrast, a middle-aged circumspectness in staring at the sun with which we reproach Victorianism.

Our age, we have long since discovered, is an age of truth-seeking and truth-telling. Plenty of smugness there is, of course, and among the enfranchised there are several conflicting counsels of perfection. But at least we do not fall under the same formula as the poet Gray. We have "spoken out," with a vengeance; nowhere, perhaps, so clearly as in the essay. The novel, the drama, poetry, it is true, choose freely their subjects and their forms; aiming at sincerity of utterance, and inevitably implying a point of view, they will be significant documents for the historian; but by the necessity of their types they are largely objective, selective, histrionic, exhibiting for art's sake a truth partial, overstressed, or uninterpreted. The essay is a more lucid medium. Hazlitt named a group of

iii

his portrait sketches *The Spirit of the Age*. In as true or a truer sense any representative anthology of twentieth century essays might bear the name. Half truths there will be among them, and histrionic poses; no doubt, too, the essayist sometimes whittles his theme to fit his period, or transfixes with a paradox another truth than his legitimate quarry. Yet a browser in the better prose of the day will be convinced that, however confusingly, the time-spirit is conveying to him its notion of reality.

The modern literary essay is notably readable; and we may hazard a guess that it will not wholly tarnish with time. Its nineteenth century predecessors may in the mass produce a greater impression of solidity and deliberateness, not to say solemnity; the majority of our literary essayists in comparison may seem lacking in seriousness and weight. But the change is more in manner than in matter; and it is not a change for the worse. Just as in the novel and in poetry, the level of technical excellence in the essay is now higher than ever before. Lamb's descent from a brilliant opening to a lame conclusion, Hunt's vapidity, Macaulay's clanking monotony, Lowell's dilute prosiness — perhaps even Carlyle's eccentric mannerism and Pater's labored felicities — the modern essayist will consciously avoid, whatever of their countervailing virtures he may miss. Set on his path, one may fancy, by the precise simplicity and firm stylistic texture of Huxley, profiting by Stevenson's luminous logic of design, catching suggestions regarding tone and attack from the little masters of the Nineties, and turning epigram and paradox from the playthings of an esthete to the weapons of Truth militant — he writes, for the most part, a consistently sound and effective prose. There is room, fortunately, for the individual — for the leisurely, the quaint, the farcical, the poetic — as well as for the earnest and the soberly urgent pen; but it remains true that in deftness, precision, and clarity, in swiftness, crispness, and wit, in general awareness and competence, the present age of essayists obscures the past. This, too, in spite of the fact that Journalism by accelerating the flow of some wits has forced them into shallows or transformed them to smartly bickering brooks. It is a question whether in any previous quarter century one could so readily as now select two score essayists whom it is a pleasure to read.

But are candor and readableness equally characteristic of American and British essayists? So far as one reader can discern, they are. One group is not more catholic in interests, more varied in convictions, than the other. On both sides the water there are shrewd and penetrating observers; on both sides lovers of poetry, of nature, of seclusion, of a good fight; on both sides radicals and conservatives. If there is a difference worth defining, it is chiefly this: that the Englishman is likely to be more allusive than the American; that his mental associations, more readily than the American's, lend his writings a pleasant color from his cultural background; that, with a gentlemanly detachment, he offers you some thoughts or feelings of his for what they are worth. The un-Anglicized American is on the whole more direct and businesslike, plainer and barer, and somewhat naïvely earnest. The Englishman is more prone to converse, the American to demonstrate; the one hopes to entertain or to interest, the other to make the world safe.

In *The Spirit of the Age* the dominant spirit is that of William Hazlitt, and in these essays that follow, the characters of the authors are plain to see. Long ago Montaigne wrote (according to John Florio): "These are but my fantasies, by which I endevour not to make things knowen, but my selfe"; and each of these pieces, though less completely personal, conveys the accent of an individual voice — usually one that charms, and always one that will interest the lover of personality. Sitting by the fire with Benson or Lucas or on the dunes with Tomlinson; listening to a new *Urn-Burial* by one of those irreverent pupils of Sir Thomas Browne, Mencken and Holliday, and to philosophies of life from such different premises as those of Belloc, Havelock Ellis, and Aldous Huxley; watching the fine play of the mind in the discriminating analyses of Paul Elmer More and Virginia Woolf and Santayana (alongside the hearty, uncritical enthusiasm of Professor Saintsbury); applauding Beerbohm's mild self-caricature, and Chesterton's broadside in favor of the joy of living, and — all the rest: from these contacts one acquires at least some materials for a gallery that Hazlitt would have liked to execute and that Guedalla may yet do.

At this point it occurs to the editor that perhaps this last suggestion may be turned against himself, and that his tastes and prejudices may be destructively analyzed on the basis of his inclusions in this book — or his exclusions. Well, that is a risk run by all anthologists, particularly those who pluck their flowers from fresh meadows, before the blooms of a day have withered. He will plead guilty to exclusion of the violently controversial, the vulgar, and the raucous, and to preference for writing with at least a touch of literary craftsmanship. But within these limits conservative, liberal, and radical speak, and a fair variety of topics are broached, some as momentous as Ike Walton's fishing basket, some as trivial as the battle of the two generations. In them all, at any rate, the modern reader may see himself in part reflected, his loves and hates, his suspicions, doubts, despairs. That is why the writing of our own time has for us all an immediacy of interest, friendly or unfriendly, which no other writing however classical can ever possess.

CONTENTS

ix

CONTENTS

CONTEMPORARY ESSAYS

.·.

GOING BACK TO SCHOOL[1]

MAX BEERBOHM

THE other evening, at about seven o'clock, I was in a swift hansom. My hat was tilted at a gay angle, and, for all I was muffled closely, my gloves betokened a ceremonious attire. I was smoking *la cigarette d'appétit*, and was quite happy. Outside Victoria my cab was stopped by a file of other cabs, that were following one another in at the main entrance of the station. I noticed, on one of them, a small hat-box, a newish trunk and a corded play-box, and I caught one glimpse of a very small, pale boy in a billicock-hat. He was looking at me through the side-window. If Envy was ever inscribed on any face, it was inscribed on the face of that very small, pale boy. "There," I murmured, "but for the grace of God, goes Max Beerbohm!"

My first thought, then, was for myself. I could not but plume me on the contrast of my own state with his. But, gradually, I became fulfilled with a very great compassion for him. I understood the boy's Envy so well. It was always the most bitter thing, in my own drive to

[1] From *More* (1899). Used by permission of Dodd, Mead and Company, Inc.

I

the station, to see other people, quite happy, as it seemed, with no upheaval of their lives; people in cabs, who were going out to dinner and would sleep in London; grown-up people! Than the impotent despair of those drives — I had exactly fifteen of them — I hope that I shall never experience a more awful emotion. Those drives have something, surely, akin with drowning. In their course the whole of a boy's home-life passes before his eyes, every phase of it standing out against the black curtain of his future. The author of *Vice-Versa* has well an-alyzed the feeling, and he is right, I think, in saying that all boys, of whatsoever temperament, are preys to it. Well do I remember how, on the last day of the holidays, I used always to rise early, and think that I had got twelve more whole hours of happiness, and how those hours used to pass me with mercifully slow feet. . . . Three more hours! . . . Sixty more minutes! . . . Five! . . . I used to draw upon my tips for a first-class ticket, that I might not be plunged suddenly among my companions, with their hectic and hollow mirth, their dreary disinter-ment of last term's jokes. I used to revel in the thought that there were many stations before G—— . . . The dreary walk, with my small bag, up the hill! I was not one of those who made a rush for the few cabs! . . . The awful geniality of the House Master! The jugs in the dormitory! . . . Next morning, the bell that woke me! The awakening!

Not that I had any special reason for hating school! Strange as it may seem to my readers, I was not un-popular there. I was a modest, good-humoured boy. It is Oxford that has made me insufferable. At school, my character remained in a state of undevelopment. I had a few misgivings, perhaps. In some respects, I was always too young, in others, too old, for a perfect relish of the convention. As I hovered, in grey knickerbockers, on a cold and muddy field, round the outskirts of a crowd that was tearing itself limb from limb for the sake of a leathern bladder, I would often wish for a nice, warm room and a good game of hunt-the-slipper. And, when we sallied forth, after dark, in the frost, to the swimming-bath, my heart would steal back to the fireside in Writing School and the plot of Miss Braddon's latest novel. Often, since, have I wondered whether a Spartan system be really well for youths who are bound mostly for Capuan Universities. It is true, certainly, that this system makes Oxford or Cambridge doubly delectable. Undergraduates owe their happiness chiefly to the consciousness that they are no longer at school. The nonsense which was knocked out of them at school is all put gently back at Oxford or Cambridge. And the discipline to which they are subject is so slight that it does but serve to accentuate their real freedom. The sudden reaction is rather dangerous, I think, to many of them.

Even now, much of my own complacency comes of having left school. Such an apparition as that boy in the hansom makes me realise my state more absolutely. Why, after all, should I lavish my pity on him and his sorrows? *Dabit deus his quoque finem.* I am at a happier point in Nature's cycle. That is all. I have suffered every one of his ordeals, and I do not hesitate to assure him, if he chance to see this essay of mine, how glad I am that I do not happen to be his contemporary. I have no construe of Xenophon to prepare for to-morrow morning, nor any ode of Horace to learn, painfully, by heart. I assure him that I have no wish nor any need to master, as he has, at this moment, the intricate absurdities of that proposition in the second book of Euclid. I have no locker, with my surname printed on it and a complement of tattered school-books. I burnt all my school-books, when I went up to Oxford. Were I to meet, now, any one of those masters who are monsters to you, my boy, he would treat me even more urbanely, it may be, than I should treat him. When he sets you a hundred lines, you write them without pleasure, and he tears them up. When I, with considerable enjoyment and at my own leisure, write a hundred lines or so, they are printed for all the world to admire, and I am paid for them enough to keep you in pocket-money for many terms. I write at a comfortable table, by a warm fire, and occupy an arm-chair, whilst you are sitting on a narrow form. My boots are not made "for school-wear," nor do they ever, like yours, get lost in a litter of other boots in a cold boot-room. In a word, I enjoy myself immensely. To-night, I am going to a theatre. Afterwards, I shall sup somewhere and drink wine. When I come home and go to bed, I shall read myself to sleep with some amusing book. . . . You will have torn yourself from your bed, at the sound of a harsh bell, have washed, quickly, in very cold water, have scurried off to Chapel, gone to first school and been sent down several places in your form, tried to master your next construe, in the interval of snatching a tepid breakfast, been kicked by a bigger boy, and had a mint of horrible experiences, long before I, your elder by a few years, have awakened, very gradually, to the tap of knuckles on the panel of my bedroom-door. I shall make a leisurely toilet. I shall descend to a warm breakfast, open one of the little budgets which my "damned good-natured friend," Romeike, is always sending me, and glance at that morning paper which appeals most surely to my sense of humour. And when I have eaten well of all the dishes on the table, I shall light a cigarette. Through the haze of its fragrant smoke, I shall think of the happy day that is before me.

THE PORTRAIT OF A CHILD [1]

HILAIRE BELLOC

In a garden which must, I think, lie somewhat apart and enclosed in one of the valleys of central England, you came across the English grass in summer beneath the shade of a tree; you were running, but your arms were stretched before you in a sort of dance and balance as though you rather belonged to the air and to the growing things about you and above you than to the earth over which you passed; and you were not three years old.

As, in jest, this charming vision was recorded by a camera which some guest had with him, a happy accident (designed, for all we know, by whatever powers arrange such things, an accident of the instrument or of the plate upon which your small, happy, advancing figure was recorded) so chanced that your figure, when the picture was printed, shone all around with light.

I cannot, as I look at it now before me and as I write these words, express, however much I may seek for expression, how great a meaning underlies that accident nor how full of fate and of reason and of suggested truth that aureole grows as I gaze. Your innocence is beatified by it, and takes on with majesty the glory which lies behind all innocence, but which our eyes can never see. Your happiness seems in that mist of light to be removed and permanent; the common world in which you are moving

[1] From *On Something* (1910), published by E. P. Dutton and Company. By permission of E. P. Dutton and Company and of Methuen and Company, Ltd.

6

passes, through this trick of the lens, into a stronger world more apt for such a sight, and one in which I am half persuaded (as I still look upon the picture) blessedness is not a rare adventure, but something native and secure.

Little child, the trick which the camera has played means more and more as I still watch your picture, for there is present in that light not only blessedness, but holiness as well. The lightness of your movement and of your poise (as though you were blown like a blossom along the tops of the grass) is shone through, and your face, especially its ready and wondering laughter, is inspired, as though the Light had filled it from within; so that, looking thus, I look not on, but through. I say that in this portrait which I treasure, there is not only blessedness, but holiness as well — holiness which is the cause of blessedness and which contains it, and by which secretly all this world is sustained.

Now there is a third thing in your portrait, little child. That accident of light, light all about you and shining through your face, is not only blessed nor only holy, but it is also sacred, and with that thought there returns to me as I look what always should return to man if he is to find any stuff or profit in his consideration of divine things. In blessedness there is joy for which here we are not made, so that we catch it only in glimpses or in adumbrations. And in holiness, when we perceive it we perceive something far off; it is that from which we came and to which we should return; yet holiness is not a human thing. But things sacred — things devoted to a purpose, things about which there lies an awful necessity of sacrifice, things devoted and necessarily suffering some doom — these are certainly of this world; that, indeed, all men know well at last, and find it part of the business through which they needs must pass. Human memories, since they are only memories; human attachments, since they are offered up and end; great human fears and hopeless human longings — these are sacred things attached to a victim and to a sacrifice; and in this picture of yours, with the light so glorifying you all round, no one can doubt who sees it but that the sacredness of human life will be yours also; that is, you must learn how it is offered up to some end and what a sacrifice is there.

I could wish, as I consider this, that the camera had played no such trick, and had not revealed in that haze of awful meaning all that lies beyond the nature of you, child. But it is a truth which is so revealed; and we may not, upon a penalty more terrible than death, neglect any ultimate truth concerning our mortal way.

Your feet, which now do not seem to press upon the lawn across which they run, have to go more miles than you can dream of, through more places than you could bear to hear, and they must be directed to a goal which will not in your very young delight be mentioned before you, or of which, if it is mentioned, you will not understand by name; and your little hands which you bear before you with the little gesture of flying things, will grasp most tightly that which can least remain and will attempt to fashion what can never be completed, and will caress that which will not respond to the caress. Your eyes, which are now so principally filled with innocence that that bright quality drowns all the rest, will look upon so much of deadly suffering and of misuse in men, that they will very early change themselves in kind; and all your face, which now vaguely remembers nothing but

8

the early vision from which childhood proceeds, will grow drawn and self-guarded, and will suffer some agonies, a few despairs, innumerable fatigues, until it has become the face of a woman grown. Nor will this sacred doom about you, which is that of all mankind, cease or grow less or be mitigated in any way; it will increase as surely and as steadily as increase the number of the years, until at last you will lay down the daylight and the knowledge of day-lit things as gladly as now you wake from sleep to see them.

For you are sacred, and all those elders about you, whose solemn demeanour now and then startles you into a pretty perplexity which soon calls back their smiles, have hearts only quite different from your quite careless heart, because they have known the things to which, in the manner of victims, they are consecrated.

All that by which we painfully may earn rectitude and a proper balance in the conduct of our short affairs I must believe that you will practise; and I must believe, as I look here into your face, seeing your confident advance (as though you were flying out from your babyhood into young life without any fear), that the virtues which now surround you in a crowd and make a sort of court for you and are your angels every way, will go along with you and will stand by you to the end. Even so, and the more so, you will find (if you read this some years hence) how truly it is written. By contrast with your demeanour, with your immortal hopes, and with your pious efforts the world about you will seem darker and less secure with every passing harvest, and in proportion as you remember the childhood which has led me so to write of you, in proportion as you remember gladness and innocence with its completed joy, in that proportion will you find at least a breaking burden in the weight of this world.

Now you may say to me, little child (not now, but later on), to what purpose is all this complaint, and why should you tell me these things?

It is because in the portrait before me the holiness, the blessedness, and therefore the sacredness are apparent that I am writing as I do. For you must know that there is a false way out and a seeming relief for the rack of human affairs, and that this way is taken by many. Since you are sacred do not take it, but bear the burden. It is the character of whatever is sacred that it does not take that way; but, like a true victim, remains to the end, ready to complete the sacrifice.

The way out is to forget that one is sacred, and this men and women do in many ways. The most of them by way of treason. They betray. They break at first uneasily, later easily, and at last unconsciously, the word which each of us has passed before He was born in Paradise. All men and all women are conscious of that word, for though their lips cannot frame it here, and though the terms of the pledge are forgotten, the memory of its obligation fills the mind. But there comes a day, and that soon in the lives of many, when to break it once is to be much refreshed and to seem to drop the burden; and in the second and the third time it is done, and the fourth it is done more easily — until at last there is no more need for a man or a woman to break that pledged word again and once again; it is broken for good and for all. This is one most common way in which the sacred quality is lost: the way of treason. Round about such as choose this kind of relief grows a habit and an air of treason.

They betray all things at last, and even common friendship is at last no longer theirs. The end of this false issue is despair.

Another way is to take refuge from ourselves in pleasures, and this is easily done, not by the worse, but by the better sort; for there are some, some few, who would never betray nor break their ancient word, but who, seeing no meaning in a sacrifice nor in a burden, escape from it through pleasure as through a drug, and this pleasure they find in all manner of things, and always that spirit near them which would destroy their sacred mark, persuades them that they are right, and that in such pursuits the sacrifice is evaded. So some will steep themselves in rhyme, some in landscapes, some in pictures, some in the watching of the complexity and change of things, some in music, some in action, some in mere ease. It seems as though the men and women who would thus forget their sacredness are better loved and better warned than those who take the other path, for they never forget certain gracious things which should be proper to the mind, nor do they lose their friends. But that they have taken a wrong path you may easily perceive from this sign: that these pleasures, like any other drug, do not feed or satisfy, but must be increased with every dose, and even so soon pall and are continued not because they are pleasures any longer, but because, dull though they have become, without them there is active pain.

Take neither the one path nor the other, but retain, I beseech you, when the time comes, that quality of sacredness of which I speak, for there is no alternative. Some trouble fell upon our race, and all of us must take upon ourselves the business and the burden. If you will attempt any way out at all it will but lead you to some worse thing. We have not all choices before us, but only one of very few, and each of those few choices is mortal, and all but one is evil.

You should remember this also, dear little child, that at the beginning — oh, only at the very beginning of life — even your reason that God gave may lead you wrong. For with those memories strong upon you of perfect will, of clear intelligence, and of harmonious beauty all about, you will believe the world in which you stand to be the world from which you have come and to which you are also destined. You have but to treat this world for but a very little while as though it were the thing you think it to find it is not so.

Do you know that that which smells most strongly in this life of immortality, and which a poet has called "the ultimate outpost of eternity," is insecure and perishes? I mean the passionate affection of early youth. If that does not remain, what then do you think can remain? I tell you that nothing which you take to be permanent round about you when you are very young is more than the symbol or clothes of permanence. Another poet has written, speaking of the chalk hills:

> Only a little while remain
> The Downs in their solemnity.

Nor is this saying forced. Men and women cannot attach themselves even to the hills where they first played.

Some men, wise but unillumined, and not conscious of that light which I here physically see shining all round and through you in the picture which is before my eyes as I write, have said that to die young and to end the business early was a great blessing. We do not know.

But we do know that to die long after and to have gone through the business must be blessed, since blessedness and holiness and sacredness are bound together in one.

But, of these three, be certain that sacredness is your chief business, blessedness after your first childhood you will never know, and holiness you may only see as men see distant mountains lifted beyond a plain; it cannot be your habitation. Sacredness, which is the mark of that purpose whose heir is blessedness, whose end is holiness, will be upon you until you die; maintain it, and let it be your chief concern, for though you neglect it, it will remain and avenge itself.

All this I have seen in your picture as you go across the grass, and it was an accident of the camera that did it. If any one shall say these things do not attach to the portrait of a child, let him ask himself whether they do not attach to the portrait that might be drawn, did human skill suffice, of the life of a woman or a man which springs from the demeanour of childhood; or let him ask himself whether, if a face in old age and that same face in childhood were equally and as by a revelation set down each in its full truth, and the growth of the one into the other were interpreted by a profound intelligence, what I have said would not be true of all that little passage of ours through the daylight.

ON GROWING OLDER [1]

ARTHUR CHRISTOPHER BENSON

THE sun flares red behind leafless elms and battlemented towers as I come in from a lonely walk beside the river; above the chimney-tops hangs a thin veil of drifting smoke, blue in the golden light. The games in the Common are just coming to an end; a stream of long-coated spectators sets towards the town, mingled with the parti-coloured, muddied figures of the players. I have been strolling half the afternoon along the river bank, watch-ing the boats passing up and down; hearing the shrill cries of coxes, the measured plash of oars, the rhythmical rat-tle of rowlocks, intermingled at intervals with the harsh grinding of the chain-ferries. Five-and-twenty years ago I was rowing here myself in one of these boats, and I do not wish to renew the experience. I cannot conceive why and in what moment of feeble good-nature or mis-applied patriotism I ever consented to lend a hand. I was not a good oar, and did not become a better one; I had no illusions about my performance, and any momentary complacency was generally sternly dispelled by the harsh criticism of the coach on the bank, when we rested for a moment to receive our meed of praise or blame. But though I have no sort of wish to repeat the process, to renew the slavery which I found frankly and consistently intolerable, I find myself looking on at the cheerful scene with an amusement in which mingles a shadow of pain,

[1] From *From a College Window* (1906). By permission of the publish-ers, G. P. Putnam's Sons and John Murray.

because I feel that I have parted with something, a certain buoyancy and elasticity of body, and perhaps spirit, of which I was not conscious at the time, but which I now realise that I must have possessed. It is with an admiration mingled with envy that I see these youthful, shapely figures, bare-necked and bare-kneed, swinging rhythmically past. I watch a brisk crew lift a boat out of the water by a boat-house; half of them duck underneath to get hold of the other side, and they march up the grating gravel in a solemn procession. I see a pair of cheerful young men, released from tubbing, execute a wild and inconsequent dance upon the water's edge; I see a solemn conference of deep import between a stroke and a coach. I see a neat, clean-limbed young man go airily up to a well-earned tea, without, I hope, a care or an anxiety in his mind, expecting and intending to spend an agreeable evening. "Oh, Jones of Trinity, oh, Smith of Queen's," I think to myself, *"tua si bona nôris!* Make the best of the good time, my boy, before you go off to the office, or the fourth-form room, or the country parish! Live virtuously, make honest friends, read the good old books, lay up a store of kindly recollections, of firelit rooms in venerable courts, of pleasant talks, of innocent festivities. Very fresh is the brisk morning air, very fragrant is the newly lighted bird's-eye, very lively is the clink of knives and forks, very keen is the savour of the roast beef that floats up to the dark rafters of the College Hall. But the days are short and the terms are few; and do not forget to be a sensible as well as a good-humoured young man!"

Thackeray, in a delightful ballad, invites a pretty page to wait till he comes to forty years: well, I have waited —

indeed, I have somewhat overshot the mark — and to-day the sight of all this brisk life, going on just as it used to do, with the same *insouciance* and the same merriment, makes me wish to reflect, to gather up the fragments, to see if it is all loss, all declension, or whether there is something left, some strength in what remains behind.

I have a theory that one ought to grow older in a tranquil and appropriate way, that one ought to be perfectly contented with one's time of life, that amusements and pursuits ought to alter naturally and easily, and not be regretfully abandoned. One ought not to be dragged protesting from the scene, catching desperately at every doorway and balustrade; one should walk off smiling. It is easier said than done. It is not a pleasant moment when a man first recognises that he is out of place in the football field, that he cannot stoop with the old agility to pick up a skimming stroke to cover-point, that dancing is rather too heating to be decorous, that he cannot walk all day without undue somnolence after dinner, or rush off after a heavy meal without indigestion. These are sad moments which we all of us reach, but which are better laughed over than fretted over. And a man who, out of sheer inability to part from boyhood, clings desperately and with apoplectic puffings to these things is an essentially grotesque figure. To listen to young men discussing one of these my belated contemporaries, and to hear one enforcing on another the amusement to be gained from watching the old buffer's manœuvres, is a lesson against undue youthfulness. One can indeed give amusement without loss of dignity, by being open to being induced to join in such things occasionally in an elderly way, without any attempt to disguise deficiencies. But that is the most that ought to be attempted. Perhaps the best way of all is to subside into the genial and interested looker-on, to be ready to applaud the game you cannot play, and to admire the dexterity you cannot rival.

What then, if any, are the gains that make up for the lack of youthful prowess? They are, I can contentedly say, many and great. In the first place, there is the loss of a quality which is productive of an extraordinary amount of pain among the young, the quality of self-consciousness. How often was one's peace of mind ruined by *gaucherie*, by shyness, by the painful consciousness of having nothing to say, and the still more painful consciousness of having said the wrong thing in the wrong way! Of course, it was all immensely exaggerated. If one went to chapel, for instance, with a straw hat, which one had forgotten to remove, over a surplice, one had the feeling for several days that it was written in letters of fire on every wall. I was myself an ardent conversationalist in early years, and, with the charming omniscience of youth, fancied that my opinion was far better worth having than the opinions of Dons encrusted with pedantry and prejudice. But if I found myself in the society of these petrified persons, by the time that I had composed a suitable remark, the slender opening had already closed, and my contribution was either not uttered at all, or hopelessly belated in its appearance. Or some deep generalisation drawn from the dark backward of my vast experience would be produced, and either ruthlessly ignored or contemptuously corrected by some unsympathetic elder of unyielding voice and formed opinions. And then there was the crushing sense, at the conclusion of one of these interviews, of having been put down as a tiresome and heavy young man. I fully believed in my own liveliness and sprightliness, but it seemed an impossible task to persuade my elders that these qualities were there. A good-natured, elderly friend used at times to rally me upon my shyness, and say that it all came from thinking too much about myself. It was as useless as if one told a man with a toothache that it was mere self-absorption that made him suffer. For I have no doubt that the disease of self-consciousness is incident to intelligent youth. Marie Bashkirtseff, in the terrible self-revealing journals which she wrote, describes a visit that she paid to some one who had expressed an interest in her and a desire to see her. She says that as she passed the threshold of the room she breathed a prayer, "O God, make me worth seeing!" How often used one to desire to make an impression, to make oneself felt and appreciated!

Well, all that uneasy craving has left me. I no longer have any particular desire for or expectation of being impressive. One likes, of course, to feel brisk and lively; but whereas in the old days I used to enter a circle with the intention of endeavouring to be felt, of giving pleasure and interest, I now go in the humble hope of receiving either. The result is that, having got rid to a great extent of this pompous and self-regarding attitude of mind, I not only find myself more at ease, but I also find other people infinitely more interesting. Instead of laying one's frigate alongside of another craft with the intention of conducting a boarding expedition, one pays a genial visit by means of the long-boat with all the circumstance of courtesy and amiability. Instead of desiring to make conquests, I am glad enough to be tolerated. I dare, too, to say what I think, not alert for any symptoms of contradiction, but fully aware that my own point of view is but one of many, and quite prepared to revise it. In the old days I demanded agreement; I am now amused by divergence. In the old days I desired to convince; I am now only too thankful to be convinced of error and ignorance. I now no longer shrink from saying that I know nothing of a subject; in old days I used to make a pretence of omniscience, and had to submit irritably to being tamely unmasked. It seems to me that I must have been an unpleasant young man enough, but I humbly hope that I was not so disagreeable as might appear.

Another privilege of advancing years is the decreasing tyranny of convention. I used to desire to do the right thing, to know the right people, to play the right games. I did not reflect whether it was worth the sacrifice of personal interest; it was all-important to be in the swim. Very gradually I discovered that other people troubled their heads very little about what one did; that the right people were often the most tiresome and the most conventional, and that the only games which were worth playing were the games which one enjoyed. I used to undergo miseries in staying at uncongenial houses, in accepting shooting invitations when I could not shoot, in going to dances because the people whom I knew were going. Of course one has plenty of disagreeable duties to perform in any case; but I discovered gradually that to adopt the principle of doing disagreeable things which were supposed to be amusing and agreeable was to misunderstand the whole situation. Now, if I am asked to stay at a tiresome house, I refuse, I decline invitations to garden parties and public dinners and dances, because I know that they will bore me; and as to games, I never play them if I can help, because I find that they do not entertain me. Of course there are occasions when one is wanted to fill a gap, and then it is the duty of a Christian and a gentleman to conform, and to do it with a good grace. Again, I am not at the mercy of small prejudices, as I used to be. As a young man, if I disliked the cut of a person's whiskers or the fashion of his clothes, if I considered his manner to be abrupt or unpleasing, if I was not interested in his subjects, I set him down as an impossible person, and made no further attempt to form acquaintance.

Now I know that these are superficial things, and that a kind heart and an interesting personality are not inconsistent with boots of a grotesque shape and even with mutton-chop whiskers. In fact, I think that small oddities and differences have grown to have a distinct value, and form a pleasing variety. If a person's manner is unattractive, I often find that it is nothing more than a shyness or an awkwardness which disappears the moment that familiarity is established. My standard is, in fact, lower, and I am more tolerant. I am not, I confess, wholly tolerant, but my intolerance is reserved for qualities and not for externals. I still fly swiftly from longwinded, pompous, and contemptuous persons; but if their company is unavoidable, I have at least learned to hold my tongue. The other day I was at a country-house where an old and extremely tiresome General laid down the law on the subject of the Mutiny, where he had fought as a youthful subaltern. I was pretty sure that he was making the most grotesque misstatements, but I was not in a position to contradict them. Next the General was a courteous, weary old gentleman, who sat with his finger-tips pressed together, smiling and nodding at intervals. Half an hour later we were lighting our candles. The General strode fiercely up to bed, leaving a company of yawning and dispirited men behind. The old gentleman came up to me and, as he took a light, said with an inclination of his head in the direction of the parting figure, "The poor General is a good deal misinformed. I didn't choose to say anything, but I know something about the subject, because I was private secretary to the Secretary for War."

That was the right attitude, I thought, for the gentlemanly philosopher; and I have learned from my old friend the lesson not to choose to say anything if a turbulent and pompous person lays down the law on subjects with which I happen to be acquainted.

Again, there is another gain that results from advancing years. I think it is true that there were sharper ecstasies in youth, keener perceptions, more passionate thrills; but then the mind also dipped more swiftly and helplessly into discouragement, dreariness, and despair. I do not think that life is so rapturous, but it certainly is vastly more interesting. When I was young there were an abundance of things about which I did not care. I was all for poetry and art; I found history tedious, science tiresome, politics insupportable. Now I may thankfully say it is wholly different. The time of youth was the opening to me of many doors of life. Sometimes a door opened upon a mysterious and wonderful place, an enchanted forest, a solemn avenue, a sleeping glade; often, too, it opened into some dusty work-a-day place, full of busy forms bent over intolerable tasks, whizzing wheels, dark gleaming machinery, the din of the factory and the workshop. Sometimes, too, a door would open into a bare and melancholy place, a hillside strewn with stones, an interminable plain of sand; worst of all, a place would sometimes be revealed which was full of suffering, anguish, and hopeless woe, shadowed with fears and sins. From such prospects I turned with groans unutterable; but the air of the accursed place would hang about me for days. These surprises, these strange surmises, crowded in fast upon me. How different the world was from what the careless forecast of boyhood had pictured it! How strange, how beautiful, and yet how terrible! As life went on the beauty increased, and a calmer, quieter beauty made itself revealed; in youth I looked for strange, impressive, haunted beauties, things that might deeply stir and move; but year by year a simpler, sweeter, healthier kind of beauty made itself felt; such beauty as lies on the bare, lightly washed, faintly tinted hillside of winter, all delicate greens and browns, so far removed from the rich summer luxuriance, and yet so austere, so pure. I grew to love different books too. In youth one demanded a generous glow, a fire of passion, a richly tinged current of emotion; but by degrees came the love of sober, subdued reflection, a cooler world in which, if one could not rest, one might at least travel equably and gladly, with a far wider range of experience, a larger, if a fainter, hope. I grew to demand less of the world, less of Nature, less of people; and behold, a whole range of subtler and gentler emotions came into sight, like the blue hills of the distance, pure and low. The whole movement of the world, past and present, became intelligible and clear. I saw the humanity that lies behind political and constitutional questions, the strong, simple forces that move like a steady stream behind the froth and foam of personality. If in youth I believed that personality and influence could sway and mould the world, in later years I have come to see that the strongest and fiercest characters are only the river-wrack, the broken boughs, the torn grasses that whirl and spin in the tongue of the creeping flood, and that there is a dim resistless force behind them that marches on unheeding and drives them in the forefront of the inundation. Things that had seemed drearily theoretical, dry, axiomatic, platitudinal, showed themselves to be great generalisations from a torrent of human effort and mortal endeavour. And thus all the mass of detail and human relation that had been rudely set aside by the insolent prejudices of youth under the generic name of business, came slowly to have an intense and living significance. I cannot trace the process in detail; but I became aware of the fulness, the energy, the matchless interest of the world, and the vitality of a hundred thoughts that had seemed to me the dreariest abstractions.

Then, too, the greatest gain of all, there comes a sort of patience. In youth mistakes seemed irreparable, calamities intolerable, ambitions realisable, disappointments unbearable. An anxiety hung like a dark impenetrable cloud, a disappointment poisoned the springs of life. But now I have learned that mistakes can often be set right, that anxieties fade, that calamities have sometimes a compensating joy, that an ambition realised is not always pleasurable, that a disappointment is often of itself a rich incentive to try again. One learns to look over troubles, instead of looking into them; one learns that hope is more unconquerable than grief. And so there flows into the gap the certainty that one can make more of misadventures, of unpromising people, of painful experiences, than one had ever hoped. It may not be, nay, it is not, so eager, so full-blooded a spirit; but it is a serener, a more interesting, a happier outlook.

And so, like Robinson Crusoe on his island, striking a balance of my advantages and disadvantages, I am inclined to think that the good points predominate. Of course there still remains the intensely human instinct, which survives all the lectures of moralists, the desire to eat one's cake and also to have it. One wants to keep the gains of middle life and not to part with the glow of youth. "The tragedy of growing old," says a brilliant writer, "is the remaining young"; that is to say, that the spirit does not age as fast as the body. The sorrows of life lie in the imagination, in the power to recall the good days that have been and the old sprightly feelings; and in the power, too, to forecast the slow overshadowing and decay of age. But Lord Beaconsfield once said that the worst evil one has to endure is the anticipation of the calamities that do not happen; and I am sure that the thing to aim at is to live as far as possible in the day and for the day. I do not mean in an epicurean fashion, by taking prodigally all the pleasure that one can get, like a spendthrift of the happiness that is meant to last a lifetime, but in the spirit of Newman's hymn —

> I do not ask to see
> The distant scene; one step enough for me.

Even now I find that I am gaining a certain power, instinctively, I suppose, in making the most of the day and hour. In old days, if I had a disagreeable engagement ahead of me, something to which I looked forward with anxiety or dislike, I used to find that it poisoned my cup. Now it is beginning to be the other way; and I find myself with a heightened sense of pleasure in the quiet and peaceful days that have to intervene before the fateful morning dawns. I used to awake in the morning on the days that were still my own before the day which I dreaded, and begin, in that agitated mood which used to accompany the return of consciousness after sleep, when the mind is alert but unbalanced, to anticipate the thing I feared, and feel that I could not face it. Now I tend to awake and say to myself, "Well, at any rate I have still to-day in my own hands"; and then the very day itself has an increased value from the feeling that the uncomfortable experience lies ahead. I suppose that is the secret of the placid enjoyment which the very old so often display. They seem so near the dark gate, and yet so entirely indifferent to the thought of it; so absorbed in little leisurely trifles, happy with a childlike happiness.

And thus I went slowly back to College in that gathering gloom that seldom fails to bring a certain peace to the mind. The porter sat, with his feet on the fender, in his comfortable den, reading a paper. The lights were beginning to appear in the court, and the firelight flickering briskly upon walls hung with all the pleasant signs of youthful life, the groups, the family photographs, the suspended oar, the cap of glory. So when I entered my book-lined rooms, and heard the kettle sing its comfortable song on the hearth, and reflected that I had a few letters to write, an interesting book to turn over, a pleasant Hall dinner to look forward to, and that, after a space of talk, an undergraduate or two were coming to talk over a leisurely piece of work, an essay or a paper, I was more than ever inclined to acquiesce in my disabilities, to purr like an elderly cat, and to feel that while I had the priceless boon of leisure, set in a framework of small duties, there was much to be said for life, and that I was a poor creature if I could not be soberly content.

Of course I know that I have missed the nearer ties of life, the hearth, the home, the companionship of a wife, the joys and interests of growing girls and boys. But if a man is fatherly and kind-hearted, he will find plenty of young men who are responsive to a paternal interest, and intensely grateful for the good-humoured care of one who will listen to their troubles, their difficulties, and their dreams. I have two or three young friends who tell me what they are doing, and what they hope to do; I have many correspondents who were friends of mine as boys, who tell me from time to time how it goes with them in the bigger world, and who like in return to hear something of my own doings.

And so I sit, while the clock on the mantel-piece ticks out the pleasant minutes, and the fire winks and crumbles on the hearth, till the old gyp comes tapping at the door to learn my intentions for the evening; and then, again, I pass out into the court, the lighted windows of the Hall gleam with the ancient armorial glass, from staircase after staircase come troops of alert, gowned figures, while overhead, above all the pleasant stir and murmur of life, hang in the dark sky the unchanging stars.

THE OLDER GENERATION [1]

RANDOLPH BOURNE

I

I read with ever-increasing wonder the guarded defenses and discreet apologies for the older generation which keep filtering through the essays of the *Atlantic*. I can even seem to detect a growing decision of tone, a definite assurance of conviction, which seems to imply that a rally has been undertaken against the accusations which the younger generation, in its self-assurance, its irreverence for the old conventions and moralities, its passion for the novel and startling, seemed to be bringing against them. The first faint twinges of conscience felt by the older generation have given place to renewed homily. There is an evident anxiety to get itself put on record as perfectly satisfied with its world, and desirous that its sons and daughters should learn anew of those peculiar beauties in which it has lived. Swept off its feet by the call to social service and social reform, it is slowly regaining its foundation, and, slightly flushed, and with garments somewhat awry, it proclaims again its belief in the eternal verities of Protestant religion and conventional New England morality.

It is always an encouraging sign when people are rendered self-conscious and are forced to examine the basis of their ideals. The demand that they explain them to

[1] From *The History of a Literary Radical*, by Randolph Bourne. New York: The Viking Press. Copyright, 1920, by B. W. Huebsch, Inc. By permission.

skeptics always makes for clarity. When the older generation is put on the defensive, it must first discover what
convictions it has, and then sharpen them to their finest
point in order to present them convincingly. There are
always too many unquestioned things in the world, and
for a person or class to have to scurry about to find reasons
for its prejudices is about as healthy an exercise as one
could wish for either of them. To be sure, the reasons are
rarely any more than *ex post facto* excuses — supports and
justifications for the prejudices rather than the causes
thereof. Reason itself is very seldom more than that.
The important point is that one should feel the need of a
reason. This always indicates that something has begun
to slide, that the world is no longer so secure as it was,
that obvious truths no longer are obvious, that the world
has begun to bristle with question marks.

One of the basic grievances of this older generation
against the younger of to-day, with its social agitation, its
religious heresy, its presumptive individuality, its economic restlessness, is that all this makes it uncomfortable.
When you have found growing older to be a process of the
reconciliation of the spirit to life, it is decidedly discon-
certing to have some youngster come along and point out
the irreconcilable things in the universe. Just as you
have made a tacit agreement to call certain things non-
existent, it is highly discommoding to have somebody
shout with strident tones that they are very real and significant. When, after much struggling and compromise,
you have got your world clamped down, it is discouraging
to have a gale arise which threatens to blow over all your
structure. Through so much of the current writing runs
this quiet note of disapprobation. These agnostic pro-

fessors who unsettle the faith of our youth, these "intellectuals who stick a finger in everybody's pie in the name of social justice," these sensation-mongers who unveil great masses of political and social corruption, these remorseless scientists who would reveal so many of our reticences — why can't they let us alone? Can they not see that God's in his heaven, all's right with the world?

II

Now I know this older generation which doth protest so much. I have lived with it for the last fifteen years, ever since I began to wonder whether all was for the best in the best of all possible worlds. I was educated by it, grew up with it. I doubt if any generation ever had a more docile pupil than I. What they taught me, I find they still believe, or at least so many of them as have not gone over to the enemy, or been captured by the militant youth of to-day. Or, as seems rather likely, they no longer precisely believe, but they want their own arguments to convince themselves. It is probable that when we really believe a thing with all our hearts, we do not attempt to justify it. Justification comes only when we are beginning to doubt it.

By this older generation I mean, of course, the mothers and fathers and uncles and aunts of the youth of both sexes between twenty and thirty who are beginning their professional or business life. And I refer of course to the comfortable or fairly comfortable American middle class. Now this older generation has had a religion, a metaphysics, an ethics, and a political and social philosophy, which have reigned practically undisputed until the appearance of the present generation. It has at least never felt called upon to justify itself. It has never been directly challenged, as it is to-day. In order to localize this generation still further, we must see it in its typical setting of the small town or city, clustered about the institutions of church and family. If we have any society which can be called "American," it is this society. Its psychology is American psychology; its soul is America's soul.

This older generation, which I have known so well for fifteen years, has a religion which is on the whole as pleasant and easy as could be devised. Though its members are the descendants of the stern and rugged old Puritans, who wrestled with the devil and stripped their world of all that might seduce them from the awful service of God, they have succeeded in straining away by a long process all the repellent attitudes in the old philosophy of life. It is unfair to say that the older generation believe in dogmas and creeds. It would be more accurate to say that it does not disbelieve. It retains them as a sort of guaranty of the stability of the faith, but leaves them rather severely alone. It does not even make more than feeble efforts to reinterpret them in the light of modern knowledge. They are useless, but necessary.

The foundation of this religion may be religious, but the superstructure is almost entirely ethical. Most sermons of to-day are little more than pious exhortations to good conduct. By good conduct is meant that sort of action which will least disturb the normal routine of modern middle-class life: common honesty in business life, faithfulness to duty, ambition in business and profession, filial obligation, the use of talents, and always and everywhere simple human kindness and love. The old Puritan ethics, which saw in the least issue of conduct a struggle between God and the devil, has become a mere code for facilitating the daily friction of conventional life.

Now one would indeed be churlish to find fault with this devout belief in simple goodness, which characterizes the older generation. It is only when these humble virtues are raised up into an all-inclusive program for social reform and into a philosophy of life, that one begins to question, and to feel afar the deep hostility of the older generation to the new faith.

Simple kindness, common honesty, filial obedience, it is evidently still felt, will solve all the difficulties of personal and social life. The most popular novels of the day are those in which the characters do the most good to each other. The enormous success with the older generation of *The Inside of the Cup*, *Queed*, and *V. V.'s Eyes*, is based primarily on the fact that these books represent a sublimated form of the good old American melodramatic moral sense. And now comes along Mr. Gerald Stanley Lee with his *Crowds* — what a funny, individualized, personal-responsibility crowd he gives us, to be sure — and his panacea for modern social ills by the old solution of applied personal virtue. Never a word about removing the barriers of caste and race and economic inequality, but only an urging to step over them. Never a trumpet-call to level the ramparts of privilege, or build up the heights of opportunity, but only an appeal to extend the charitable hand from the ramparts of heaven, or offer the kindly patronage to the less fortunate, or—most dazzling of all — throw away, in a frenzy of abandonment, life and fortune. Not to construct a business organization where dishonesty would be meaningless, but to be utopianly honest against the business world. In other words, the older generation believes in getting all the luxury of the virtue of goodness, while conserving all the advantages of being in a vicious society.

If there is any one characteristic which distinguishes the older generation, it is this belief that social ills may be cured by personal virtue. Its highest moral ideals are sacrifice and service. But the older generation can never see how intensely selfish these ideals are, in the most complete sense of the word selfish. What they mean always is, "I sacrifice myself for you," "I serve you," not, "We coöperate in working ceaselessly toward an ideal where all may be free and none may be served or serve." These ideals of sacrifice and service are utterly selfish, because they take account only of the satisfaction and moral consolidation of the doer. They enhance his moral value; but what of the person who is served or sacrificed for? What of the person who is done good to? If the feelings of sacrifice and service were in any sense altruistic, the moral enhancement of the receiver would be the object sought. But can it not be said that for every individual virtuous merit secured by an act of sacrifice or service on the part of the doer, there is a corresponding depression on the part of the receiver? Do we not universally recognize this by calling a person who is not conscious of this depression, a parasite, and the person who is no longer capable of depression, a pauper? It is exactly those free gifts, such as schools, libraries, and so forth, which are impersonal or social, that we can accept gratefully and gladly; and it is exactly because the ministrations of a Charity Organization Society are impersonal and businesslike that they can be received willingly and without moral depression by the poor.

The ideal of duty is equally open to attack. The great complaint of the younger against the older generation has to do with the rigidity of the social relationships into which the younger find themselves born. The world seems to be full of what may be called canalized emotions. One is "supposed" to love one's aunt or one's grandfather in a certain definite way, at the risk of being "unnatural." One gets almost a sense of the quantitative measurement of emotion. Perhaps the greatest tragedy of family life is the useless energy that is expended by the dutiful in keeping these artificial channels open, and the correct amount of current running. It is exactly this that produces most infallibly the rebellion of the younger generation. To hear that one ought to love this or that person; or to hear loyalty spoken of, as the older generation so often speaks of it, as if it consisted in an allegiance to something which one no longer believes in — this is what soonest liberates those forces of madness and revolt which bewilder spiritual teachers and guides. It is those dry channels of duty and obligation through which no living waters of emotion flow that it is the ideal of the younger generation to break up. They will have no network of emotional canals which are not brimming, no duties which are not equally loves.

But when they are loves, you have duty no longer meaning very much. Duty, like sacrifice and service, always implies a personal relation of individuals. You are always doing your duty to somebody or something. Always the taint of inequality comes in. You are morally superior to the person who has duty done to him. If that duty is not filled with good-will and desire, it is morally hateful, or at very best, a necessary evil — one of those compromises with the world which must be made in order to get through it at all. But duty without goodwill is a compromise with our present state of inequality, and to raise duty to the level of a virtue is to consecrate that state of inequality forevermore.

III

It is the same thing with service. The older generation has attempted an insidious compromise with the new social democracy by combining the words "social" and "service." Under cover of the ideal of service it tries to appropriate to itself the glory of social work, and succeeds in almost convincing itself and the world that its Christianity has always held the same ideal. The faithful are urged to extend their activities. The assumption is that, by doing good to more individuals, you are thereby becoming social. But to speak of "social democracy," which of course means a freely coöperating, freely reciprocating society of equals, and "service," together, is a contradiction of terms. For, when you serve people or do good to them, you thereby render yourself unequal with them. You insult the democratic ideal. If the service is compulsory, it is menial and you are inferior. If voluntary, you are superior. The difference, however, is only academic. The entire Christian scheme is a clever but unsuccessful attempt to cure the evils of inequality by transposing the values. The slave serves gladly instead of servilely. That is, he turns his master into a slave. That is why good Christian people can never get over the idea that Socialism means simply the triumph of one class over another. To-day the proletarian is down, the capitalist up. To-morrow the proletarian will be up and the capitalist down. To pull down the mighty from their seats and exalt them of low degree is the highest pitch to which Christian ethics ever attained. The failure of the older generation to recognize a higher ethic, the ethic of democracy, is the cause of all the trouble.

The notorious Victorian era, which in its secret heart this older generation still admires so much, accentuated all the latent individualism of Christian ethics, and produced a code which, without the rebellion of the younger generation, would have spiritually guaranteed forever all moral caste divisions and inequalities of modern society. The Protestant Church, in which this exaggerated ethic was enshrined, is now paying heavily the price of this debauch of ethical power. Its rapidly declining numbers show that human nature has an invincible objection to being individually saved. The Catholic Church, which saves men as members of the Beloved Community, and not as individuals, flourishes. When one is saved by Catholicism, one becomes a democrat, and not a spiritual snob and aristocrat, as one does through Calvinism. The older generation can never understand that superb loyalty which is loyalty to a community — a loyalty which, paradoxical as it may seem, nourishes the true social personality in proportion as the individual sense is lessened. The Protestant Church in its tenacious devotion to the personal ideal of a Divine Master — the highest and most popular Christian ideal of to-day — shows how very far it still is away from the ideals and ethics of a social democracy, a life lived in the Beloved Community.

The sense of self-respect is the very keystone of the personality in whose defence all this individualistic philosophy has been carefully built up. The Christian virtues date from ages when there was a vastly greater number of morally depressed people than there is now. The tenacious survival of these virtues can be due only to the fact that they were valuable to the moral prestige of some class. Our older generation, with its emphasis on duty, sacrifice, and service, shows us very clearly what those interests were. I deliberately accuse the older generation of conserving and greatly strengthening these ideals, as a defensive measure. Morals are always the product of a situation; they reflect a certain organization of human relations which some class or group wishes to preserve. A moral code or set of ideals is always the invisible spiritual sign of a visible social grace. In an effort to retain the *status quo* of that world of inequalities and conventions in which they most comfortably and prosperously live, the older generation has stamped, through all its agencies of family, church and school, upon the younger generation, just those seductive ideals which would preserve its position. These old virtues upon which, however, the younger generation is already making guerilla warfare are simply the moral support with which the older generation buttresses its social situation.

The natural barriers and prejudices by which our elders are cut off from a freely flowing democracy are thus given a spiritual justification, and there is added for our elders the almost sensual luxury of leaping, by free grace, the barriers and giving themselves away. But the price has to be paid. Just as profits, in the socialist philosophy, are taken to be an abstraction from wages, through the economic power which one class has over another, so the virtues of the older generation may be said to be an ab-

36

straction from the virtue of other classes less favorably situated from a moral or personal point of view. Their swollen self-respect is at the expense of others.

How well we know the type of man in the older generation who has been doing good all his life! How his personality has thriven on it! How he has ceaselessly been storing away moral fat in every cranny of his soul! His goodness has been meat to him. The need and depression of other people has been, all unconsciously to him, the air which he has breathed. Without their compensating misfortune or sin, his goodness would have wilted and died. If good people would earnestly set to work to make the world uniformly healthy, courageous, beautiful, and prosperous, the field of their vocation would be constantly limited, and finally destroyed. That they so stoutly resist all philosophies and movements which have these ends primarily in view is convincing evidence of the fierce and jealous egoism which animates their so plausibly altruistic spirit. One suspects that the older generation does not want its vocation destroyed. It takes an heroic type of goodness to undermine all the foundations on which our virtue rests.

If then I object to the ethical philosophy of the older generation on the ground that it is too individualistic, and, under the pretense of altruism, too egoistic, I object to its general intellectuality as not individual enough. Intellectually the older generation seems to me to lead far too vegetative a life. It may be that this life has been lived on the heights, that these souls have passed through fires and glories, but there is generally too little objective evidence of this subjective fact. If the intuition which accompanies experience has verified all the data regarding

God, the soul, the family, and so forth — to quote one of the staunchest defenders of the generation — this verification seems to have been obtained rather that the issues might be promptly disposed of and forgotten. Certainly the older generation is rarely interested in the profounder issues of life. It never speaks of death — the suggestion makes it uncomfortable. It shies in panic at hints of sex-issues. It seems resolute to keep life on as objective a plane as possible. It is no longer curious about the motives and feelings of people. It seems singularly to lack the psychological sense. If it gossips, it recounts actions, effects; it rarely seeks to interpret. It tends more and more to treat human beings as moving masses of matter instead of as personalities filled with potent influence, or as absorbingly interesting social types, as I am sure the younger generation does.

The older generation seems no longer to generalize, although it gives every evidence of having once prodigiously generalized, for its world is all hardened and definite. There are the good and the criminal, and the poor, the people who can be called nice, and the ordinary people. The world is already plotted out. Now I am sure that the generalizations of the truly philosophical mind are very fluid and ephemeral. They are no sooner made than the mind sees their insufficiency and has to break them up. A new cutting is made, only in turn to be shaken and rearranged. This keeps the philosopher thinking all the time, and it makes his world a very uncertain place. But he at least runs no risk of hardening, and he has his eyes open to most experience.

I am often impressed with the fact that the older generation has grown weary of thinking. It has simply put up the bars in its intellectual shop-windows and gone off home to rest. It may well be that this is because it has felt so much sorrow that it does not want to talk about sorrow, or so much love that to interpret love tires it, or repulsed so many rude blows of destiny that it has no interest in speaking of destiny. Its flame may be low for the very reason that it has burned so intensely. But how many of the younger generation would eagerly long for such interpretations if the older would only reveal them! And how little plausible is that experience when it is occasionally interpreted! No, enthusiasm, passion for ideas, sensuality, religious fervor — all the heated weapons with which the younger generation attacks the world, seem only to make the older generation uneasy. The spirit, in becoming reconciled to life, has lost life itself.

As I see the older generation going through its daily round of business, church, and family life, I cannot help feeling that its influence is profoundly pernicious. It has signally failed to broaden its institutions for the larger horizon of the time. The church remains a private club of comfortable middle-class families, while outside there grows up without spiritual inspiration a heterogeneous mass of people without ties, roots, or principles. The town changes from a village to an industrial center, and church and school go through their time-honored and listless motions. The world widens, society expands, formidable crises appear, but the older generation does not broaden, or if it does, the broadening is in no adequate proportion to our needs. The older generation still uses the old ideas for the new problem. Whatever new wine it finds must be poured into the old bottles.

Where are the leaders among the older generation in

America who, with luminous faith and intelligence, are rallying around them the disintegrated numbers of idealistic youth, as Bergson and Barrès and Jaurès have done in France? A few years ago there seemed to be a promise of a forward movement toward Democracy, led by embattled veterans in a war against privilege. But how soon the older generation became wearied in the march! What is left now of that shining army and its leader? Must the younger generation eternally wait for the sign?

The answer is, of course, that it will not wait. It must shoulder the gigantic task of putting into practice its ideals and revolutionary points of view as wholeheartedly and successfully as our great-grandfathers applied theirs and tightened the philosophy of life which imprisons the older generation. The shuddering fear that we in turn may become weary, complacent, evasive, should be the best preventive of that stagnation. We shall never have done looking for the miracle, that it shall be given us to lighten, cheer, and purify our "younger generation," even as our older has depressed and disintegrated us.

THE SARGASSO SEA[1]

VAN WYCK BROOKS

I

"THE fiddles are tuning as it were all over America."
This is a remark of the best, the youngest, and the most
Irish of all good Americans, Mr. J. B. Yeats. It is true
that under the glassy, brassy surface of American jocosity
and business there is a pulp and a quick, and this pulpy
quick, this nervous and acutely self-critical vitality, is in
our day in a strange ferment. A fresh and more sensitive
emotion seems to be running up and down even the old
Yankee backbone — that unblossoming stalk.

I am speaking myself as a thoroughgoing Yankee to
other thoroughgoing Yankees — as a "little American"
(to adopt a phrase which, as time goes on, will prove
more and more useful). For to find this ferment in the
immigrant folk of one, two, or three generations is in itself
only natural and the effect of a more vivid, instinctive,
and vital civilization in their own past. The importation
of radical ideas and the ferment of radical ideas which
have been imported scarcely touch, it seems to me, the
centre of the American problem. So far as we are concerned, the sea-crossing, to begin with, has a very damp-
ening effect on the gunpowder contained in them. Trans-
planted they have at once the pleasing remoteness of literature and the stir of an only half-apprehended actual-

[1] From *America's Coming-of-Age*, by Van Wyck Brooks. New York:
The Viking Press. Copyright, 1915, by B. W. Huebsch, Inc. By permission.

ity; they become admirably safe, they become even delightful. In the American mind Nietzsche and A. C.
Benson — the lion and the lamb — lie down quite peacefully together, chewing the cud of culture. To get civilization out of the Yankee stock — *ex forte dulcitudo* — is
the more arduous and the more inspiriting enterprise. Is
it possible? Is it in process? The signs are anything but
obvious: one has to keep quite still and hold one's ear
close to the ground to hear the sap stirring and the little
half-inconsequential voices that whisper and breathe in
the intervals of bombast and business. For there is nothing so shy and so puzzled as the fine Puritan temperament face to face with a free world.

If something vibrates in the air it is without doubt the
expectation of a social ideal that shall act upon us as the
sun acts upon a photographic plate, that shall work as a
magnet upon all these energies which are on the point of
being released. But the formulation of a social ideal can
only be the work of a wiser head and a riper heart than
we have yet seen; and we have had, meanwhile, quite
enough of the egoism which, with foolish head and unripe
heart, has undertaken this intoxicating function.

If it is for the State to weed out the incentives to private
gain, it is for us meanwhile simultaneously to build up
other incentives to replace them. These incentives must
be personal. They must not spring from floating, evanescent ideals, political, spiritualistic, or other; they must
touch the primitive instincts which are touched by the
incentives they replace. Emerson gave us the Over-
Soul; Catholicism gave us the Madonna and the Bambino;
— which has really touched the religious sense of mankind?

II

America is like a vast Sargasso Sea — a prodigious welter of unconscious life, swept by ground-swells of half-conscious emotion. All manner of living things are drifting in it, phosphorescent, gayly colored, gathered into knots and clotted masses, gelatinous, unformed, flimsy, tangled, rising and falling, floating and merging, here an immense distended belly, there a tiny rudimentary brain (the gross devouring the fine) — everywhere an unchecked, uncharted, unorganized vitality like that of the first chaos. It is a welter of life which has not been worked into an organism, into which fruitful values and standards of humane economy have not been introduced, innocent of those laws of social gravitation which, rightly understood and pursued with a keen faith, produce a fine temper in the human animal.

Now as everybody knows there was a time when the actual Sargasso Seas were, to the consciousness of science, just in this uncharted state. The creatures they contain, instead of being studied with reference to an organic unity of which they were all modifications, were divided into certain fixed subkingdoms according as they superficially resembled one another; here a group with soft bodies, there a group whose organs were disposed about a centre, and the like. It was, I think, Huxley who first exposed the superficiality of this method and who began the grouping of creatures according to real identity in structure.

American society, so to speak, is in this pre-Darwinian state. It is filled with "groups" which have long ceased to mean anything, which do not stand for living issues, which do not engage personal energies. A Democrat is no more a genuine type than one of the pre-Darwinian Mollusca, so called because they had soft bodies; a Republican is no more a genuine type than the Radiata, so called because their organs were disposed about a centre. The superficial characteristics of the types remain — that is to say, Democrats generally *have* soft bodies, and Republicans *do* believe in centralization — but the fruitful elements of a group have departed from them: they no longer touch personal instincts, they no longer possess the life which impels to personal action.

The recognized divisions of opinion, the recognized issues, the recognized causes in American society are extinct. And although Patriotism, Democracy, the Future, Liberty are still the undefined, unexamined, unapplied catchwords over which the generality of our public men dilate, enlarge themselves, and float (careful thought and intellectual contact still remaining on the level of engineering, finance, advertising, and trade) — while this remains true, every one feels that the issues represented by them are no longer genuine or adequate.

The most striking American spectacle to-day is a fumbling about after new issues which no one as yet has been able to throw into relief. We have seen one President advocating a "New Nationalism," another President advocating a "New Freedom," a well-known novelist talking about a "New Patriotism" — phrases which illustrate just this vague fumbling, this acute consciousness of the inadequacy of the habitual issues, this total inability to divine and formulate new issues that really are issues. With us the recognized way of pinning down something that is felt to be in the air is to adopt some cast-off phrase and tack the word "New" before it. A pleasant thrill then runs over the country, something which is vaguely felt to be new having been recognized and labeled as new, and the issue itself is quietly smothered (or springs forth divinely haloed as a Currency Bill).

The truth is that it signifies nothing for politicians to import social issues into the plane of politics, even if they import the whole of socialism into politics, so long as they and we fail to recognize that the centre of gravity in American affairs has shifted wholly from the plane of politics to the plane of psychology and morals. So long as we fail to recognize this, politics can only continue the old endless unfruitful seesaw of corruption and reform. That is why catchwords like the "New Nationalism" and the "New Freedom" are really so much farther from the centre of gravity than catchwords like "Highbrow" and "Lowbrow," or "Bromide" and "Sulphite." The latter lead nowhither, but they at least explain things. "Are you a Bromide?" may be a silly vulgar question, but it is by no means a silly vulgar fact that a whole population should go about putting that question. It is a fact that grows in meaning when you consider that not so much as a remnant of the American people can go about *thinking* any question that stands for a social and psychological issue which cuts deeper than that.

It is pathetic, it is very nearly tragic. How much hunger is represented by all these "New" things which give the American public such a quantity of gaseated water to stay their appetites? How much of a real psychological curiosity miscarries at the outset in questions like "Are you a Bromide?" American slang in general, alive with psychological interest in a rudimentary state, is the most mournful tribute to a vitality in the American people, missing fire in a million trivialities, because it has not been engaged by issues which really touch home in the personality, because — to put it the other way round — the catchwords of American society are not themselves personal.

For it may as well be understood that the human race will have catchwords and will not budge without them. Consequently it makes all the difference to a people and an age whether its catchwords really do or do not correspond with convictions, and whether these convictions really do or do not reach down among the real problems of personal and social life — whether they really *catch* at the bottom of things, like a dredging-machine, or whether they merely scrape along the bottom or stir up the water or ruffle the surface. "Home Rule," "No Taxation without Representation," the "Right of Private Judgment," the "Three Unities," are catchwords which have played an immense part in the world of thought and action, because they have stood for genuine causes, genuine issues in religion, in politics, in art. The rank and file who grasp the idea behind them incompletely and in varying degrees and who, if they depended on their understanding of the idea, would be at sixes and sevens, grasp the catchword and unite on a common platform which, if the catchword is a worthy one, educates them through action. Every leader will have his catchword: his philosophy will be a "Synthetic" philosophy, his ideal will be the "Superman," his *bête noire* will be the "Servile" state, and the generality of men will fall in line according to whether the connotations of these catchwords do or do not strike home to their own personal preferences. For generations the test of a living society, a living philosophy or art, will be whether or not the catchwords it flings forth really correspond with profound divisions of type, deeply felt issues, genuine convictions, in whichever field, between — I was going to say — some good and some evil. But these words are so unfashionable that if I use them I shall certainly alienate any Advanced Person who honors these pages with a glance.

But it makes no difference how many games of pea-and-thimble philosophy may play, wherever the thimble is put down the problem of good and evil is the pea that lies under it; and the happiest excitement in life is to be convinced that one is fighting for all one is worth on behalf of some clearly seen and deeply felt good and against some greatly scorned evil. To quicken and exhilarate the life of one's own people — as Heine and Nietzsche did in Germany, as Matthew Arnold, William Morris, and H. G. Wells have done in England — is to bring, not peace, but a sword. With Heine the warfare was between philistinism and enlightenment, with Nietzsche between master-morality and slave-morality, with Matthew Arnold between Hebraism and Hellenism, with Morris between machinery and handicraft, with Wells between muddle-headedness and fine thinking. There are five distinct conceptions of good and five distinct conceptions of evil. And each of these pairs of opposed catchwords stands for a conceivable interpretation of society, a cleavage in things like the cleavage of the Red Sea. Accept them or not as you choose, they go down so deep that you can walk with dry feet between them.

To this happy excitement of urgent issues is due the happy excitement of European thought, the muscular and earthy sense of opposition under which personality becomes aware of itself and grows with a certain richness. I do not know how much dull pain, poverty, and chagrin are responsible for these manifestations of high pressure: but certainly it is a pressure of this kind which forces the European to define his position, to form his own micro-cosm, and by virtue of which the catchwords that cor-respond with issues defined really represent something and are apt, relatively speaking, to cut deep. And certain it is that while European literature grows ever closer and denser and grapples to life more and more, American literature grows only windier and windier. You will find in H. G. Wells, for example, what seems at times as ir-responsible a mysticism as that of any American. But while the American tendency is to begin in the air and re-main in the air, you will scarcely find a European thinker who has not earned his right to fly by serving an appren-ticeship with both feet on the ground; — if he leaves the earth it is because he has been pressed from it and he carries flesh and blood and clods of earth with him. You cannot have too much mysticism; but on the other hand you cannot have enough good human mud for ballast. The pressure which actuates the European mind is due no doubt to a vast deal of dull pain, poverty, and chagrin. But are we Americans very much happier? In America, I think, pain, poverty, and chagrin are at last very nearly as imminent as elsewhere, and so far we have devised no compensation for them.

Self-fulfillment is the immemorial compensation for having eaten of the fruit of good and evil, and under the conditions of modern life self-fulfillment has to be a some-what artificial thing. In a world of instincts blunted by trade, system, and machinery, the sweat of the brow, the resurgence of the seasons, the charm of perfect color and of pure form are not for the generality of men sufficient. The exhilarating sense of conflict and of rest from conflict which together make up the meaning of life, no longer universally possible on the plane of instinct, have largely come to exist in the more contagious, the more gregarious, the more interdependent world of the intelligence. In that world the majority are lost and astray unless the tune has been set for them, the key given them, the lever and the fulcrum put before them, the spring of their own personalities touched from the outside.

In the midst of the machine age, as everybody knows, it was the contagious personality of William Morris which opposed the ideal of craftsmanship to the ideal of cheapest work and largest money and substituted for the inhumane stimulus of competition the humane stimulus of fellowship. No doubt this was only a drop in the bucket. But, speaking relatively, picture to yourself what might have been the inner mind even of the average artisan — to adopt the method of patent-medicine advertising — Before and After the William Morris treatment. One contagious personality, one clear shadowing forth of opposed issues — a good and an evil, a humane and an inhumane — touched the spring of personality in how many workingmen! and gave them how rich and how adequate a reason to turn over this world of ours, as a spade turns over a clod of earth. It is of no use to talk about Reform. Society will be very obedient when the myriad personalities that compose it have, and are aware that they have, an object in living.

How can one speak of progress in a people like our own that so sends up to heaven the stench of atrophied personality? How can one speak of progress in a people whose main object is to climb, peg by peg, up a ladder which leads to the impersonal ideal of private wealth? How can the workingman have any reality or honesty of outlook when he regards his class merely as an accidental, temporary group of potential capitalists? And the university man — the man, that is to say, who has had the fullest opportunity to seek and find a disinterested end in living, an end to which the machinery of self-preservation however compelling remains yet in subservience — the man who has within him a world of ineffectual dreams and impotent ideals — what has he to actuate him but a confused and moralized instinct that somehow he must make a lot of money?

It is not a question of blame. You cannot blame the individual, even as a citizen, though as a citizen he overtly upholds the conception of society which is responsible for his helplessness as an individual. His personality, his latent energies go to waste just as the personalities of so many artisans would have gone to waste if there had been no William Morris. The way has not been made straight for him, the waters of the sea of good and evil have not been divided for him; he flounders in the mud and the waves, until at last, if he is exceptionally fortunate, he drowns in a million dollars. It is the economic individualist himself who blames people; socialism has the charity of science.

III

Issues which really make the life of a society do not spring spontaneously out of the mass. They exist in it — a thousand potential currents and cross-currents; but they have to be discovered like principles of science, they have almost to be created like works of art. A people is like a ciphered parchment which has to be held up to the fire before its hidden significances come out. Once the divisions that have ripened in a people have been discerned and articulated, its beliefs and convictions are brought into play, the real evils that have been vaguely surmised spring into the light, the real strength of what is intelligent and sound becomes a measureable entity. To cleanse politics is of the least importance if the real forces of the people cannot be engaged in politics; and they cannot be so engaged while the issues behind politics remain inarticulate.

In spite of their frequent show of strength and boldness no ideas in America are really strong or bold — not because the talents are wanting but because the talents and the mass have not been brought into conflict. No serious attempt has been made to bring about the necessary contraposition of forces, to divine them, to detach them, to throw them into relief; the real goats and the real sheep have not been set apart. There has not in fact been one thinker strong enough to create a resisting background in the vague element of American life.

To create this resisting background must be the first work for our thinkers. It is incomparably difficult, for it is like standing on clouds and attempting to gain purchase for a lever. The vast, vague movements of sentiment in the democracy directly produce the conventionality of our ideas, for there is no clinch in things, nothing to brace the feet against, no substance against which ideas can assume a bold relief. "To preserve the freedom of the will in such expansion," says Victor Hugo (who had reason to know), "is to be great"; and certainly the man who can throw American life into relief will be a man out of ninety million.

But how shall we know him when he comes? — we who have invented the phrase "any old thing," we whose watchword has always been "just about as good," we who delight in plausible mediocrity and are always ready with tinkling cymbals to greet the sounding brass? To leave behind the old Yankee self-assertion and self-sufficiency, to work together, think together, feel together, to believe so fervently in the quality of standards that we delight in prostrating our work and our thoughts before them — all that is certainly in the right direction. "My belief becomes indefinitely more certain to me as soon as another shares it" is the true catholic observation of a German poet, which all good Americans ought to ponder; for intimate feeling, intimate intellectual contact, even humor — that rich, warm, robust and all-dissolving geniality which never, I think, quite reached the heart of Mark Twain — it is these we chiefly lack. These are the enemies of that base privateness which holds the string of what we call publicity; these promote that right, free, disinterested publicity which the real gentleman, the real craftsman, the real civil servant has always had in his blood.

Socialism flows from this as light flows from the sun. And socialism is based on those three things in the world which, of all things, have the most dignity — hunger, science, and good will. Is it "against human nature"? The foolish socialist laughs in his sleeve when he hears this, convinced as he is that human nature is the sport of circumstance and that when the time is right human nature will fall in line as the trees fall in line through the process of the seasons. Only the foolish socialist stops there. To be a sheer determinist is in all probability to have behind one the authority of the intellect. But human nature is an elusive magical thing which has the faculty of submitting its intellect to all manner of sea-changes. Determinism, which at one moment appears to enslave man, may at the next become the slave of man. There is a free will within determinism by which, as it were, men can cheat nature, convincing themselves — and with a whole heart — that what nature wills is what they will: and if they will it enough, which is master of the situation? We Americans ought to know, for we have produced one of the greatest of determinists, and one of the greatest of all transmuters of determinism:

My foot is tenoned and mortised in granite,
I laugh at what you call dissolution,
And I know the amplitude of time.

All forces have been steadily employed to complete
and delight me;
Now on this spot I stand with my robust soul.

IV

All Americans are good — this to me is an axiom; but we are good as the Germans used to be a hundred years ago, as good, that is, as bread which is baked without yeast. We are good and we are humble. We have so schooled ourselves in humility that nobody in the world more carefully, more steadily (and more unjustly) takes down our pretensions than the educated American. In the end it may be our humility that saves us. But the

acquisition of culture and the acquisition of money —
"Highbrow" and "Lowbrow" — are equally impersonal,
equally extraneous to the real matter, equally incapable
of arousing the one thing needful. When the women of
America have gathered together all the culture in the
world and the men have collected all the money there is —
who knows? — perhaps the dry old Yankee stalk will
begin to stir and send forth shoots and burst into a storm
of blossoms. Strange things happen. I have heard of
seeds which, either planted too deep or covered with ac-
cretions of rubble, have kept themselves alive for generations until by chance they have been turned up once more
to the friendly sun. And after all humanity is older than
Puritanism.

LIFE, THE COPY CAT[1]

HEYWOOD BROUN

EVERY evening when dusk comes in the Far West, little groups of men may be observed leaving the various ranch houses and setting out on horseback for the moving-picture shows. They are cowboys and they are intent on seeing Bill Hart in Western stuff. They want to be taken out of the dull and dreary routine of the world in which they live.

But somehow or other the films simply cannot get very far away from life, no matter how hard or how fantastically they try. As we have suggested, the cowboy who struts across the screen has no counterpart in real life, but imitation is sure to bridge the gap. Young men from the cattle country, after much gazing at Hart, will begin to be like him. The styles which the cowboys are to wear next year will be dictated this fall in Hollywood.

It has generally been recognized that life has a trick of taking color from literature. Once there were no flappers and then F. Scott Fitzgerald wrote *This Side of Paradise* and created them in shoals. Germany had a fearful time after the publication of Goethe's *Werther*, because striplings began to contract the habit of suicide through the influence of the book and went about dying all over the place. And all Scandinavia echoed with slamming doors for years just because Ibsen sent Nora

[1] From *Pieces of Hate*, by Heywood Broun. Copyright, 1922, George H. Doran Company, publishers.

out into the night. In fact the lock on that door has never worked very well since. When *Uncle Tom's Cabin* was written, things came to such a pass that a bloodhound couldn't see a cake of ice without jumping on it and beginning to bay.

If authors and dramatists can do so much with their limited public, think of the potential power of the maker of films, who has his tens of thousands to every single serf of the writing man. The films can make us a new people and we rather think they are doing it. Fifteen years ago Americans were contemptuous of all Latin races because of their habit of talking with gestures. It was considered the part of patriotic dignity to stand with your hands in your pockets and to leave all expression, if any, to the voice alone.

Watch an excited American to-day and you will find his gestures as sweeping as those of any Frenchman. As soon as he is jarred in the slightest degree out of calm, he immediately begins to follow subconscious promptings and behave like his favorite motion-picture actor. Nor does the resemblance end necessarily with mere externals. Hiram Johnson, the Senator from California, is reported to be the most inveterate movie fan in America, and it is said that he never takes action on a public question without first asking himself, "What would Mary Pickford do under similar circumstances?" In other words, the Senator's position on the proposal to increase the import tax on nitrates may be traced directly to the fact that he spent the previous evening watching *Little Lord Fauntleroy*.

Even the speaking actors, most contemptuous of all motion-picture critics, are slaves of the screen. At an audible drama in a theater the other day we happened to see a young actor who had once given high promise of achievement in what was then known as the legitimate. Eventually he went into motion pictures, but now he was back for a short engagement. We were shocked to observe that he tried to express every line he uttered with his features and his hands regardless of the fact that he had words to help him. He spoke the lines, but they seemed to him merely incidental. We mean that when his part required him to say, "It is exactly nineteen minutes after two," he tried to do it by gestures and facial expression. This is a difficult feat, particularly as most young players run a little fast or a little slow and are rather in need of regulating. When the young man left the theater at the close of the performance, we sought him out and reproached him bitterly on the ground of his bad acting.

"Where do you get that stuff?" we asked.

"In the movies," he admitted frankly enough.

There was no dispute concerning facts. We merely could not agree on the question of whether or not it was true that he had become a terrible actor. Life came into the conversation. Something was said by somebody (we can't remember which one of us originated it) about holding the mirror up to nature. The actor maintained that everyday common folk talked and acted exactly like characters in the movies whenever they were stirred by emotion. We made a bet and it was to be decided by what we observed in an hour's walk. At the southwest corner of Thirty-Seventh Street and Third Avenue, we came upon two men in an altercation. One had already laid a menacing hand upon the coat collar of the other.

We crowded close. The smaller man tried to shake himself loose from the grip of his adversary. And he said, "Unhand me." He had met the movies and he was theirs.

The discrepancy in size between the two men was so great that my actor friend stepped between them and asked, "What's all this row about?" The big man answered: "He has spoken lightly of a woman's name."

That was enough for us. We paid the bet and went away convinced of the truth of the actor's boast that the movies have already bent life to their will. At first it seemed to us deplorable, but the longer we reflected on the matter the more compensations crept in.

Somehow or other we remembered a tale of Kipling's called *The Finest Story in the World*, which dealt with a narrow-chested English clerk, who, by some freak or other, remembered his past existences. There were times when he could tell with extraordinary vividness his adventures on a Roman galley and later on an expedition of the Norsemen to America. He told all these things to a writer who was going to put them into a book, but before much material had been supplied the clerk fell in love with a girl in a tobacconist's and suddenly forgot all his previous existences. Kipling explained that the lords of life and death simply had to step in and close the doors of the past as soon as the young man fell in love because love-making was once so much more glorious than now that we would all be single if only we remembered.

But love-making is likely to have its renaissance from now on since the movies have come into our lives. Douglas Fairbanks is in a sense the rival of every young man in America. And likewise no young woman can hope to touch the fancy of a male unless she is in some ways more fetching than Mary Pickford. In other words, pace has been provided for lovers. For ten cents we can watch courtship being conducted by experts. The young man who has been to the movies will be unable to avail himself of the traditional ineptitude under such circumstances. Once upon a time the manly thing to do was mumble and make a botch of it. The movies have changed all that. Courtship will come to have a technique. A young man will no more think of trying to propose without knowing how than he would attempt a violin concert without ever having practiced. The phantom rivals of the screen will be all about him. He must win to himself something of their fire and gesture. Love-making is not going to be as easy as it once was. Those who have already wed before the competition grew so acute should consider themselves fortunate. Consider for instance the swain who loves a lady who has been brought up on the picture plays of Bill Hart. That young man who hopes to supplant the shadow idol will have to be able to shoot Indians at all ranges from four hundred yards up, and to ride one hundred thousand miles without once forgetting to keep his face to the camera.

THE AMERICAN TRADITION [1]

HENRY SEIDEL CANBY

I REMEMBER a talk in Dublin with an Irish writer whose English prose has adorned our period. It was 1918, and the eve of forced conscription, and his indignation with English policy was intense. "I will give up their language," he said, "all except Shakespeare. I will write only Gaelic." Unfortunately, he could read Gaelic much better than he could write it. In his heart, indeed, he knew how mad he would have been to give up the only literary tradition which, thanks to language, could be his own; and in a calmer mood since he has enriched that tradition with admirable translations from the Irish. He was suffering from a mild case of Anglomania.

Who is the real Anglomaniac in America? Not the now sufficiently discredited individual with a monocle and a pseudo-Oxford accent, who tries to be more English than the English. Not the more subtly dangerous American who refers his tastes, his enthusiasms, his culture, and the prestige of his compatriots to an English test before he dare assert them. The real Anglomaniac is the American who tries to be less English than his own American tradition. He is the man who is obsessed with the fear of "Anglo-Saxon domination."

How many Anglomaniacs by this definition are at large in America each reader may judge for himself. Person-

[1] From *Definitions: First Series*, by Henry S. Canby. Copyright, 1922, by Harcourt, Brace and Company, Inc. By permission.

ally, I find them extraordinarily numerous, and of so
many varieties, from the mere borrower of opinions to
the deeply convinced zealot, that it seems wiser to
analyze Anglomania than to discuss the various types
that possess it. And in this analysis let us exclude from
the beginning such very real, but temporary, grievances
against the English as spring from Irish oppressions,
trade rivalries, or the provocations which always arise
between allies in war. All such causes of anti-English
and anti-"Anglo-Saxon" sentiment belong in a different
category from the underlying motives which I propose to
discuss.

These new Anglomaniacs, with their talk of Anglo-
Saxon domination, cannot mean English domination.
That would be absurd, although even absurdities are current coin in restless years like these. At least one Irishman of my acquaintance *knows* that King George cabled
Wilson to bring America into the war, and that until that
cable came Wilson dared not act. I can conceive of an
English influence upon literature that is worth attacking,
and also worth defending. I can conceive of a far less
important English influence upon our social customs.
But in neither case, domination. That England domi-
nates our finance, our industry, our politics, is just now,
especially, the suspicion of a paranoiac, or the idea of an
ignoramus.

"Anglo-Saxon domination," even in an anti-British
meeting, cannot and does not mean English domination;
it can mean only control of America by the so-called
"Anglo-Saxon" element in our population. The quarrel
is local, not international. The "Anglo-Saxon" three
thousand miles away who cannot hit back is a scapegoat,

a whipping boy for the so-called "Anglo-Saxon" American at home.

What is an "Anglo-Saxon" American? Presumably he is the person familiar in "want" advertisements: "American family wants boarder for the summer. References exchanged." But this does not help us much. He is certainly not English. Nothing is better established than the admixture of bloods since the earliest days of our nationality. That I, myself, for example, have ancestral portions of French, German, Welsh, and Scotch, as well as English blood in my veins, makes me, by any historical test, characteristically more rather than less American. Race, indeed, within very broad limits, is utterly different from nationality, and it is usually many, many centuries before the two become even approximately identical. The culture I have inherited, the political ideals I live by, the literature which is my own, most of all the language that I speak, are far more important than the ultimate race or races I stem from, obviously more important, since in thousands of good Americans it is impossible to determine what races have gone to their making. There is no such thing as an "Anglo-Saxon" American — and so few English Americans that they are nationally insignificant.

An American with a strong national individuality there certainly is, and it is true that his traditions, irrespective of the race of his forbears, are mainly English; from England he drew his political and social habits, his moral ideas, his literature, and his language. This does not make him a "slave to England," as our most recent propagandists would have it; it does not put him in England's debt. We owe no debt to England. Great

Britain, Canada, Australia, New Zealand, South Africa, and ourselves are deeply in debt to our intellectual, our spiritual, our æsthetic ancestors who were the moulders of English history and English thought, the interpreters of English emotion, the masters of the developing English *mores* that became our *mores*, and have since continued evolution with a difference. Chaucer, Shakespeare, Spenser, and Milton, Wycliffe, Bunyan, Fox, and Wesley, Elizabeth, Cromwell, and the great Whigs, these made the only tradition that can be called Anglo-Saxon, and if we have an American tradition, as we assuredly have, here are its roots. This is our "Anglo-Saxon domination."

But if the roots of this tradition are English, its trunk is thoroughly American, seasoned and developed through two centuries of specifically American history. As we know it to-day it is no longer "Anglo-Saxon," it is as American as our cities, our soil, our accent upon English. If we are going to discuss "domination" let us be accurate and speak of the domination of American tradition. It is against the American tradition that the new Anglomaniac actually protests.

Dominating this American tradition is, dominating, almost tyrannical, for one reason only, but that a strong one, a fact not a convention, a factor, not a mere influence — dominating because of the English language.

In our century language has become once again as powerful as in the Roman Empire — and its effects, thanks to printing and easy transportation, are far more quickly attained. Hordes from all over Europe have swarmed into the domain of English. They have come to a country where the new language was indispensable. They have learned it, or their children have learned it.

English has become their means of communication with their neighbors, with business, with the State. Sooner or later even the news of Europe has come to them through English, and sometimes unwillingly, but more often unconsciously, they have come under the American, the real "Anglo-Saxon" domination.

For a language, of course, is more than words. It is a body of literature, it is a method of thinking, it is a definition of emotions, it is the exponent and the symbol of a civilization. You cannot adopt English without adapting yourself in some measure to the English, or the Anglo-American tradition. You cannot adopt English political words, English literary words, English religious words, the terms of sport or ethics, without in some measure remaking your mind on a new model. If you fail or refuse, your child will not. He is forcibly made an American, in ideas at least, and chiefly by language.

I submit that it is impossible for an alien *thoroughly* to absorb and understand Lincoln's *Gettysburg Speech* or Hawthorne's *Scarlet Letter* without working a slight but perceptible transformation in the brain, without making himself an heir of a measure of English tradition. And the impact of English as a spoken tongue, and the influence of its literature as the only read literature, are great beyond ordinary conception. Communities where a foreign language is read or spoken only delay the process, they cannot stop it.

The foreigner, it is true, has modified the English language precisely as he has modified the American tradition. Continental Europe is audible in the American tongue, as it is evident in the American mind; but it is like the English or the Spanish touch upon the Gothic style in architecture — there is modification, but not fundamental change.

Many a foreign-born American has been restless under this domination. The letters and memoirs of the French immigrants from revolutionary France express discomfort freely. The Germans of '48, themselves the bearers of a high civilization, have often confessed an unwilling assimilation. The Germans of earlier migrations herded apart like the later Scandinavians, in part to avoid the tyranny of tongue.

Imagine a German coming here in early manhood. His tradition is not English; he owes nothing to a contemporary England that he but dimly knows. Speaking English, perhaps only English, he grows impatient with a tongue every concept of which has an English coloring. The dominance of the language, and especially of its literature, irks him. He no longer wants to think as a German; he wants to think as an American; but the medium of his thought must be English. His anger often enough goes out against English history, English literature. He is easily irritated by England. But it is the American past that binds and is converting him. Such consciousness of the power of environment is perhaps rare, but the fact is common. In our few centuries of history millions have been broken into English, with all that implies. Millions have experienced the inevitable discomfort of a foreign tradition which makes alien their fatherlands, and strangers of their children. This is an "Anglo-Saxon" domination. But it is useless to struggle against it.

There is a similar discomfort among certain American authors, especially just now, when, for the first time since the Civil War and the materialism that succeeded it, we are finding our national self once again in literature. Mr. Mencken and Mr. Dreiser have vigorously expressed this annoyance with American tradition. They wish to break with it — at least Mr. Dreiser does — break with it morally, spiritually, æsthetically. Let the dotards, he says, bury their dead.

Mr. Mencken wishes to drive us out of Colonialism. He says that Longfellow has had his day, and that it is time to stop imitating Addison, time to be ashamed of aping Stevenson, Kipling, or John Masefield. He is right.

But when it comes to disowning English literature and the past of American literature (as many a writer directly or by implication would have us) in order to become one hundred per cent American, let us first take breath long enough to reflect that, first, such a madcap career is eminently undesirable, and, second, utterly impossible. It is a literature which by general admission is now the richest and most liberal in the world of living speech. English is a tongue less sonorous than Italian, less fine than French, less homely than German, but more expressive, more flexible, than these and all others. Its syntax imposes no burdens, its traditions are weighty only upon the vulgar and the bizarre. Without its literary history, American literature in general, and usually in particular, is not to be understood. That we have sprung from a Puritanical loin, and been nourished in the past from the breast of Victorianism, is obvious. In this we have been not too much, but too narrowly, English. We have read Tennyson when it might have been better to have read Shakespeare or Chaucer. But to wish to break with English literature in order to become altogether American is like desiring to invent an entirely new kind of clothes. I shall not give up trousers because my fourth great-grandfather, who was a Yorkshireman, wore them, and his pattern no longer fits my different contour. I shall make me a pair better suiting my own shanks — yet they shall still be trousers. But in any case, language binds us.

Indeed, in this welter of newcomers here in America, whose children learn, read, write only English, the tradition of Anglo-American literature is all that holds us by a thread above chaos. If we could all be made to speak German, or Italian, or Spanish, there would be cause, but no excuse, for an attempted revolution. But English is dominant here and will remain so. Could we hope to make an American literary language without dependence on English literature, a protective tariff on home-made writing, or an embargo against books more than a year old, or imported from across the Atlantic, would be worth trying; but the attempts so far are not encouraging. This has not been the way in the past by which original literatures have been made. They have sucked nourishment where it could best be found, and grown great from the strength that good food gave them.

One can sympathize with the desire to nationalize our literature at all costs; and can understand lashings out at the tyranny of literary prestige which England still exercises. But the real question is: shall the English of Americans be good English or bad English; shall a good tradition safeguard change and experiment, or shall we have chaotic vulgarity like the Low Latin of the late Roman Empire?

The truth is that our language *is* tradition, for it holds tradition in solution like iron in wine. And here lie the secret and the power of American, "Anglo-Saxon" domination.

What is to be done about it? Shall anything be done about it? The Anglomaniac is helpless before the fact of language. The most he can do is to attack, and uproot if he can, the American tradition.

There is nothing sacrosanct in this American tradition. Like all traditions it is stiff, it will clasp, if we allow it, the future in the dead hand of precedent. It can be used by the designing to block progress. But as traditions go it is not conservative. Radicalism, indeed, is its child. Political and religious radicalism brought the Pilgrims to New England, the Quakers to Pennsylvania; political and economic radicalism made the Revolution against the will of American conservatives; political and social radicalism made the Civil War inevitable and gave it moral earnestness. Radicalism, whether you like it or not, is much more American than what some people mean by "Americanism" to-day. And its bitterest opponents in our times would quite certainly have become Nova Scotian exiles if they had been alive and likeminded in 1783.

Nor is this American tradition impeccable in the political ideas, the literary ideals, the social customs it has given us. We must admit a rampant individualism in our political practices which is in the very best Anglo-American tradition, and yet by no means favorable to coöperative government. We admit also more Puritanism in our standard literature than art can well digest; and more sentiment than is good for us; nor is it probable that the traditions and the conventions which govern American family life are superior to their European equivalents. We should welcome (I do not say that we do) liberalizing, broadening, enriching influences from other traditions. And whether we have welcomed them or not, they have come, and to our great benefit. But to graft upon the plant is different from trying to pull up the roots.

We want better arguments than the fear of "Anglo-Saxon" domination before the root-pulling begins. We wish to know what is to be planted. We desire to be convinced that the virtue has gone out of the old stock. We want examples of civilized nations that have profited by borrowing traditions wholesale, or by inventing them. We wish to know if a cultural, a literary *sans-culottism* is possible, except with chaos as a goal. Most of all, we expect to fight for and to hold our Anglo-American heritage.

It is not surprising that discontent with our own ultimately English tradition has expressed itself by a kind of Freudian transformation in anti-English sentiment. Every vigorous nation strains and struggles with its tradition, like a growing boy with his clothes, and this is particularly true of new nations with old traditions behind them. Our pains are growing pains — a malady we have suffered from since the early eighteenth century at the latest. Tradition, our own tradition, pinches us; but you cannot punch tradition for pinching you, or call it names to its face, especially if it proves to be your father's tradition, or your next-door neighbor's. Therefore, since that now dim day when the Colonies acquired a self-consciousness of their own, many good Americans have chosen England and the English to symbolize whatever irked them in their own tradition. It is from England and the English that we have felt ourselves growing away, from which we had to grow away in order to be ourselves and not a shadow — imitators, second-bests, Colonials. England and the English have had our vituperation whenever the need to be American has been greatest. And when an English government like Palmerston's, or Salisbury's, or Lloyd George's, offends some group or race among us, a lurking need to assert our individuality, or prove that we are not Colonials, leads thousands more to join in giving the lion's tail an extra twist.

This may be unfortunate, but it argues curiously enough respect and affection rather than the reverse, and it is very human. It is a fact, like growing, and is likely to continue until we are fully grown. It will reassert itself vehemently until upon our English tradition we shall have built an American civilization as definitely crystallized, a literature as rich and self-sufficing, as that of France and England to-day. Three quarters of our national genius went into the creating of our political system. Three quarters of our national genius since has gone into the erecting of our economic system. Here we are independent — and thick skinned. But a national civilization and a national literature take more time to complete.

Cool minds were prepared for a little tail-twisting after the Great War, even though they could not foresee the unfortunate Irish situation in which a British government seemed determined to make itself as un-English as possible. If there had not been the patriotic urge to assert our essential Americanism more strongly than ever, there still would have been a reaction against all the pledging and the handshaking, the pother about blood and water, the purple patches in every newspaper asserting Anglo-Saxonism against the world. I remember my own nervousness when, in 1918, after the best part of a year in England, in England's darkest days, I came back full of admiration for the pluck of all England and the enlightenment of her best minds in the great struggle, to hear men who knew little of England orating of enduring friendship, and to read writers who had merely read of England, descanting of her virtues. I felt, and many felt, that excess of ignorant laudation which spells certain reaction into ignorant dispraise. No wonder that Americans whose parents happened to be Germans, Italians, Jews, or Irish grew weary of hearing of the essential virtues of the Anglo-Saxon race. There never was such a race. It was not even English blood, but English institutions that created America; but Liberty Loan orators had no time to make fine distinctions of that kind. They talked, and even while the cheers were ringing and the money rolled in dissent raised its tiny head.

Dissent was to be expected; antagonism against a tradition made by English minds and perpetuated in English was natural after a war in which not merely nationalism, but also every racial instinct, has been quickened and made sensitive. But *tout comprendre, c'est tout pardonner*, is only partly true in this instance. We should understand, and be tolerant with, the strainings against tradition of folk to whom it is still partly alien; we should diagnose our own growing pains and not take them too seriously. Nevertheless, the better more violent movements of race and national prejudice are understood, the less readily can they be pardoned, if by pardon one means easy tolerance.

It is not inconceivable that we shall have to face squarely a split between those who prefer the American tradition and those who do not, although where the cleavage line would run, whether between races or classes, is past guessing. There are among us apparently men and women who would risk wars, external or internal, in order to hasten the discordant day; although just what they expect as a result, whether an Irish-German state organized by German efficiency and officered by graduates of Tammany Hall, or a pseudo-Russian communism, is not yet clear. In any case, the time is near when whoever calls himself American will have to take his stand and do more thinking, perhaps, than was necessary in 1917. He will need to know what tradition is, what his own consists of, and what he would do without it. He will need especially to rid himself of such simple and fallacious ideas as that what was good enough for his grandfather is good enough for him; or that, as some of our more reputable newspapers profess to think, the Constitution has taken the place once held by the Bible, and contains the whole duty of man and all that is necessary for his welfare. He will need to think less of one hundred per cent Americanism, which, as it is commonly used, means not to think at all, and more of how he himself is moulding American tradition for the generation that is to follow. If he is not to be a pawn merely in the struggle for American unity, he must think more clearly and deeply than has been his habit in the past.

But whatever happens in America (and after the sad experiences of prophets in the period of war and reconstruction, who would prophesy), let us cease abusing England whenever we have indigestion in our own body politic. It is seemingly inevitable that the writers of vindictive editorials should know little more of England as she is to-day than of Russia or the Chinese Republic; inevitable, apparently, that for them the Irish Policy of the Tory group in Parliament, Indian unrest, and Lloyd George, are all that one needs to know about a country whose liberal experiments in industrial democracy since the war, and whose courage in reconstruction, may well make us hesitate in dispraise. But it is not inevitable that Americans who are neither headline and editorial writers, nor impassioned orators, regardless of facts, should continue to damn the English because their ancestors and ours founded America.

OMAR AND THE SACRED VINE [1]

GILBERT K. CHESTERTON

A NEW morality has burst upon us with some violence in
connection with the problem of strong drink; and enthusiasts in the matter range from the man who is violently
thrown out at twelve-thirty, to the lady who smashes
American bars with an axe.   In these discussions it is almost always felt that one very wise and moderate position is to say that wine or such stuff should only be drunk
as a medicine.   With this I should venture to disagree
with a peculiar ferocity.   The one genuinely dangerous
and immoral way of drinking wine is to drink it as a
medicine.   And for this reason.   If a man drinks wine in
order to obtain pleasure, he is trying to obtain something
exceptional, something he does not expect every hour of
the day, something which, unless he is a little insane, he
will not try to get every hour of the day.   But if a man
drinks wine in order to obtain health, he is trying to get
something natural; something, that is, that he ought not
to be without; something that he may find it difficult to
reconcile himself to being without.   The man may not be
seduced who has seen the ecstasy of being ecstatic; it is
more dazzling to catch a glimpse of the ecstasy of being
ordinary.   If there were a magic ointment, and we took
it to a strong man, and said, "This will enable you to jump
off the Monument," doubtless he would jump off the

[1] From *Heretics* (1905).   By permission of the author and of his publishers, Dodd, Mead and Company, and John Lane: The Bodley Head:
Limited.

Monument, but he would not jump off the Monument all day long to the delight of the City. But if we took it to a blind man, saying, "This will enable you to see," he would be under a heavier temptation. It would be hard for him not to rub it on his eyes whenever he heard the hoof of a noble horse or the birds singing at daybreak. It is easy to deny one's self festivity; it is difficult to deny one's self normality. Hence comes the fact which every doctor knows, that it is often perilous to give alcohol to the sick even when they need it. I need hardly say that I do not mean that I think the giving of alcohol to the sick for stimulus is necessarily unjustifiable. But I do mean that giving it to the healthy for fun is the proper use of it, and a great deal more consistent with health.

The sound rule in the matter would appear to be like many other sound rules — a paradox. Drink because you are happy, but never because you are miserable. Never drink when you are wretched without it, or you will be like the grey-faced gin-drinker in the slum; but drink when you would be happy without it, and you will be like the laughing peasant of Italy. Never drink because you need it, for this is rational drinking, and the way to death and hell. But drink because you do not need it, for this is irrational drinking, and the ancient health of the world.

For more than thirty years the shadow and glory of a great Eastern figure has lain upon our English literature. Fitzgerald's translation of Omar Khayyám concentrated into an immortal poignancy all the dark and drifting hedonism of our time. Of the literary splendour of that work it would be merely banal to speak; in few other of the books of men has there been anything so combining

the gay pugnacity of an epigram with the vague sadness
of a song. But of its philosophical, ethical, and religious
influence, which has been almost as great as its brilliancy,
I should like to say a word, and that word, I confess, one
of uncompromising hostility. There are a great many
things which might be said against the spirit of the
Rubáiyát, and against its prodigious influence. But one
matter of indictment towers ominously above the rest — a
genuine disgrace to it, a genuine calamity to us. This is
the terrible blow that this great poem has struck against
sociability and the joy of life. Some one called Omar
"the sad, glad old Persian." Sad he is; glad he is not, in
any sense of the word whatever. He has been a worse foe
to gladness than the Puritans.

A pensive and graceful Oriental lies under the rose-tree
with his wine-pot and his scroll of poems. It may seem
strange that any one's thoughts should, at the moment of
regarding him, fly back to the dark bedside where the doctor doles out brandy. It may seem stranger still that
they should go back to the grey wastrel shaking with gin
in Houndsditch. But a great philosophical unity links the
three in an evil bond. Omar Khayyám's wine-bibbing is
bad, not because it is wine-bibbing. It is bad, and very
bad, because it is medical wine-bibbing. It is the drinking of a man who drinks because he is not happy. His is
the wine that shuts out the universe, not the wine that
reveals it. It is not poetical drinking, which is joyous
and instinctive; it is rational drinking, which is as prosaic
as an investment, as unsavoury as a dose of camomile.
Whole heavens above it, from the point of view of sentiment, though not of style, rises the splendour of some old
English drinking-song —

> Then pass the bowl, my comrades all,
> And let the zider vlow.

For this song was caught up by happy men to express the worth of truly worthy things, of brotherhood and garrulity, and the brief and kindly leisure of the poor. Of course, the great part of the more stolid reproaches directed against the Omarite morality are as false and babyish as such reproaches usually are. One critic, whose work I have read, had the incredible foolishness to call Omar an atheist and a materialist. It is almost impossible for an Oriental to be either; the East understands metaphysics too well for that. Of course, the real objection which a philosophical Christian would bring against the religion of Omar, is not that he gives no place to God, it is that he gives too much place to God. His is that terrible theism which can imagine nothing else but deity, and which denies altogether the outlines of human personality and human will.

> The ball no question makes of Ayes or Noes,
> But Here or There as strikes the Player goes;
> And He that tossed you down into the field,
> He knows about it all — he knows — he knows.

A Christian thinker, such as Augustine or Dante, would object to this because it ignores free-will, which is the valour and dignity of the soul. The quarrel of the highest Christianity with this scepticism is not in the least that the scepticism denies the existence of God; it is that it denies the existence of man.

In this cult of the pessimistic pleasure-seeker the *Rubáiyát* stands first in our time; but it does not stand alone. Many of the most brilliant intellects of our time have urged us to the same self-conscious snatching at a rare delight. Walter Pater said that we were all under sentence of death, and the only course was to enjoy exquisite moments simply for those moments' sake. The same lesson was taught by the very powerful and very desolate philosophy of Oscar Wilde. It is the *carpe diem* religion; but the *carpe diem* religion is not the religion of happy people, but of very unhappy people. Great joy does not gather the rosebuds while it may; its eyes are fixed on the immortal rose which Dante saw. Great joy has in it the sense of immortality; the very splendour of youth is the sense that it has all space to stretch its legs in. In all great comic literature, in *Tristram Shandy* or *Pickwick*, there is this sense of space and incorruptibility; we feel the characters are deathless people in an endless tale.

It is true enough, of course, that a pungent happiness comes chiefly in certain passing moments; but it is not true that we should think of them as passing, or enjoy them simply "for those moments' sake." To do this is to rationalize the happiness, and therefore to destroy it. Happiness is a mystery like religion, and should never be rationalized. Suppose a man experiences a really splendid moment of pleasure. I do not mean something connected with a bit of enamel, I mean something with a violent happiness in it — an almost painful happiness. A man may have, for instance, a moment of ecstasy in first love, or a moment of victory in battle. The lover enjoys the moment, but precisely not for the moment's sake. He enjoys it for the woman's sake, or his own sake. The warrior enjoys the moment, but not for the sake of the moment; he enjoys it for the sake of the flag. The cause which the flag stands for may be foolish and fleeting; the love may be calf-love, and last a week. But the patriot thinks of the flag as eternal; the lover thinks of his love as something that cannot end. These moments are filled with eternity; these moments are joyful because they do not seem momentary. Once look at them as moments after Pater's manner, and they become as cold as Pater and his style. Man cannot love mortal things. He can only love immortal things for an instant.

Pater's mistake is revealed in his most famous phrase. He asks us to burn with a hard, gem-like flame. Flames are never hard and never gem-like — they cannot be handled or arranged. So human emotions are never hard and never gem-like; they are always dangerous, like flames, to touch or even to examine. There is only one way in which our passions can become hard and gem-like, and that is by becoming as cold as gems. No blow then has ever been struck at the natural loves and laughter of men so sterilizing as this *carpe diem* of the æsthetes. For any kind of pleasure a totally different spirit is required; a certain shyness, a certain indeterminate hope, a certain boyish expectation. Purity and simplicity are essential to passions — yes, even to evil passions. Even vice demands a sort of virginity.

Omar's (or Fitzgerald's) effect upon the other world we may let go, his hand upon this world has been heavy and paralyzing. The Puritans, as I have said, are far jollier than he. The new ascetics who follow Thoreau or Tolstoy are much livelier company; for, though the surrender of strong drink and such luxuries may strike us as an idle negation, it may leave a man with innumerable natural pleasures, and, above all, with man's natural power of happiness. Thoreau could enjoy the sunrise without a cup of coffee. If Tolstoy cannot admire marriage, at least he is healthy enough to admire mud. Nature can be enjoyed without even the most natural luxuries. A good bush needs no wine. But neither nature nor wine nor anything else can be enjoyed if we have the wrong attitude towards happiness, and Omar (or Fitzgerald) did have the wrong attitude towards happiness. He and those he has influenced do not see that if we are to be truly gay, we must believe that there is some eternal gaiety in the nature of things. We cannot enjoy thoroughly even a *pas-de-quatre* at a subscription dance unless we believe that the stars are dancing to the same tune. No one can be really hilarious but the serious man. "Wine," says the Scripture, "maketh glad the heart of man," but only of the man who has a heart. The thing called high spirits is possible only to the spiritual. Ultimately a man cannot rejoice in anything except the nature of things. Ultimately a man can enjoy nothing except religion.

Once in the world's history men did believe that the stars were dancing to the tune of their temples, and they danced as men have never danced since. With this old pagan eudæmonism the sage of the *Rubáiyát* has quite as little to do as he has with any Christian variety. He is no more a Bacchanal than he is a saint. Dionysius and his church was grounded on a serious *joie-de-vivre* like that of Walt Whitman. Dionysius made wine, not a medicine, but a sacrament. Jesus Christ also made wine, not a medicine, but a sacrament. But Omar makes it, not a sacrament, but a medicine. He feasts because life is not joyful; he revels because he is not glad. "Drink," he says, "for you know not whence you come nor why. Drink, for you know not when you go nor where. Drink, because the stars are cruel and the world as idle as a humming-top. Drink, because there is nothing worth trusting, nothing worth fighting for. Drink, because all things are lapsed in a base equality and an evil peace." So he stands offering us the cup in his hand. And at the high altar of Christianity stands another figure, in whose hand also is the cup of the vine. "Drink," he says, "for the whole world is as red as this wine, with the crimson of the love and wrath of God. Drink, for the trumpets are blowing for battle and this is the stirrup-cup. Drink, for this my blood of the new testament that is shed for you. Drink, for I know of whence you come and why. Drink, for I know of when you go and where."

PREFACE, *THE NIGGER OF THE NARCISSUS*[1]

JOSEPH CONRAD

A WORK that aspires, however humbly, to the condition of art should carry its justification in every line. And art itself may be defined as a single-minded attempt to render the highest kind of justice to the visible universe, by bringing to light the truth, manifold and one, underlying its every aspect. It is an attempt to find in its forms, in its colours, in its light, in its shadows, in the aspects of matter and in the facts of life what of each is fundamental, what is enduring and essential — their one illuminating and convincing quality — the very truth of their existence. The artist, then, like the thinker or the scientist, seeks the truth and makes his appeal. Impressed by the aspect of the world the thinker plunges into ideas, the scientist into facts — whence, presently, emerging they make their appeal to those qualities of our being that fit us best for the hazardous enterprise of living. They speak authoritatively to our common-sense, to our intelligence, to our desire of peace or to our desire of unrest; not seldom to our prejudices, sometimes to our fears, often to our egoism — but always to our credulity. And their words are heard with reverence, for their concern is with weighty matters: with the cultivation of our minds and the proper care of our bodies, with the attainment of

[1] From *The Nigger of the Narcissus* (1897). Published by Doubleday, Page and Company. By permission.

our ambitions, with the perfection of the means and the glorification of our precious aims.

It is otherwise with the artist.

Confronted by the same enigmatical spectacle the artist descends within himself, and in that lonely region of stress and strife, if he be deserving and fortunate, he finds the terms of his appeal. His appeal is made to our less obvious capacities: to that part of our nature which, because of the warlike conditions of existence, is necessarily kept out of sight within the more resisting and hard qualities — like the vulnerable body within a steel armour. His appeal is less loud, more profound, less distinct, more stirring — and sooner forgotten. Yet its effect endures forever. The changing wisdom of successive generations discards ideas, questions facts, demolishes theories. But the artist appeals to that part of our being which is not dependent on wisdom; to that in us which is a gift and not an acquisition — and, therefore, more permanently enduring. He speaks to our capacity for delight and wonder, to the sense of mystery surrounding our lives; to our sense of pity, and beauty, and pain; to the latent feeling of fellowship with all creation — and to the subtle but invincible conviction of solidarity that knits together the loneliness of innumerable hearts, to the solidarity in dreams, in joy, in sorrow, in aspirations, in illusions, in hope, in fear, which binds men to each other, which binds together all humanity — the dead to the living and the living to the unborn.

It is only some such train of thought, or rather of feeling, that can in a measure explain the aim of the attempt, made in the tale which follows, to present an unrestful episode in the obscure lives of a few individuals out of all

the disregarded multitude of the bewildered, the simple
and the voiceless. For, if any part of truth dwells in the
belief confessed above, it becomes evident that there is
not a place of splendour or a dark corner of the earth
that does not deserve, if only a passing glance of wonder
and pity. The motive, then, may be held to justify the
matter of the work; but this preface, which is simply an
avowal of endeavour, cannot end here — for the avowal
is not yet complete.

Fiction — if it at all aspires to be art — appeals to
temperament. And in truth it must be, like painting,
like music, like all art, the appeal of one temperament to
all the other innumerable temperaments whose subtle
and resistless power endows passing events with their true
meaning, and creates the moral, the emotional atmosphere of the place and time. Such an appeal to be effective must be an impression conveyed through the
senses; and, in fact, it cannot be made in any other way,
because temperament, whether individual or collective,
is not amenable to persuasion. All art, therefore, appeals primarily to the senses, and the artistic aim when
expressing itself in written words must also make its
appeal through the senses, if its high desire is to reach the
secret spring of responsive emotions. It must strenu-
ously aspire to the plasticity of sculpture, to the colour
of painting, and to the magic suggestiveness of music —
which is the art of arts. And it is only through complete, unswerving devotion to the perfect blending of form
and substance; it is only through an unremitting never-
discouraged care for the shape and ring of sentences
that an approach can be made to plasticity, to colour, and
that the light of magic suggestiveness may be brought

to play for an evanescent instant over the commonplace surface of words: of the old, old words, worn thin, defaced by ages of careless usage.

The sincere endeavour to accomplish that creative task, to go as far on that road as his strength will carry him, to go undeterred by faltering, weariness or reproach, is the only valid justification for the worker in prose. And if his conscience is clear, his answer to those who in the fulness of a wisdom which looks for immediate profit, demand specifically to be edified, consoled, amused; who demand to be promptly improved, or encouraged, or frightened, or shocked, or charmed, must run thus: — My task which I am trying to achieve is, by the power of the written word to make you hear, to make you feel — it is, before all, to make you *see*. That — and no more, and it is everything. If I succeed, you shall find there according to your deserts: encouragement, consolation, fear, charm — all you demand — and, perhaps, also that glimpse of truth for which you have forgotten to ask.

To snatch in a moment of courage, from the remorseless rush of time, a passing phase of life, is only the beginning of the task. The task approached in tenderness and faith is to hold up unquestioningly, without choice and without fear, the rescued fragment before all eyes in the light of a sincere mood. It is to show its vibration, its colour, its form; and through its movement, its form, and its colour, reveal the substance of its truth — disclose its inspiring secret: the stress and passion within the core of each convincing moment. In a single-minded attempt of that kind, if one be deserving and fortunate, one may perchance attain to such clearness of sincerity that at last the presented vision of regret or pity, of terror or mirth, shall awaken in the hearts of the beholders that feeling of unavoidable solidarity; of the solidarity in mysterious origin, in toil, in joy, in hope, in uncertain fate, which binds men to each other and all mankind to the visible world.

It is evident that he who, rightly or wrongly, holds by the convictions expressed above cannot be faithful to any one of the temporary formulas of his craft. The enduring part of them — the truth which each only imperfectly veils — should abide with him as the most precious of his possessions, but they all: Realism, Romanticism, Naturalism, even the unofficial sentimentalism (which like the poor, is exceedingly difficult to get rid of,) all these gods must, after a short period of fellowship, abandon him — even on the very threshold of the temple — to the stammerings of his conscience and to the outspoken consciousness of the difficulties of his work. In that uneasy solitude the supreme cry of Art for Art itself, loses the exciting ring of its apparent immorality. It sounds far off. It has ceased to be a cry, and is heard only as a whisper, often incomprehensible, but at times and faintly encouraging.

Sometimes, stretched at ease in the shade of a roadside tree, we watch the motions of a labourer in a distant field, and after a time, begin to wonder languidly as to what the fellow may be at. We watch the movements of his body, the waving of his arms, we see him bend down, stand up, hesitate, begin again. It may add to the charm of an idle hour to be told the purpose of his exertions. If we know he is trying to lift a stone, to dig a ditch, to uproot a stump, we look with a more real interest at his efforts; we are disposed to condone the jar of his agitation

upon the restfulness of the landscape; and even, if in a
brotherly frame of mind, we may bring ourselves to forgive his failure. We understood his object, and, after all,
the fellow has tried, and perhaps he had not the strength
— and perhaps he had not the knowledge. We forgive,
go on our way — and forget.

And so it is with the workman of art. Art is long and
life is short, and success is very far off. And thus, doubtful of strength to travel so far, we talk a little about the
aim — the aim of art, which, like life itself, is inspiring,
difficult — obscured by mists. It is not in the clear logic
of a triumphant conclusion; it is not in the unveiling of
one of those heartless secrets which are called the Laws
of Nature. It is not less great, but only more difficult.

To arrest, for the space of a breath, the hands busy
about the work of the earth, and compel men entranced
by the sight of distant goals to glance for a moment at the
surrounding vision of form and colour, of sunshine and
shadows; to make them pause for a look, for a sigh, for a
smile — such is the aim, difficult and evanescent, and reserved only for a very few to achieve. But sometimes,
by the deserving and the fortunate, even that task is accomplished. And when it is accomplished — behold! —
all the truth of life is there: a moment of vision, a sigh,
a smile — and the return to an eternal rest.

UNSEASONABLE VIRTUES[1]

SAMUEL McCHORD CROTHERS

THERE are certain philosophers who have fallen into the habit of speaking slightingly of Time and Space. Time, they say, is only a poor concept of ours corresponding to no ultimate reality, and Space is little better. They are merely mental receptacles into which we put our sensations. We are assured that could we get at the right point of view we should see that real existence is timeless. Of course we cannot get at the right point of view, but that does not matter.

It is easy to understand how philosophers can talk in that way, for familiarity with great subjects breeds contempt; but we of the laity cannot dismiss either Time or Space so cavalierly. Having once acquired the time-habit, it is difficult to see how we could live without it. We are accustomed to use the minutes and hours as stepping-stones, and we pick our way from one to another. If it were not for them, we should find ourselves at once beyond our depth. It is the succession of events which makes them interesting. There is a delightful transitoriness about everything, and yet the sense that there is more where it all comes from. To the unsophisticated mind Eternity is not the negation of Time; it is having all the time one wants. And why may not the unsophisticated mind be as nearly right in such matters as any other?

In a timeless existence there would be no distinction

between now and then, before and after. Yesterdays and to-days would be merged in one featureless Forever. When we met one another it would be impertinent to ask, "How do you do?" The chilling answer would be: "I do not do; I am." There would be nothing more to say to one who had reduced his being to such bare metaphysical first principles.

I much prefer living in Time, where there are circumstances and incidents to give variety to existence. There is a dramatic instinct in all of us that must be satisfied. We watch with keen interest for what is coming next. We would rather have long waits than to have no shifting of the scenes, and all the actors on the stage at once, doing nothing.

An open-minded editor prints the following question from an anxious reader in regard to a serial story appearing in his paper: "Does it make any difference in reading the serial whether I begin with Saturday's chapter and read backward toward Monday, or should the tale be read as the chapters appear?"

The editor assures his subscriber that the story is of such uniform excellence that it would read well in either direction. In practical affairs our dramatic instinct will not allow us this latitude. We insist upon certain sequences. There is an expectancy that one thing will lead up to another. We do not take kindly to an anti-climax or to an anachronism. The Hebrew sage declares, "He hath made everything beautiful in his time." That is in the right time, but alas for the beautiful thing that falls upon the wrong time! It is bewitched beyond all recognition by the old necromancer who has power to make "ancient good uncouth."

It is just here that charity requires that we should discriminate. There is a situation that demands the services of a kind-hearted indulgencer. Ethics has to do with two kinds of offenses: one is against the eternal and unchanging standards of right and wrong, and the other against the perpetually varying conditions of the passing day. We are continually confusing the two. We visit upon the ancient uncouth good which comes honestly stumbling on its belated journey toward the perfect, all the condemnation that properly belongs to willful evil. It is lucky if it gets off so easily as that, for we are likely to add the pains and penalties which belong to hypocritical pretense. As for a premature kind of goodness coming before there is time properly to classify it, that must expect martyrdom. Something of the old feeling about strangers still survives in us. We think it safer to treat the stranger as an enemy. If he survives our attacks we may make friends with him.

Those good people who, in their devotion to their own ideals, have ignored all considerations of timeliness, have usually passed through sore tribulations. They have been the victims of cruel misunderstandings. Such, for example, was Saint Cerbonius. Cerbonius is one of the October saints. October is a good month for saints. The ecclesiastical calendar gives us a sense of spiritual mellowness and fruitfulness. The virtues celebrated are without the acidity which belongs to some other seasons: witness Saint Francis of Assisi, Saint Teresa, Saint Luke, the beloved physician, Saint John Capistran, of whom it is written, "he had a singular talent for reconciling inveterate enemies and inducing them to love one another." Cerbonius has a modest place in this autumnal brotherhood; indeed, in some *Lives of the Saints*, he is not even mentioned, and yet he had the true October spirit. Nevertheless, his good was evil spoken of, and he came near to excommunication, and all because of his divergence from popular custom in the matter of time.

It seems that he lived towards the end of the sixth century, and that he was Bishop of Piombino. Very soon a great scandal arose, for it was declared that the bishop was neglecting his duties. At the accustomed hour the citizens came to the cathedral for their devotions, only to find the chancel devoid of clergy. Cerbonius and his priests were at that moment comfortably seated at breakfast. Each succeeding morning witnessed the same scene. The bishop was evidently an infidel scoffing at the rites of religion. Appeal was made to Rome, and legates were appointed who confirmed the astounding rumors. At last Cerbonius went to Rome to plead his cause; but only by a special miracle was his character cleared. The miracle induced the authorities to look into the matter more carefully, and it was found that Cerbonius, instead of neglecting his duties, had been carried away by holy zeal. While the people of Piombino were still in their beds, Cerbonius and his clergy would be celebrating mass. As for breakfast, that was quite late in the day.

It is easy to be wise after the event, and now that the matter has been cleared up it is evident that all the religion was not on one side. Taking a large view of the subject, we see that in the course of the twenty-four hours the bishop spent as much time in the church as the most scrupulous parishioner could ask. But it was just this large view that they were unwilling to take. With them it was now or never. They judged his character by the cross-section which they took at one particular hour.

I suppose that, had I lived in Piombino, I should have been a moderate anti-Cerbonian. Cerbonius was in error, but not in mortal sin. He was guilty of a heresy that disturbed the peace of the church, — that of early rising. So long as early rising is held only as a creed for substance of doctrine and set forth as a counsel of perfection, it may be tolerated, but when the creed becomes a deed it awakens fanatical opposition. This breeds schism. A person cannot be popular who gets the reputation of being a human alarm clock. The primitive instinct in regard to an alarm clock is to stop it. If Cerbonius had possessed the tact necessary to a man in his position, he would not only have done his duty, but he would have done it at the time most convenient to the greatest number. His virtue was unseasonable; but between a man of unseasonable virtue and an abandoned character who has no virtue at all, there is a great difference. It is just this difference which the majority of people will not see. They make no distinction between one who deliberately offends against the eternal verities and one who accidentally tramples upon a temporary verity that he didn't know was there.

Most of our quarrels do not concern absolute right and wrong; they arise from disputes about the time of day. Two persons may have the same qualities and convictions and yet never agree. An ironical fate sets them at cross purposes and they never meet without irritating contradictions. It is all because their moods do not synchronize. One is always a little too slow, the other a little too fast. When one is in fine fettle the other is just beginning to get tired. They are equally serious, but never on the same occasion, and so each accuses the other of

heartless frivolity. They have an equal appreciation of
a pleasantry, but they never see it at the same instant.
One gives it an uproarious welcome when the other is
speeding the parting guest.

Two quick-tempered people may live together very
comfortably so long as they lose their tempers simultaneously; they are then ready to make up at the same
time. They get on like an automobile, by a series of
small explosions accurately timed. But when a quick-
tempered person is unequally yoked with one who is slow
to wrath, the case is difficult. The slowness causes continual apprehension. The fuse burns so deliberately that
it seems to have gone out and then the explosion comes.
In such cases there can be no adequate explanation. The
offender would apologize if he could remember what the
offense was, and he doesn't dare to ask.

Said one theologian to another: "The difference between us is that your God is my Devil." This involved
more than the mere matter of nomenclature. It upset
the spiritual time-table and caused disastrous collisions.
When one good man set forth valiantly to fight the
Devil, the other would charge him with disturbing his
worship.

The fact that one man's work is another man's play is
equally fruitful in misunderstandings. The proverbial
irritability of the literary and artistic tribes arises in part
from this cause. They feel that they are never taken
seriously. When we go to a good play we find it so easy
to be amused that we do not realize what hard work
it is for those whose business it is to be amusing. The
better the work, the more effortless it seems to us. On a
summer afternoon we take up a novel in a mood which

to the conscientious novelist seems sacrilege. He has thrown all the earnestness of his nature into it, and he wants his message to be received in the same spirit. We have earnestness of nature too, but we have expended it in other directions. Having finished our work, we take our rest by reading his. It is a pleasant way to pass the time. This enrages the novelist, and he writes essays to rebuke us. He calls us Philistines and other hard names, and says that we are incapable of appreciating literary art.

But what is our offense? We have used his work for our own purpose, which was to rest our minds. We got out of it what at the time we needed. Does he not act in very much the same way? Did we not see him at the town-meeting when a very serious question concerning the management of the town poor-house was to be settled? It was a time when every good citizen should have shown his interest by speaking an earnest word. Unmindful of all this, he sat through the meeting with the air of an amused outsider. He paid little attention to the weighty arguments of the selectmen, but noted down all their slips in grammar. He confessed unblushingly that he attended the meeting simply to get a little local color. What is to become of the country when a tax-payer will take the duties of citizenship so lightly?

These recriminations go on endlessly. Because we do not see certain qualities in action, we deny their existence. The owl has a reputation for sedentary habits and unpractical wisdom, simply because he keeps different business hours from those to which we are accustomed. Could we look in on him during the rush time, we would find him a hustling fellow. He has no time to waste on unremunerative meditation. This is his busy night. How ridiculous is the sleepiness of the greater part of the animal world! There is the lark nodding for hours on his perch. They say he never really wakes up — at least, nobody has seen him awake.

There is a pedagogical theory according to which each individual in his early life repeats quite accurately the history of mankind up to date. He passes through all the successive stages in the history of the race, with a few extra flourishes now and then to indicate the surprises which the future may have in store for us. The history of civilization becomes, for the initiated, the rehearsal of the intensely interesting drama of the nursery and the schoolroom. It lacks the delicacy of the finished performance, but it presents the arguments clearly enough and suggests the necessary stage business. The young lady who attempts to guide a group of reluctant young cave-dwellers from one period in human culture to another is not surprised at any of their tantrums. Her only anxiety is lest some form of barbarism appropriate to their condition may have been skipped. Her chief function is like that of the chorus in the Greek tragedy, to explain to the audience each dramatic situation as it unfolds.

I should not like to take the responsibility of running such an excellent theory into the ground, yet it does seem to me that it might be carried further. Granted that childhood is innocent savagery and that adolescence is gloriously barbaric, what is the matter with mature life? Does it not have any remnants of primitiveness? Does not Tennyson write of "the gray barbarian"?

The transitions from primitive savagery to civilization which took the race centuries to accomplish are repeated by the individual, not once but many times. After we get the knack of it, we can run over the alphabet of human progress backwards as well as forwards.

Exit Troglodyte. Enter Philosopher discoursing on disinterested virtue. Reënter Troglodyte. Such dramatic transformations may be expected by merely changing the subject of the conversation.

I remember sitting, one Sunday afternoon, on a vine-covered piazza reading to a thoughtful and irascible friend. The book was Martineau's *Endeavors after the Christian Life*. In the middle of the second discourse my friend's dog rushed into the street to attack the dog of a passer-by. It was one of those sudden and unpredictable antipathies to which the members of the canine race are subject. My friend, instead of preserving a dignified neutrality, rushed into the fray in the spirit of offensive partisanship, and instantly became involved in an altercation with the gentleman on the sidewalk. Canes were brandished, fierce threats were exchanged, and only by the greatest efforts were the Homeric heroes separated. Returning to his chair, my friend handed me the book, saying, "Now let us go on with our religion." The religion went on as placidly as aforetime. There was no sense of confusion. The wrath of Achilles did not disturb the calm spirituality of Martineau. Each held the center of the stage for his own moment, and there was no troublesome attempt to harmonize them. Why should there be? Martineau was not talking about dogs.

I know no greater luxury than that of thinking well of my fellow-men. It is a luxury which a person in narrow circumstances, who is compelled to live within the limits of strict veracity, sometimes feels to be beyond his means. Yet I think it no harm to indulge in a little extravagance in this direction. The best device for seeing all sorts and conditions of men to advantage is to arrange them in their proper chronological order.

For years it was the custom to speak disparagingly of the "poor whites" of our Southern mountains. Shut off from the main currents of modern life, they seemed unpardonably unprogressive. They were treated as mere degenerates. At last, however, a keener and kindlier observer hit upon a happy phrase. These isolated mountaineers, he said, have retained the characteristic habits of a former generation. They are our "contemporary ancestors." Instantly everything was put in a more favorable light; for we all are disposed to see the good points in our ancestors. After all, the whole offense with which these mountain people are charged is that they are behind the times. In our *bona-fide* contemporaries this is a grave fault, but in our ancestors it is pardonable. We do not expect them to live up to our standards, and so we give them credit for living up to their own.

In this case we agree to consider fifty miles of mountain roads, if they be sufficiently bad, as the equivalent of rather more than a hundred years of time. Behind the barrier the twentieth century does not yet exist. Many things may still be winked at for which the later generation may be sternly called to repentance. Then, too, the end of the eighteenth century has some good points of its own. These contemporary ancestors of ours are of good old English stock, and we begin to look upon them with a good deal of family pride.

But when we once accept poor roads as the equivalent of the passage of time, putting people at the other end into another generation, there is no knowing what we may come to in our charitable interpretations. For there are other equally effective non-conductors of thought. By the simple device of not knowing how to read, a man cuts off some thousands of culture years and saves himself from no end of intellectual distractions. He becomes the contemporary of "earth's vigorous, primitive sons." If to his illiteracy he adds native talent and imagination, there is a chance for him to make for himself some of those fine old discoveries which we lose because we got the answer from some blabbing book before we had come to the point of asking the question. Of course the danger is that if he has native talent and imagination he will learn to read, and it must be confessed that for this reason we do not get such a high order of illiterates as formerly.

I once made the acquaintance of an ancient Philosopher. His talents were for cosmogony, and his equipment would have been deemed ample in the days when cosmogony was the fashion. He had meditated much on the genesis of things and had read nothing, so that his speculations were uncontaminated by the investigations of others. He was just the man to construct a perfectly simple and logical theory of the universe, and he did it. His universe was not like that of which our sciences give us imperfect glimpses, but it was very satisfactory to him. He was very fair in dealing with facts; he explained all that could be explained by his system. As the only criterion of a fact which he recognized was that it agreed with his system, there was none left over to trouble him. His manner of thought was so foreign to that of our time that his intellectual ability was not widely appreciated; yet had his birth not been so long delayed, he might have been the founder of a school and have had books written about him. For so far as I could learn, his views of the four elements of earth, air, fire, and water, were very much like those of the early Greek physicists. Had I taken him as a fellow American, I should have dismissed him as not up to date; but considering him in the light of an ancient sage, I found much in him to admire.

Once upon the coast of Maine I came upon a huge wooden cylinder. Within it was a smaller one, and in the center, seated upon a swinging platform, was the owner of the curious contrivance. He was a mild-eyed, pleasant-spoken man, whom it was a pleasure to meet. He explained that this was "The Amphibious Vehicle," and that it would move equally well on land or sea.

"You know," said he, "what the prophet Ezekiel said about the 'wheel in the middle of a wheel'?"

"Yes," I answered.

"Well, this is it."

There was something convincing in this matter-of-fact statement. The "wheel within a wheel" had been to me little more than a figure of speech, but here it was made out of good pine lumber, with a plank in the middle for the living creature to sit on. It was as if I had fallen through a trap door into another age. Here was a literal-minded contemporary of Ezekiel, who, having heard of the wheel within a wheel, had proceeded at once to make one. I ascended into the precarious seat, and we conversed upon the spiritual and temporal possibilities of the vehicle. I found that on the scriptural argument he was clearly ahead of me, being able to quote chapter and verse with precision, while my references were rather vague. In the field of mechanics he was also my superior. I could not have made the vehicle, having not yet emerged beyond the stone age. As we talked I forgot that we were at the mouth of the Penobscot. We were on the "river of Chebar," and there was no knowing what might happen.

The belated philosophers and inventors, who think the thoughts of the ancient worthies after them, live peaceful lives. What matters it that they are separated by a millennium or two from the society in which they were fitted to shine? They are self-sufficing, and there are few who care to contradict them. It is not so with one who is morally belated. There is something pathetic in the condition of one who cherishes the ambition of being a good man, but who has not informed himself of the present "state of the art."

Now and then an ethical revolution takes place. New ideals are proclaimed, and in their light all things are judged. The public conscience becomes sensitive in regard to courses of conduct which heretofore had been unchallenged. Every such advance involves a waste in established reputations. There are always excellent men who are not aware of what has been going on. They keep on conforming scrupulously to the old standards, being good in the familiar ways that were commended in their youth. After a time they find themselves in an alien world, and in that world they are no longer counted among the best people. The tides of moral enthusiasm are all against them. The good man feels his solid ground of goodness slipping away from under him. Time has played false with his moral conventionalities. He is like a polar bear on a fast-diminishing iceberg, growling at the Gulf Stream.

When a great evil has been recognized by the world, there is a revision of all our judgments. A new principle of classification is introduced, by which we differentiate the goats from the sheep. It is hard after that to revive the old admirations. The temperance agitation of the last century has not abolished drunkenness, but it has made the conception of a pious, respectable drunkard seem grotesque. It has also reduced the business of liquor-selling to a decidedly lower place in the esteem of the community. When we read to-day of the horrors of the slave trade, we reconstruct in our imagination the character of the slave trader — and a brutal wretch he is. But in his day the Guinea captain held his own with the best. He was a good husband and father, a kind neighbor, a generous benefactor. President Ezra Stiles of Yale College, in his *Literary Diary*, describes such a beautiful character. It was when Dr. Stiles was yet a parish minister in Newport that one of his parishioners died, of whom he wrote: "God had blessed him with a good Estate and he and his Family have been eminent for Hospitality to all and Charity to the poor and afflicted. At his death he recommended Religion to his Children and told them that the world was nothing. The only external blemish on his Character was that he was a little addicted to the marvelous in stories of what he had seen in his Voyages and Travels. But in his Dealings he was punctual, upright, and honest, and (except as to the

Flie in the Oynment, the disposition to tell marvelous
Stories of Dangers, Travels, &c.), in all other Things he
was of a sober and good moral character, respected and
beloved of all, so as to be almost without enemies. He
was forward in all the concerns of the Church and Congregation, consulting its Benefit and peaceably falling in
with the general sense without exciting quarrels, parties,
&c., and even when he differed from his Brethren he so
differed from them that they loved him amidst the differences. He was a peaceable man and promoted Peace."

It was in 1773 that this good man died in the odor of
sanctity. It is quite incidentally that we learn that "he
was for many years a Guinea captain, and had no doubt
of the slave trade." His pastor suggests that he might
have chosen another business than that of "buying and
selling the human species." Still, in 1773, this did not
constitute an offense serious enough to be termed a fly
in the ointment. In 1785, Dr. Stiles speaks of the slave
trade as "a most iniquitous trade in the souls of men."
Much may happen in a dozen years in changing one's
ideas of moral values. In another generation the civilized
world was agreed that the slave trade was piracy. After
that there were no fine Christian characters among the
slave traders.

There is evidence that at the present time there is an
awakening of the social conscience that threatens as great
a revolution as that which came with the abolition of the
slave trade. Business methods which have been looked
upon as consistent with high moral character are being
condemned as "the sum of all villainies." The condemnation is not yet universal, and there are still those
who are not conscious that anything has happened. The

Christian monopolist, ruthlessly crushing out his competitors and using every trick known to the trade, has no more doubts as to the rightfulness of his proceedings than had the good Newport captain in regard to the slave trade.

It is a good time to have his obituary written. His contemporaries appreciate his excellent private virtues, and have been long accustomed to look leniently on his public wrong-doing. The new generation, having agreed to call his methods robbery, may find the obituary eulogies amusing.

RED–BLOODS AND "MOLLYCODDLES"[1]

G. LOWES DICKINSON

I AM staying at a pleasant place in New Hampshire. The country is hilly and wooded, like a larger and wilder Surrey, and through it flows what, to an Englishman, seems a large river, the Connecticut. Charming villas are dotted about, well designed and secluded, in pretty gardens. I mention this because, in my experience of America, it is unique. Almost everywhere the houses stare blankly at one another and at the public roads, ugly, unsheltered, and unashamed, as much as to say, "Every one is welcome to see what goes on here. We court publicity. See how we eat, drink, and sleep. Our private life is the property of the American people." It was not, however, to describe the country that I began this letter, but to elaborate a generalisation developed by my host and myself as a kind of self-protection against the gospel of "strenuousness."

We have divided men into Red-bloods and Mollycoddles. "A Red-blood man" is a phrase which explains itself, "Mollycoddle" is its opposite. We have adopted it from a famous speech of Mr. Roosevelt, and redeemed it — perverted it, if you will — to other uses. A few examples will make the notion clear. Shakspere's Henry V is a typical Red-blood; so was Bismarck; so was Palmerston; so is almost any business man. On the other hand,

[1] From *Appearances*, by G. Lowes Dickinson. Copyright, 1914, by G. Lowes Dickinson. Published by Doubleday, Page and Company. By permission of the author and the publishers.

typical Mollycoddles were Socrates, Voltaire, and Shelley. The terms, you will observe, are comprehensive, and the types very broad. Generally speaking, men of action are Red-bloods. Not but what the Mollycoddle may act, and act efficiently. But, if so, he acts from principle, not from the instinct of action. The Red-blood, on the other hand, acts as the stone falls, and does indiscriminately anything that comes to hand. It is thus he that carries on the business of the world. He steps without reflection into the first place offered him and goes to work like a machine. The ideals and standards of his family, his class, his city, his country, and his age, he swallows as naturally as he swallows food and drink. He is therefore always "in the swim"; and he is bound to "arrive," because he has set before himself the attainable. You will find him everywhere, in all the prominent positions. In a military age he is a soldier, in a commercial age a business man. He hates his enemies, and he may love his friends; but he does not require friends to love. A wife and children he does require, for the instinct to propagate the race is as strong in him as all other instincts. His domestic life, however, is not always happy; for he can seldom understand his wife. This is part of his general incapacity to understand any point of view but his own. He is incapable of an idea and contemptuous of a principle. He is the Samson, the blind force, dearest to Nature of her children. He neither looks back nor looks ahead. He lives in present action. And when he can no longer act, he loses his reason for existence. The Red-blood is happiest if he dies in the prime of life; otherwise, he may easily end with suicide. For he has no inner life; and when the outer life fails, he can only fail with it. The instinct that animated him being dead, he dies, too. Nature, who has blown through him, blows elsewhere. His stops are dumb; he is dead wood on the shore.

The Mollycoddle, on the other hand, is all inner life. He may indeed act, as I said, but he acts, so to speak, by accident; just as the Red-blood may reflect, but reflects by accident. The Mollycoddle in action is the Crank: it is he who accomplishes reforms; who abolished slavery, for example, and revolutionised prisons and lunatic asylums. Still, primarily, the Mollycoddle is a critic, not a man of action. He challenges all standards and all facts. If an institution is established, that is a reason why he will not accept it; if an idea is current, that is a reason why he should repudiate it. He questions everything, including life and the universe. And for that reason Nature hates him. On the Red-blood she heaps her favours; she gives him a good digestion, a clear complexion, and sound nerves. But to the Mollycoddle she apportions dyspepsia and black bile. In the universe and in society the Mollycoddle is "out of it" as inevitably as the Red-blood is "in it." At school, he is a "smug" or a "swat," while the Red-blood is captain of the Eleven. At college, he is an "intellectual," while the Red-blood is in the "best set." In the world, he courts failure while the Red-blood achieves success. The Red-blood sees nothing; but the Mollycoddle sees through everything. The Red-blood joins societies; the Mollycoddle is a non-joiner. Individualist of individualists, he can only stand alone, while the Red-blood requires the support of a crowd. The Mollycoddle engenders ideas, and the Red-blood exploits them. The Mollycoddle discovers, and the Red-blood invents. The whole structure of civilisation rests on foundations laid by Mollycoddles; but all the building is done by Red-bloods. The Red-blood despises the Mollycoddle; but, in the long run, he does what the Mollycoddle tells him. The Mollycoddle also despises the Red-blood, but he cannot do without him. Each thinks he is master of the other, and, in a sense, each is right. In his lifetime the Mollycoddle may be the slave of the Red-blood; but after his death, he is his master, though the Red-blood know it not.

Nations, like men, may be classified roughly as Red-blood and Mollycoddle. To the latter class belong clearly the ancient Greeks, the Italians, the French, and probably the Russians; to the former the Romans, the Germans, and the English. But the Red-blood nation *par excellence* is the American; so that, in comparison with them, Europe as a whole might almost be called Mollycoddle. This characteristic of Americans is reflected in the predominant physical type — the great jaw and chin, the huge teeth and predatory mouth; in their speech, where beauty and distinction are sacrificed to force; in their need to live and feel and act in masses. To be born a Mollycoddle in America is to be born to a hard fate. You must either emigrate or succumb. This, at least, hitherto has been the alternative practised. Whether a Mollycoddle will ever be produced strong enough to breathe the American atmosphere and live, is a crucial question for the future. It is the question whether America will ever be civilised. For civilisation, you will have perceived, depends on a just balance of Red-bloods and Mollycoddles. Without the Red-blood there would be no life at all, no stuff, so to speak, for the Mollycoddle to work upon; without the Mollycoddle, the stuff would remain shapeless and chaotic. The Red-blood is the matter, the Mollycoddle the form; the Red-blood the dough, the Mollycoddle the yeast. On these two poles turns the orb of human society. And if, at this point, you choose to say that poles are points and have no dimensions, that strictly neither the Mollycoddle nor the Red-blood exist, and that real men contain elements of both mixed in different proportions, I have no quarrel with you except such as one has with the man who states the obvious. I am satisfied to have distinguished the ideal extremes between which the Actual vibrates. The detailed application of the conception I must leave to more patient researchers.

One point more before I close. This Dichotomy, so far as I can see, applies only to man. Woman appears to be a kind of hybrid. Regarded as a creature of instinct, she resembles the Red-blood, and it is to him that she is first attracted. The hero of her youth is the athlete, the soldier, the successful man of business; and this predilection of hers accounts for much of human history, and in particular for the maintenance of the military spirit. On the other hand, as a creature capable of and craving sympathy, she has affinities with the Mollycoddle. This dual nature is the tragedy of her life. The Red-blood awakens her passion, but cannot satisfy it. He wins her by his virility, but cannot retain her by his perception. Hence the fact, noted by a cynic, that it is the Mollycoddle who cuckolds the Red-blood. For the woman, married to the Red-blood, discovers too late that she is to him only a trophy, a scalp. He hangs her up in the hall, and goes about his business. Then comes the Mollycoddle, divining all, possessing and offering all. And if the Red-blood is an American, and the Mollycoddle an European, then the situation is tense indeed. For the American Red-blood despises woman in his heart as profoundly as he respects her in outer observance. He despises her because of the Mollycoddle he divines in her. Therefore he never understands her; and that is why European Mollycoddles carry off American women before the very eyes of the exasperated Red-blood. "Am I not clean?" he cries. "Am I not healthy? Am I not athletic and efficient?" He is, but it does not help him, except with young girls. He may win the body, but he cannot win the soul. Can it be true then that most women would like two husbands, one Red-blood, the other Mollycoddle, one to be the father of their children, the other to be the companion of their souls? Women alone can answer; and, for the first time in history, they are beginning to be articulate.

HUMOR AND TRUTH[1]

MAX EASTMAN

LAUGHTER has perhaps a more elementary — or at least a more strong and spasmodic — connection with states of triumphant lust and battle cruelty than with any other satisfactions except those of the social instinct itself. And hence that peculiar loon-like, hysterical, crying giggle that comes out of some people whenever in joking either of these springs is touched. It is not humor, but glee, that makes them whoop so loud at cruel gibes and obscene quips and mimicries. And glee, while it may be a rank and ringing kind of pleasure, is of no more special pertinence to the art of joking than any other pleasure toward which we have a commonly unsatisfied hunger. So much indeed of what is real and strong and tasting of good earth in every direction is pressed down and out of our conscious or conversational selves by various acquired tricks of virtue and decorum, that we may properly place Truth herself beside sex and sudden glory as a chief source of the joy motive in popular jokes. We are always hungry for the simple truth.

Not only the proprieties of civilization but the more inward postulates of self-consciousness — consistency and good faith and loyalty and emotional stability and resolute adherence — all these excellent presumptions insulate us from the flux of reality even through the portals of our own hearts. We are not free to experience the

[1] From *The Sense of Humor*. Copyright, 1921, by Charles Scribner's Sons. By permission of the publishers.

world's being, or even our own beings within it. We are prisoners in a mist of pretense. And to shock us with the playful precipitation of that mist, and yet in the very shock to warm us with a clear serious glimpse of the naked movement of life, is a universal and joyful way of joking. We can all be honest playfully and for half a second. And to be honest without fear is an experience that may fitly be placed in comparison with the ecstasies of the saints. It is a most wholesome way to be redeemed — to be purged, in these forever-recurring quick flashes, from the original sin of self-consciousness. I can say, for instance, that if there is one thing I cannot endure about the learned, it is the information they possess. And I offer you there a little absurdity conjoined with the glimpse of a considerable interior truth. But to set down in serious and cold visibility the substance of that truth — which is certainly of the color neither of sex nor sudden glory — would exceed the strength of my candor.

Aristophanes, the slap-stick comedian of the Acropolis, boasted that he was after all "the best of poets, the one who was reckless enough to speak truth among the Athenians." He spoke truth among the Athenians to such point of uproar that he was arrested during the Peloponnesian War and tried for sedition. We do not know what the charge was in that early misadventure, but we have the copy of a later play in which his comic hero negotiated for himself and family a "separate peace" with Sparta, his reason being that he was not interested in international politics, and wanted to go home. That was an absurd performance, to be sure, a shattering of all the tragic prepossessions of the hour — but was not half the value of that absurdity its truth to what lay covered up through all those dark days in the hearts of the Athenian people? One of our own comedists, Art Young, was arrested and tried for the same crime as Aristophanes during our own war of the worlds. And when he was put upon the witness-stand and asked in a terrible voice of accusation, "What did you *mean*, Mr. Young, by those pictures?" he who had so long delighted us with the originality of his humor, could only look down with a kind of bewildered belligerence in his good gray eyes and answer: "I meant nothing but what everybody *knows!*"

It is not usually, indeed, a new truth, or truth as the result of any high intellectual analysis, whose force the humorist calls in to help us enjoy a playful shock. It is just the simple reality of feeling or sagacity of judgment that was already lurking in us. He may have no motive to instruct us, or improve our morals, or try to mix honesty with politics. His motive may be only to make good, strong, enduring, universal jokes. But the opportunity afforded by this contrast between the simple and eternal things in our hearts, and the grand procession of hysterical and temporary banner and flapdoodle parading through our minds as thoughts, he cannot possibly resist. As an artist he is compelled to drop bombs of honesty in that procession.

It is not a correct statement, however, of the relation between these two things to say that "humor is truth." Humor is often the last weapon in the hands of those who are menaced by a truth. Lacking the force or shamelessness to stand off truth's champions in sober combat, these skulking jokers — among whom I am afraid we often find the celebrated Doctor Johnson — have the trick of getting behind a joke and disappearing. What they do is to meet a serious thrust with a flatly frivolous and irrelevant rebuff, which would not be tolerated at all if it did not conceal also the serious satisfaction of some *other* interest than the one involved — perhaps an interest in some other truth — and thus permit the listener's attention to slide off in a new direction and find rest. That is what Cicero meant when he advised his pupils in oratory that joking "very often disposes of extremely ugly matters that will not bear to be cleared up by proofs." And for those orators who may find themselves on the side of the proofs, I offer this corresponding advice: Do not try to match wits with a Ciceronian joker, for you are retained and he is free; enjoy his joke as a perfectly frivolous pleasure, and then return with a reluctant force to serious speech, reserving your own wit until you are again in command. You will thus rob him of the appearance of having parried and thrust, when all he did was to jump out of the way of the wound.

Humor is not truth — but truth, under the terms of this elaborate process we call civilized life, is humorous. And those who are not satisfied with the classical authority upon this point will be interested to know that Charlie Chaplin has the same thing to say of his art as Aristophanes.

"It is telling them the plain truth of things," he replied instantly, when I asked him what it is that he does to people when he makes them laugh. "It is bringing home to them by means of a shock the sanity of a situation which they think is insane. When I walk up and slap a fine lady, for instance, because she gave me a contemptuous look, it is really right! They won't admit it, but it's right, and that is why they laugh.

"I make them *conscious of life*. 'You think this is it, don't you?' I say, 'Well, it isn't, but *this* is, see?' And then they laugh."

I doubt if any joker ever gave a more penetrating analysis of his art. Its lovers will agree — and the lovers of every deeply moving art of humor — that it is full of the sudden uncoverings of a simple, original, and more purely burning element of reality, from which we have all somehow got intricately lost, and from which we still hold ourselves aloof, so that when his relentlessly playful hand uncovers it, our very gesture of the moment has been baffled, and yet our deepest wish drinks deep.

There are people, of course, who lack altogether these deeper wishes, or have them so well stifled that they seem really satisfied to dwell forever in the false fronts of decorum. I suppose they cannot come down to the face of reality even alone in the bathtub. And these people are resentful of the humor that reveals, because it shakes their confidence and frightens them. They call it "levity," and wish to have it segregated and rendered irrelevant, confined to the "funny page," or the "comic paper," included in parentheses, or at least stigmatized with an exclamation-point, or a pointed voice, or something else to indicate that it is not to be taken seriously or allowed to spread. Stanton called it "levity" when Abraham Lincoln endeavored to bring a little of the light of sagacious laughter into those stern meetings of the war cabinet.

People who manifest this asperity or uncouth stupor at the play of humor through the serious enterprises of life must be either heavy of interest, so that they cannot shift within the time required from some end they were bent upon, to the new and perhaps greater one, or else they are shallow and timorous and unaccustomed to dwell with these greater ends — the passions and realities — even in their own hearts. A man whose interest is agile, and whose converse with life and death is mature, does not have to have a bell rung and a flag put up every time anything is to be taken humorously. He does not regard humor as an interlude. He is continually in hope that a bit of the framework will break back and something real look through the stucco front of our culture, and when not hoping that it will, he is contriving that it shall. For although he may be too fond of his own comfort to attack the sham and superficialities of man with anger and riot, he could not quite endure them if they were not continually shot through with humorous acknowledgments to the source and reality of life. To him seriousness in these weak exploits and waterish matters of conversation and business is the interlude, and humor the real engagement. A true joke is a reverence that we do to Nature, an expiation for having so denied and betrayed her in our lives. It is at once a glad acceptance of failure in the puny enterprise upon which our mind is bent and a grateful acknowledgment of some greater good that she was holding out in her hands.

FORGOTTEN ROADS[1]

WALTER PRICHARD EATON

To find and follow an abandoned road is to read a half-obliterated record of the past, full of gaps inviting speculation, and alluring, if wistful, revelations of a vanished day, it may be even a vanished society and manner of life. Our Berkshire Hills are pathetically rich in such abandoned roads, and they make to-day by far the pleasantest trails for the tramper — that semi-extinct species of biped who still exists in isolated specimens and spends his vacations slyly avoiding the traveled ways and the eyes of motorists. Occasionally he is even found in small groups, or herds of as many as three or four, most commonly, perhaps, in the White Mountains, but even at times in our part of the world. Even when in a herd, however, he is a shy animal, consulting his contour maps frequently to discover the worst and consequently least frequented roads, and rejoicing more over the one village that is lost and never found again by summer residents than over the ninety and nine which boast palatial inns. For him these scattered records of our forgotten roads. His feet, and his alone, are worthy to brush their grasses and his hands alone to part their meeting alder screens.

My first acquaintance with a forgotten road in western Massachusetts was made twenty years ago, when, in my college days, I was on a tramping trip through the so-called Beacon Hills which lie just to the east of the Hoosac

[1] From *In Berkshire Fields* (1920). By permission of the author and of the publishers, W. A. Wilde Company.

Tunnel, between the gorge of the Deerfield River and
Vermont. The villages amid these hills are far above sea-
level — is not the cemetery in West Heath said to be
"the highest point of cultivated ground in Massachusetts"? — and reached by highways which lead up
from the river and railroad over thank-you-marm rapids
and beside tumbling brooks. The road from Monroe
Bridge to Rowe rises something like a thousand feet in
one mile, which is considered a bit of a grade, even in
those parts. It is not abandoned — but it ought to be.
Before the Mohawk Trail state highway over Hoosac
Mountain was built, the descent into North Adams was
nearly as severe. From the eastern mouth of the Hoosac
Tunnel there is an abandoned road which leads north-
eastward toward Rowe. It runs past a cellar hole or two,
climbing steeply, and suddenly walks into the back dooryard of a farm, apparently entering the house. But if
you go around the corner you discover that it has done
the same thing, and then become a living highway,
though a grassy one. It keeps on past several upland
farms, growing less grassy with each, till it comes down
the hill and over the brook to the front porch of the Rowe
general store and post-office.

When I got to the Rowe store, twenty years ago, I
bought Boston crackers and sage cheese (both of which
could still be procured in those happy days), and entered
into a conversation which resulted in my spending two
weeks in that delightful sky village, where a hundred
years before Preserved Smith had preached in the "old
center" farther on up the hill, discoursing liberalism and
dispensing with the covenant for almost a generation before he was found out by the orthodox down on the plains

and called to account. The "old center" discloses, like so many of our hill towns, plentiful evidence of a vanished prosperity and comfort. Up there are two fine Colonial dwellings, one of them with arched ceilings, and a ruined town house and church, each of which could seat, with room to spare, the entire present population of the township. Long ago the town got its name because a Mr. Rowe, merchant, of Boston, offered a bell to the church if the citizens would rename their town after him. Previously the name had been Myrafield, said to be a "corruption" of My-rye-field. A settler in Charlemont, a town down in the Deerfield gorge (the birthplace of Charles Dudley Warner), cleared a patch of beaver meadow up in the hills, where he planted rye. When asked where he was going he would reply, "Up to my rye-field." Hence, when other settlers followed and built houses up here on the pleasant hills, the name clung. Such, at least, I was told in the Rowe general store and post-office, and I like to think it is true.

Between Rowe and Charlemont, in the direct line, lies a mountain, Mount Adams, something over two thousand feet high, and noted for its blueberries and raspberries. One day the then successor to the Reverend Preserved Smith asked me if I would like to see how the first settlers went to and from Charlemont, and thence down the river to Deerfield, and so on to Boston. It was, I well remember, a lovely late September day, almost October, and we set out directly for the mountain, over a steep pasture and through an orchard full of Porter apple trees. For a time it seemed doubtful if I should ever get any farther, for a ripe Porter, sun-kissed and exuding its incomparable odor, is like nothing else on earth. Also, it makes by far the best apple jelly, as all old-time housewives knew. Yet, to-day, I cannot find it stocked by any nursery, presumably because the fruit does not pack and ship well — as if we were to grow no apples for our own home use!

But I digress. Even to-day the mere thought of a Porter apple delays me, as the apples themselves did that morning. Ultimately, however, we got started again, and entered the woods on the mountain-side, by what seemed at that time a very old and well-made logging-road. It headed straight up for the ridge, missing the peak of the mountain by only two or three hundred feet, and dropping down on the other side into a beautiful and then heavily timbered erosion "cove" (as it would be called in the Cumberlands), a kind of amphitheater cut into the mountain, with a green meadow at the bottom, and out through the open end a view of far blue hills. This was not a logging-road; it was the ancient road for man and beast from Charlemont to Rowe. Up it came mahogany furniture, tea, molasses, silks, and Bibles; down it went wool and syrup and grain. Why make a six-mile detour to follow the grade of Pelham Brook, when the straight line lay right here, with nothing but Mount Adams in the way? The ancient road-bed was carpeted deep with moss and purpled with magnificent fringed gentians. It finally descended to farms and became once more a living highway. I well remember, however, that in the yard of the first farm we came to stood a large cage, of wood with an iron-barred door, and inside snapped and spit an extremely peevish wildcat with huge, restless paws.

The town of Sheffield, where I now live, is in the south-

western corner of Massachusetts, on the plain of the
Housatonic River. It is bounded on the west by the
long rampart of Mount Everett, or "the Dome," as we
call it, which rises in a sheer leap for a thousand feet
directly from the level, and then slopes back more gradually till the dominating summit ascends to a total height
of twenty-six hundred feet, the second highest mountain
in the State. Sheffield was settled in the first half of the
eighteenth century, among the earliest inhabitants being
a certain Dutch family named Spoor (since changed to
Spurr), who had a large grant of land on the western side
of the township, lying on, and at the base of, the mountain. They came from the Hudson Valley, presumably
over the mountain. My farm is a part of their grant, and
just beyond my north boundary, entering first the
grounds of the Berkshire School, is an ancient road, leading west from the state highway. It makes directly for
the mountain wall, which is here almost precipitous in
places, and it can still be followed to the summit of the
ridge, an air-line distance of considerably less than a mile,
but a rise of almost a thousand feet. You would naturally suppose that it would have to resort to frequent
switchbacks in order to make the ascent, more than half
of which is contained in the last few hundred yards, yet
the switchbacks are few. It makes a long swing to the
north, and then a long swing to the south, getting in behind a pine-clad promontory we call the Fiddler's Elbow,
and suddenly emerging triumphant from the pines into
the hardwoods of the level shoulder-top. From this point
it goes straight west, by a more gradual ascent, passing
just north of the summit cone, and beside Guilder Pond.
This little pond, the highest in the State, is over two

thousand feet above the sea. It is perhaps a third of a mile long, its shallow water over a leafy bottom a rich, dark-brown color, its banks indented with rocky coves and toothed with jutting ledges, each sentineled by hemlocks which show the first signs of storm-dwarfing in their twisted growth. (It is a curious fact that on Mount Everett timber-line is practically reached at twenty-five hundred feet. Graylock, fifty miles to the north, does not reach it at thirty-five hundred and it is at something like four thousand feet in the White Mountains.) The rocky shore-line, too, is pink and picturesque with laurel in early July, and the calm brown mirror of the pond holds the reflection of the summit cone. It is a true mountain pond, and, fortunately, is now a part of the Mount Everett State Reservation. From its shores the old road, regraded by the State at this point, drops down three hundred feet to the township of Mount Washington, a hamlet now boasting fourteen voters (some may have died since this was written), and situated on a high plateau which again plunges down, on the western side, past the wild and beautiful Bash Bish Falls, to Copake Iron Works in New York State. At present, to reach Mount Washington, except on foot, I must either go nine miles south or five miles north, to get around the ridge of Mount Everett and find a road up. Even these roads will be steep and long, and half the year impassable for motors. But in the old days there was no such roundabout journeyings, no, sir. You got to Mount Washington by heading straight for Mount Washington, and a mere thousand-foot wall did not deter you. Nor has this old road been so long abandoned, as time runs. Our village doctor can remember driving down it once in a buggy a mere forty years ago, and on the less steep portion, above the shoulder, the crown and side ditches are still detectable here and there, while the trees have not always closed across it nor the shrubs badly grown in.

Five miles south, almost exactly on the Connecticut state line, another road leads up the cliff into Sage's Ravine and then to Plantain Pond and Mount Washington. It is still on the maps, too, and I have been frequently asked if it can be traveled in a motor, but not, unfortunately, as yet by anybody whom I particularly dislike. As no author dislikes his readers, I hasten to assure you that it cannot. It has been used of late years exclusively by a periodic brook, which is almost as destructive to a road surface as the town scraper in the hands of our selectmen. Not far up this road are the cellar hole, the clearings, the dilapidated orchard, of an old-time farm, and the dooryard is still riotous with spiræa and day-lilies, which have successfully stood off the goldenrod, the blackberries, the hardhack, and the seedling maples.

On the opposite side of the Housatonic Valley, from the Connecticut line northward, is a wall of hills leading to a high, broken plateau which extends eastward for many miles, till it begins to break down into the valley of the Connecticut River. Through this region, not through the city of Pittsfield, the stage-coach line from Boston to Albany used to pass, *via* Hartford and the Farmington River gorge. It is a pathetic region of high pastures going back to scrub wilderness, of once prosperous villages with beautiful Colonial houses, some of them belonging to the riper third period, slowly being abandoned to decay (or Polish Jews), of eloquent cellar holes, gray,

ruined barns, the "No trespassing" signs of game preserves owned by non-residents, of course, and of forgotten
roads that once led past prosperous farms, from town to
town, and now lead past nothing but encroaching forest
and are only to be discovered by the initiated.

I well remember one such road, if only for the human
associations it disclosed, though the day was crisp and
fair when we tramped it, the woods were putting on their
autumn glory, and two does, with a fawn behind them,
looked at us over a tumbled-down wall. This road, we
learned, was young in forgetfulness, having been abandoned but fifteen years, though for a generation before
that it could have seen but little travel. The rows of
sugar-maples, planted a century ago, the open fields, the
still visible stone walls, proclaimed the proximity of a
farm, and over a rocky crest, which commanded a wide
prospect, we came to the dwelling. It still stood four
square to the winds, with both main chimneys intact and
telling us it belonged to a later period than the type of
house built around a central chimney. The front door
and windows were boarded up, but the rear door was
entirely gone, and we entered the kitchen, where we had
evidently been preceded in past years by wandering cattle. Here was a great fireplace, with paneling over it,
and large panels on either side. The two front rooms
boasted hand-worked window-trim, and each had its excellent mantel, with considerable cabinet-work upon it,
and a curiously flat-molded chair-rail all around, in excellent preservation. Endeavoring to pry a piece of this
rail loose, we discovered that it was not applied over the
lathing, but was molded on the face of studding which was
built into the frame and went clean through to the outer

sheathing, which in turn was nailed to it. There is construction for you! It must have added many days or even weeks of labor. The floors of this house were composed of maple planks from twelve to twenty-four inches wide. And everywhere was the scum and litter left behind by a gang of lumberjacks who had occupied it a few years before while the near-by pine woods were being slaughtered.

We left it presently, and followed the old road down a slope into a swampy reach where huge alders met over our heads and the road-bed had long ago been absorbed by the muck. Emerging on the farther side and climbing a hill where the chestnut burs littered the grassy way, we once more came upon the roadside maples in golden procession, with the remnants of a clearing over the tumbled-down stone wall, and knew that another house was once, at least, near by. In a moment we reached what was left of it — the great foundation and first-story fireplaces (two smaller ones on the sides and a huge one behind) of the stone chimney rising out of a rotting mass of bricks, plaster, and woodwork, with nothing else left standing except a portion of one side wall, to the second-story beams, with two window openings still intact. Yes, there was something else! Half against this wall, in what was once a corner of the room, turned gray and furry by the weather, rose the frame of a corner cupboard, the base split away by the collapse of the floor and standing by a seeming miracle, but the fluted pilasters on either side, and the connecting cap and cornice, apparently intact. The lower portion of the cupboard had once been inclosed by a door; the upper part had evidently always been open, with four gracefully curved shelves.

There it stood, above the mournful ruins, like a gray ghost of the departed domestic life. It seemed almost as if the wraiths of a luster pitcher and a blue-china tea-set would appear upon its shelves.

We made our way to it, over the débris pile in the cellar hole, and with all the gentleness possible disengaged it from the side wall and the single rotted joist which upheld it at the back. But, in spite of our tenderness, it fell quite to pieces. The carved keystone cap and cornice moldings, rotted by water from above, separated into their component parts or even disintegrated into a brown powder, leaving scarcely enough for a reconstruction model. The shelves were rotted to a kind of damp punk. Only the fluted side pieces, or pilasters, could ever be used again (with reconstructed capitals). And they are going to be. The rest of the tramp down that forgotten road was under the shouldered burden of them, and when the alders met overhead there was less rejoicing than before.

So we emerged, at length, into a road which we knew was not abandoned, chiefly because we detected the track of a motor tire, and in time swung the circle home, or to our own waiting motor, rather, because in these days you go on a tramp by riding as far as you can, and walking only when you are sure no cars will follow you.

The total length of this particular abandoned road was, I suppose, about six miles. It ran north and south. By employing here and there a few back-country high-ways to bridge the gaps, I think it would be possible, how-ever, to walk from Connecticut to Vermont, across west-ern Massachusetts, or from the Housatonic Valley to the brook-heads of the Connecticut Valley, on practically abandoned and in places virtually forgotten roads. I have never done it; one no longer has time for such amiable or wistful wanderings in these latter days. But I am sure it could be done, with sufficient zigzagging, consultation of ancient gazetteers, and consultation with ancient gossips. The ancient gazetteers alone are interesting; the ancient gossips more so. Some day I shall try it. It is my Carcassonne. And, who knows, I may find another corner cupboard? They once lived well on our forgotten roads, with fires that roared on marble hearthstones, to send back reflections from blue-china bowls and glints from the white paint on wide pine panels, worked by hand. Now, even more than their roads, they, the people, are forgotten — a vanished race. I come down from our hills sometimes as if I were descending from a dream of dead days. In the cellar hole of the Sandisfield church, I think, lies buried the grace and the strength and the bitter iron of an old theology, and in the sagging ruins of the splendid colonial abode beyond this cellar hole move the ghosts of men and women who dared cheerfully to conquer a wilderness, a wilderness that is now driving the last of their descendants down to the plain once more. The old order changeth, indeed; but it is by no means certain that it is the good customs which corrupt the world.

TRADITION AND THE INDIVIDUAL TALENT [1]

T. S. ELIOT

I

In English writing we seldom speak of tradition, though we occasionally apply its name in deploring its absence. We cannot refer to "the tradition" or to "a tradition"; at most, we employ the adjective in saying that the poetry of So-and-So is "traditional" or even "too traditional." Seldom, perhaps, does the word appear except in a phrase of censure. If otherwise, it is vaguely approbative, with the implication, as to the work approved, of some pleasing archæological reconstruction. You can hardly make the word agreeable to English ears without this comfortable reference to the reassuring science of archæology.

Certainly the word is not likely to appear in our appreciations of living or dead writers. Every nation, every race, has not only its own creative, but its own critical turn of mind; and is even more oblivious of the shortcomings and limitations of its critical habits than of those of its creative genius. We know, or think we know, from the enormous mass of critical writing that has appeared in the French language the critical method or habit of the French; we only conclude (we are such unconscious people) that the French are "more critical" than we, and sometimes even plume ourselves a little

[1] From *The Sacred Wood* (1920). By permission of the publishers, Methuen and Company, Ltd.

with the fact, as if the French were the less spontaneous. Perhaps they are; but we might remind ourselves that criticism is as inevitable as breathing, and that we should be none the worse for articulating what passes in our minds when we read a book and feel an emotion about it, for criticizing our own minds in their work of criticism. One of the facts that might come to light in this process is our tendency to insist, when we praise a poet, upon those aspects of his work in which he least resembles any one else. In these aspects or parts of his work we pretend to find what is individual, what is the peculiar essence of the man. We dwell with satisfaction upon the poet's difference from his predecessors, especially his immediate predecessors; we endeavour to find something that can be isolated in order to be enjoyed. Whereas if we approach a poet without his prejudice we shall often find that not only the best, but the most individual parts of his work may be those in which the dead poets, his ancestors, assert their immortality most vigorously. And I do not mean the impressionable period of adolescence, but the period of full maturity.

Yet if the only form of tradition, of handing down, consisted in following the ways of the immediate generation before us in a blind or timid adherence to its successes, "tradition" should positively be discouraged. We have seen many such simple currents soon lost in the sand; and novelty is better than repetition. Tradition is a matter of much wider significance. It cannot be inherited, and if you want it you must obtain it by great labour. It involves, in the first place, the historical sense, which we may call nearly indispensable to any one who would continue to be a poet beyond his twenty-fifth year; and the historical sense involves a perception, not only of the pastness of the past, but of its presence; the historical sense compels a man to write not merely with his own generation in his bones, but with a feeling that the whole of the literature of Europe from Homer and within it the whole of the literature of his own country has a simultaneous existence and composes a simultaneous order. This historical sense, which is a sense of the timeless as well as of the temporal and of the timeless and of the temporal together, is what makes a writer traditional. And it is at the same time what makes a writer most acutely conscious of his place in time, of his contemporaneity.

No poet, no artist of any art, has his complete meaning alone. His significance, his appreciation is the appreciation of his relation to the dead poets and artists. You cannot value him alone; you must set him, for contrast and comparison, among the dead. I mean this as a principle of æsthetic, not merely historical, criticism. The necessity that he shall conform, that he shall cohere, is not one-sided; what happens when a new work of art is created is something that happens simultaneously to all the works of art which preceded it. The existing monuments form an ideal order among themselves, which is modified by the introduction of the new (the really new) work of art among them. The existing order is complete before the new work arrives; for order to persist after the supervention of novelty, the *whole* existing order must be, if ever so slightly, altered; and so the relations, proportions, values of each work of art toward the whole are readjusted; and this is conformity between the old and the new. Whoever has approved this idea of order, of the form of European, of English literature, will not find it preposterous that the past should be altered by the present as much as the present is directed by the past. And the poet who is aware of this will be aware of great difficulties and responsibilities.

In a peculiar sense he will be aware also that he must inevitably be judged by the standards of the past. I say judged, not amputated, by them; not judged to be as good as, or worse or better than, the dead; and certainly not judged by the canons of dead critics. It is a judgment, a comparison, in which two things are measured by each other. To conform merely would be for the new work not really to conform at all; it would not be new, and would therefore not be a work of art. And we do not quite say that the new is more valuable because it fits in; but its fitting in is a test of its value — a test, it is true, which can only be slowly and cautiously applied, for we are none of us infallible judges of conformity. We say: it appears to conform, and is perhaps individual, or it appears individual, and may conform; but we are hardly likely to find that it is one and not the other.

To proceed to a more intelligible exposition of the relation of the poet to the past: he can neither take the past as a lump, an indiscriminate bolus, nor can he form himself wholly on one or two private admirations, nor can he form himself wholly upon one preferred period. The first course is inadmissible, the second is an important experience of youth, and the third is a pleasant and highly desirable supplement. The poet must be very conscious of the main current, which does not at all flow invariably through the most distinguished reputations. He must be quite aware of the obvious fact that art never improves, but that the material of art is never quite the same. He must be aware that the mind of Europe — the mind of his own country — a mind which he learns in time to be much more important than his own private mind — is a mind which changes, and that this change is a development which abandons nothing *en route*, which does not superannuate either Shakespeare, or Homer, or the rock drawing of the Magdalenian draughtsmen. That this development, refinement perhaps, complication certainly, is not, from the point of view of the artist, any improvement. Perhaps not even an improvement from the point of view of the psychologist or not to the extent which we imagine; perhaps only in the end based upon a complication in economics and machinery. But the difference between the present and the past is that the conscious present is an awareness of the past in a way and to an extent which the past's awareness of itself cannot show.

Some one said: "The dead writers are remote from us because we *know* so much more than they did." Precisely, and they are that which we know.

I am alive to a usual objection to what is clearly part of my programme for the *metier* of poetry. The objection is that the doctrine requires a ridiculous amount of erudition (pedantry), a claim which can be rejected by appeal to the lives of poets in any pantheon. It will even be affirmed that much learning deadens or perverts poetic sensibility. While, however, we persist in believing that a poet ought to know as much as will not encroach upon his necessary receptivity and necessary laziness, it is not desirable to confine knowledge to whatever can be put into a useful shape for examinations, drawing-rooms, or the still more pretentious modes of publicity. Some can absorb knowledge, the more tardy must sweat for it. Shakespeare acquired more essential history from Plutarch than most men could from the whole British Museum. What is to be insisted upon is that the poet must develop or procure the consciousness of the past and that he should continue to develop this consciousness throughout his career.

What happens is a continual surrender of himself as he is at the moment to something which is more valuable. The progress of an artist is a continual self-sacrifice, a continual extinction of personality.

There remains to define this process of depersonalization and its relation to the sense of tradition. It is in this depersonalization that art may be said to approach the condition of science. I shall, therefore, invite you to consider, as a suggestive analogy, the action which takes place when a bit of finely filiated platinum is introduced into a chamber containing oxygen and sulphur dioxide.

II

Honest criticism and sensitive appreciation is directed not upon the poet but upon the poetry. If we attend to the confused cries of the newspaper critics and the susurrus of popular repetition that follows, we shall hear the names of poets in great numbers; if we seek not Bluebook knowledge but the enjoyment of poetry, and ask for a poem, we shall seldom find it. In the last article I tried to point out the importance of the relation of the poem to other poems by other authors, and suggested the conception of poetry as a living whole of all the poetry that has ever been written. The other aspect of this Impersonal theory of poetry is the relation of the poem to its author. And I hinted, by an analogy, that the mind of the mature poet differs from that of the immature one not precisely in any valuation of "personality," not being necessarily more interesting, or having "more to say," but rather by being a more finely perfected medium in which special, or very varied, feelings are at liberty to enter into new combinations.

The analogy was that of the catalyst. When the two gases previously mentioned are mixed in the presence of a filament of platinum, they form sulphurous acid. This combination takes place only if the platinum is present; nevertheless the newly formed acid contains no trace of platinum, and the platinum itself is apparently unaffected; has remained inert, neutral, and unchanged. The mind of the poet is the shred of platinum. It may partly or exclusively operate upon the experience of the man himself; but, the more perfect the artist, the more completely separate in him will be the man who suffers and the mind which creates; the more perfectly will the mind digest and transmute the passions which are its material.

The experience, you will notice, the elements which enter the presence of the transforming catalyst, are of two kinds: emotions and feelings. The effect of a work of art upon the person who enjoys it is an experience different in kind from any experience not of art. It may be formed out of one emotion, or may be a combination of several; and various feelings, inhering for the writer in particular words or phrases or images, may be added to compose the final result. Or great poetry may be made without the direct use of any emotion whatever: composed out of feelings solely. Canto XV of the *Inferno* (Brunetto

Latini) is a working up of the emotion evident in the situation; but the effect, though single as that of any work of art, is obtained by considerable complexity of detail. The last quatrain gives an image, a feeling attaching to an image, which "came," which did not develop simply out of what precedes, but which was probably in suspension in the poet's mind until the proper combination arrived for it to add itself to. The poet's mind is in fact a receptacle for seizing and storing up numberless feelings, phrases, images, which remain there until all the particles which can unite to form a new compound are present together.

If you compare several representative passages of the greatest poetry you see how great is the variety of types of combination, and also how completely any semi-ethical criterion of "sublimity" misses the mark. For it is not the "greatness," the intensity, of the emotions, the components, but the intensity of the artistic process, the pressure, so to speak, under which the fusion takes place, that counts. The episode of Paolo and Francesca employs a definite emotion, but the intensity of the poetry is something quite different from whatever intensity in the supposed experience it may give the impression of. It is no more intense, furthermore, than Canto XXVI, the voyage of Ulysses, which has not the direct dependence upon emotion. Great variety is possible in the process of transmutation of emotion: the murder of Agamemnon, or the agony of Othello, gives an artistic effect apparently closer to a possible original than the scenes from Dante. In the *Agamemnon*, the artistic emotion approximates to the emotion of an actual spectator; in *Othello* to the emotion of the protagonist himself. But the difference between art and the event is always absolute; the combination which is the murder of Agamemnon is probably as complex as that which is the voyage of Ulysses. In either case there has been a fusion of elements. The ode of Keats contains a number of feelings which have nothing particular to do with the nightingale, but which the nightingale, partly, perhaps, because of its attractive name, and partly because of its reputation, served to bring together.

The point of view which I am struggling to attack is perhaps related to the metaphysical theory of the substantial unity of the soul: for my meaning is, that the poet has, not a "personality" to express, but a particular medium, which is only a medium and not a personality, in which impressions and experiences combine in peculiar and unexpected ways. Impressions and experiences which are important for the man may take no place in the poetry, and those which become important in the poetry may play quite a negligible part in the man, the personality.

I will quote a passage which is unfamiliar enough to be regarded with fresh attention in the light — or darkness — of these observations:

> And now methinks I could e'en chide myself
> For doating on her beauty, though her death
> Shall be revenged after no common action.
> Does the silkworm expend her yellow labours
> For thee?   For thee does she undo herself?
> Are lordships sold to maintain ladyships
> For the poor benefit of a bewildering minute?
> Why does yon fellow falsify highways,
> And put his life between the judge's lips,
> To refine such a thing — keeps horse and men
> To beat their valours for her? . . .

In this passage (as is evident if it is taken in its context) there is a combination of positive and negative emotions: an intensely strong attraction toward beauty and an equally intense fascination by the ugliness which is contrasted with it and which destroys it. This balance of contrasted emotion is in the dramatic situation to which the speech is pertinent, but that situation alone is inadequate to it. This is, so to speak, the structural emotion, provided by the drama. But the whole effect, the dominant tone, is due to the fact that a number of floating feelings, having an affinity to this emotion by no means superficially evident, have combined with it to give us a new art emotion.

It is not in his personal emotions, the emotions provoked by particular events in his life, that the poet is in any way remarkable or interesting. His particular emotions may be simple, or crude, or flat. The emotion in his poetry will be a very complex thing, but not with the complexity of the emotions of people who have very complex or unusual emotions in life. One error, in fact, of eccentricity in poetry is to seek for new human emotions to express: and in this search for novelty in the wrong place it discovers the perverse. The business of the poet is not to find new emotions, but to use the ordinary ones and, in working them up into poetry, to express feelings which are not in actual emotions at all. And emotions which he has never experienced will serve his turn as well as those familiar to him. Consequently, we must believe that "emotion recollected in tranquillity" is an inexact formula. For it is neither emotion, nor recollection, nor, without distortion of meaning, tranquillity. It is a concentration, and a new thing resulting from the concentration, of a very great number of experiences which to the practical and active person would not seem to be experiences at all; it is a concentration which does not happen consciously or of deliberation. These experiences are not "recollected," and they finally unite in an atmosphere which is "tranquil" only in that it is a passive attending upon the event. Of course this is not quite the whole story. There is a great deal, in the writing of poetry, which must be conscious and deliberate. In fact, the bad poet is usually unconscious where he ought to be conscious, and conscious where he ought to be unconscious. Both errors tend to make him "personal." Poetry is not a turning loose of emotion, but an escape from emotion; it is not the expression of personality, but an escape from personality. But, of course, only those who have personality and emotions know what it means to want to escape from these things.

III

ὁ δὲ νοῦς ἴσως θειότερόν τι καὶ ἀπαθές ἐστιν [1]

This essay proposes to halt at the frontier of metaphysics or mysticism, and confine itself to such practical conclusions as can be applied by the responsible person interested in poetry. To divert interest from the poet to the poetry is a laudable aim: for it would conduce to a juster estimation of actual poetry, good and bad. There are many people who appreciate the expression of sincere emotion in verse, and there is a smaller number of people who can appreciate technical excellence. But very few know when there is expression of *significant* emotion,

[1] "But perhaps Mind is rather divine, and not subject to impressions from without."

emotion which has its life in the poem and not in the history of the poet.   The emotion of art is impersonal.   And the poet cannot reach this impersonality without surrendering himself wholly to the work to be done.   And he is not likely to know what is to be done unless he lives in what is not merely the present, but the present moment of the past, unless he is conscious, not of what is dead, but of what is already living.

IMPRESSIONS AND COMMENTS[1]

HAVELOCK ELLIS

THE SIGNIFICANCE OF TECHNIQUE

March 26, [1913.] — I have lately been hearing Busoni play Chopin, and absorbing an immense joy from the skill with which that master-player evokes all the virile and complex power of Chopin, the power and the intellect which Pachmann, however deliciously he catches the butterflies fluttering up from the keys, for the most part misses.

All the great artists, in whatever medium, take so rare a delight, now and again, in interpreting some unutterable emotion, some ineffable vision, in mere terms of technique. In Chopin, in Rodin, in Besnard, in Rossetti — indeed in any supreme artist — again and again I have noted this. Great simple souls for the most part, inarticulate except through an endless power over the medium of their own art, they all love to take some insignificant little lump of that medium, to work at that little lump, with all their subtlest skill and power, in the production of what seemingly may be some absolutely trivial object or detail, and yet, not by what it obviously represents, but by the technique put into it, has become a reality, a secret of the soul, and an embodiment of a vision never before seen on earth.

Many years ago I realised this over Rossetti's poem

[1] From *Impressions and Comments* (Three Series, 1914, 1921, 1924). By permission of the publishers, Houghton Mifflin Company.

Cloud Confines. It is made out of a little lump of tawdry material which says nothing, is, indeed, mere twaddle. Yet it is wrought with so marvellous a technique that we seem to catch in it a far-away echo of voices that were heard when the morning stars sang together, and it clings tremulously to the memory forever.

Technique is the art of so dealing with matter — whether clay or pigment or sounds or words — that it ceases to affect us in the same way as the stuff it is wrought out of originally affects us, and becomes a Transparent Symbol of a Spiritual Reality. Something that was always familiar and commonplace is suddenly transformed into something that until that moment eye had never seen or ear heard, and that yet seems the revelation of our hearts' secret.

It is an important point to remember. For one sometimes hears ignorant persons speak of technique with a certain supercilious contempt, as though it were a mere negligible and inferior element in an artist's equipment and not the art itself, the mere virtuosity of an accomplished fiddler who seems to say anything with his fiddle, and has never really said anything in his whole life. To the artist technique is another matter. It is the little secret by which he reveals his soul, by which he reveals the soul of the world. Through technique the stuff of the artist's work becomes the stuff of his own soul moulded into shapes that were never before known. In that act Dust is transubstantiated into God. The Garment of the Infinite is lifted, and the aching human heart is pressed for one brief moment against the breast of the Ineffable Mystery.

PAUL AND VIRGINIA

September 9, [1913.] — As I sit basking in the sunshine
on this familiar little rocky peninsula in the centre of the
bay, still almost surrounded by the falling tide, I note a
youth and a girl crossing the sands below me, where the
gulls calmly rest, to the edge of dry beach. Then she
sits down and he stands or bends tenderly over her. This
continues for some time, but the operation thus deliberately carried out, it ultimately becomes clear, is simply
that of removing her shoes and stockings. At last it is accomplished, he raises her, swiftly harmonises his costume
to hers, and forthwith conducts her through some shallow
water to an island of sand. The deeper passage to my
peninsula still remains to be forded, and the feat requires
some circumspection. In less than half an hour it will be
easy to walk across dry-shod, and time is evidently no
object. But so prosaic a proceeding is disdained by Paul
and Virginia. He wades carefully forward within reach
of the rocks, flings boots, white stockings, and other
cumbersome belongings on to the lowest ledge of rock,
returns to the island, and lifts her up, supporting her body
with one arm as she clasps his neck, while with the other
he slowly and anxiously feels his way with his stout stick
among the big seaweed-grown stones in the surf. I see
them clearly now, a serious bespectacled youth of some
twenty-one years and a golden-haired girl, some two or
three years younger, in a clinging white dress. The
young Saint Christopher at last deposits his sacred
burden at the foot of the peninsula, which they climb, to
sit down on the rocks, and in the same deliberate, happy,
self-absorbed spirit complete their toilet and depart.

I know not what relation of tender intimacy unites

them, but when they have gone their faces remain in my memory. I seem to see them thirty years hence, that honest, faithful, straightforward face of the youth, transformed into the rigid image of an eminently worthy and wholly undistinguished citizen, and the radiant, meaningless girl a stout and careful Mrs. Grundy with a band of children around her. Yet the memory of to-day will still perhaps be enshrined in their hearts.

CHRISTMAS THOUGHTS

Christmas Day, [1917.] — The great recurring Festivals of the Year, each one more than the last, like the tolling of a bell, remind me how I am nearer than ever before to the last stroke of midnight, the final rhythmic flutter of the swallow's wing. Often recurs to memory the saying of the pagan Anglo-Saxon chief that we know no more of our life than that it is like the flight of a swallow which enters the hall at one end and passes out at the other. Only to me — who love the open air, and to see the world from a height, and to dream — it is not quite so that I picture my swallow's flight. Rather I seem to be taking my course from unknown mists to unknown mists over the clear lake in the valley below upon which all the shows of life are mirrored. When I set out the lake all lay before me and my dreams were ever of the life I seemed to see mirrored ahead. But now there is little to see before me, and all my dreams, beautiful or sad, are no longer of the future but of the past, that is receding into the mist now fast swallowing the whole scene.

SPRING

April 12, [1918.] — It is one of the first days of Spring, and I sit once more in the Old Garden where I hear no faintest echo of the obscene rumbling of the London streets which are yet so little away. Here the only movement I am conscious of is that of the trees shooting forth their first sprays of bright green, and of the tulips expanding the radiant beauty of their flaming globes, and the only sound I hear is the blackbird's song — the liquid softly gurgling notes that seem to well up spontaneously from an infinite Joy, an infinite Peace, at the Heart of Nature, and to bring a message not from some remote Heaven of the Sky or the Future but the Heaven that is Here, beneath our feet, even beneath the exquisite texture of our own skins, the Joy, the Peace, at the heart of the mystery which is Man. For Man alone can hear the Revelation that lies in the blackbird's song.

These years have gone by, I scarcely know how, and the heart has often been crushed and heavy, life has seemed to recede into the dimness behind, and one's eyes have been fixed on the End that crowns all. Yet on the first days of Spring, and this Spring more than those of the late years that passed over us, soft air and sunshine lap me around and I indeed see again the solemn gaiety of the tulip and hear the message in the blackbird's low and serenely joyous notes, my heart is young again, and the blood of the world is in my veins, and a woman's soul is beautiful, and her lips are sweet.

BEAUTY THE END OF LIVING

May 6, [1918.] — Yesterday, here in London, the sky was dark. The rain dropped continuously, one's spirit was dismal. To-day the air has been washed clean, the sky is bright, the trees burst into fresh green. Here, as

I sit in the Old Garden, the flowers flash with warm radiance beneath the sun, and I hear the deepest wisdom of the world slowly, quietly, melodiously voiced in the throat of the blackbird. I understand. I see the World as Beauty.

To see the World as Beauty is the whole End of Living. I cannot say it is the aim of living. Because the greatest ends are never the result of aiming; they are infinite and our aims can only be finite. We can never go beyond the duty of Saul, the Son of Kish, who went forth to seek his father's asses and found a Kingdom. It is only so that the Kingdom of Beauty is won. There is that element of truth in the contention of Bergson, no intellectual striving will bring us to the heart of things, we can only lay ourselves open to the influences of the world, and the living intuition will be born in its own due time.

Beauty is the end of living, not Truth. When I was a youth, by painful struggle, by deliberate courage, by intellectual effort, I won my way to what seemed to be Truth. It was not the end of living. It brought me no joy. Rather, it brought despair; the universe seemed empty and ugly. Yet in seeking the Asses of Truth I had been following the right road.

One day, by no conscious effort of my own, by some inspiration from without, by some expiration from within, I saw that empty and ugly Universe as Beauty, and was joined to it in an embrace of the spirit. The joy of that Beauty has been with me ever since and will remain with me till I die. All my life has been the successive quiet realisations in the small things of the world of that primary realisation in the greatest thing of the world. I know that no striving can help us to attain it, but, in so far as we attain, the end of living is reached and the cup of joy runs over.

So I know at such a moment as this, to-day, as I sit here, alone, in the warm sunshine, while the flowers flame into colour and the birds gurgle their lazy broken message of wisdom, however my life may be shadowed by care, and my heart laden with memories, the essential problems are solved.

THE DOCTRINE OF PROGRESS

June 7, [1918.] — It is a perpetual wonder and delight to watch how during the last twenty years the whole Prehistory of the world is being slowly revealed to us, with fresh marvels at every stage of the revelation. It is not long since the date of the world's creation was fixed at a few thousand years ago; now it extends to hundreds of millions, and even the age of Man himself is beginning to be thought of as running into millions. It is but thirty years ago that Virchow, the greatest authority of his time, could believe that the solitary Neanderthal skull of Palæolithic man was merely a pathological specimen. Now Neanderthal Man is a genus with many species, a being with a skull sometimes as capacious as our own, and with pioneering and inventive powers as great as our own, while behind Neanderthal Man there are other more vaguely seen beings who were yet already Man. Then there was the Magdalenian Age, the climax of a later type of Palæolithic Man's development, the race of cave-men, who were such artists that they even neglected the fine perfection of the implements of daily life in seeking to perfect the manifestation of their æsthetic sensibility. Then, again, there was the subsequent Azilian Age with its yet unsolved problems. And then, during some eight thousand or so years, there followed the revolutionary Neolithic Age which laid the solid foundations on which we still live, for little of importance has been added since. There was the Bronze Age, with its seemingly new cult of Woman. There was finally Crete with its vastly long Minoan civilisation, almost as modern to our eyes as our own to-day, and the flashing moment of its aftermath in Greece; and there was that long reverberating Decline and Fall of Rome, in the trail of which we still live, since Christianity was but a Roman filtrate of the Near East.

We cherish the popular doctrine of Progress — I have sometimes cherished it myself — yet I sometimes wonder if we have not made a huge mistake. Might it not be better if we cherished the doctrine in a reversed form? Might it not be better if we looked upon Progress as backwards? Was not the classic world — which was in a better position to know—wiser when it placed the Golden Age in the past and not, as we, doubtless influenced by the pessimistic conceptions of Christianity, in the impossible future of another world, first in the skies and then on earth? So we should indeed be trailing great clouds of glory along with us instead of being engaged in the painful task of searching for them in an uncertain future. Indeed the whole cosmic conception would fall into a new and more satisfying harmony. As things now are, we are compelled to believe that the earth is slowly decaying towards a final catastrophe, while Man, its most conspicuous inhabitant, is slowly marching towards the height of ideal Perfection. It is a painful clash of absurdly contradictory conceptions, only, it would seem, to be resolved when we attain to the faith that Man and the Earth, after their

long and agitated career, surely unique in the cosmos for
fantastic charm, are at length declining together towards
their sorely needed and infinite Rest.

Would not some such large and harmonising conception as this revolutionise and revitalise morals? Nothing
has so intoxicated and maddened the men of the latest
period of world-history as that doctrine of Progress towards a great future which they were passionately striving to achieve. (We may see it even in the present war.)
In the great Pacification of the tender bonds of a common
Fate, in the dying down of contentions which have grown
out of date, in the growth of a Toleration at length made
possible, in a new vision of Fellowship and Joy among
Comrades doomed in the same Great War, we attain to a
morality which a genuinely realised faith in the Final
Death of Man can perhaps alone render possible.

THE REAL JESUS

January 20, [1919.] — I have often wished that some
disciple of Jesus had proved a Boswell. To be able to
catch the precise definite outline of that figure as it impressed itself on the eyes, to know how this man met the
ordinary routine of daily life, what he said in casual intercourse, the tones of his voice, and all those little manner-
isms of conduct which reveal so much — how nearer
we should be brought to that unique person, and what
devastation so scandalous a Fifth Gospel would have
wrought beforehand in the ranks of the orthodox! Still
one knows they would save themselves by declaring that
it was a blasphemous forgery.

I still wish for a Boswell of Jesus, but I realise now more
than ever what a supreme work of art we already possess

in the Gospels. That is not to say that the history of
Jesus is a myth. The theory is scarcely credible. To
suppose that the religion of Jesus differed from all the
other religions which came into the world about that
time — the religion of Confucius, the religion of Buddha,
the religion of Mahomet — by crystallising round a
figure of the imagination, would be to confer on it a
supreme distinction one would hesitate to recognise.
Religion, like love in Stendhal's famous analogy, must always crystallise round some twig of the tree of life.
Apart from such aprioristic considerations, Binet-Sanglé
— though the orthodox refuse to recognise his existence
and the unorthodox cross the road to pass him by on the
other side — seems to have placed Jesus on a pedestal of
solid pathological human reality from which it will be
hard to tear him down.

There was a real Jesus, impossible as it will ever be even
for the concentrated vision of a Binet-Sanglé to discern
all his features. Yet around that concealed human person it is really the Imagination of Man which has built
up the lovely crystal figure we see. An innumerable
company of men, who had a few of them seen Jesus and
most of them only heard of him, aided in this task. Each
threw into it his highest inspiration, his deepest insight,
with the sublime faith — based on that deep human impulse, seen even in our dreams, to exteriorise our own
feelings — that this divine moment of his own soul could
only be the truthful expression of a Saviour and liberator
of Man.

It was the peculiar virtue of the personality of Jesus
that all these inspirations and insights could adhere to it
and drew together into a congruous whole. At the same

time a reversed process was evidently in movement. All the facts of the hero's life, actual or alleged, and all his sayings, real or apocryphal, were sifted and filtered through the human imagination, so purged that not a single trivial, ignoble, or even ordinary crude unpleasing statement has come down to us. At once by putting in and by taking out, with an art like that of the painter and the sculptor in one, under some rare combination of favouring conditions, the human imagination, out of the deepest impulses of the human heart, has unconsciously wrought this figure of Jesus, purified of dross and all gold, tragic in its sublimity and tremulously tender in its loving-kindness. So that now when I open and turn over with reverent joy the leaves of the Gospels, I feel that here is enshrined the highest achievement of Man the Artist, a creation to which nothing can be added, from which nothing can be taken away.

IMMORTALITY AS AN IDEAL

January 6, [1920.] — Life is not worth living, I read today in a thoughtful article in a thoughtful journal, unless it is continued beyond death. I have read that statement so often. It seems to be an idea passionately cherished by so many people. Life is nothing to them, they think, unless they are to live for ever. Everything else in the world is born and blossoms and grows lovely and fades and dies. They must go on for ever! To feel like that is to feel an alien in the world, to be divorced from Nature, to be to oneself a rigid and dead thing — for only such things persist, and even they undergo a constant subtle change — in a Universe that is in magnificent movement, for ever and for ever renewed in immortal youth, where there is in a deeper sense no Death because all Death is Life.

There must be strong reasons why that alien feeling is widespread among men. The result of tradition? No doubt, but of a tradition that goes far back in human history, even, it may be, in the history of earlier species of Man than ours. The Mousterian, who so carefully buried his dead, must have felt the same. It is a faith like the faith of those who believed that the sun travels round the earth, a faith so firm that no tortures were too precious to bestow on those who refused to share it.

Yet the faith in the fixity of the soul, like the faith in the fixity of the earth, will not work out even as an ideal conception. One may leave aside the question of it as a fact. As a fact we should be ready to accept it when it came, while still affirming, with the dying Thoreau: "One world at a time, if you please!" But as an ideal it is less easy to accept than these good people think. It is not merely that to live a full and rich life in this wonderful world, among these fascinating beings, not even excluding human beings, and to fade away when — or better, before — one has exhausted all one's power of living, should surely be a fate splendid enough for the greatest. What has always come home to me is that with the dissolution of the body the reasons for desiring the non-dissolution of the soul fall away. If I am to begin a new life, let me begin it washed clean from all my defects and errors and failures in this life, freed from the disillusioning results of all my accumulated experiences, unburdened of all my sad and delicious memories. But so to begin a new life is to annihilate the old life. The new self would be a self that is not me: what has happened to me would mean nothing to it: what happens to it can mean nothing to me.

Then again, it seems to me, and surely to many, that the supreme reason for desiring to live beyond this life is to rejoin those whom here we loved. But what would be left of them when we met again? It is the human presence of the beloved, the human weakness, the human tenderness, that are entwined round our hearts, and it is these that we crave to see and to touch again. But if they are gone — and could I be so cruel as to desire that they should be perpetuated for ever? — and if I myself no longer have eyes to see or hands to touch or a heart to throb, what can the beloved be to me or I to the beloved?

One may amuse oneself with supposing all sorts of powers of perception transcending our powers here; yet the more they transcend them the more surely they would destroy all that we now count precious, just as, it is most certain, whatever transcending powers we received on coming into the world have totally annihilated from our existence all knowledge of the powers we may or may not have possessed before we entered it.

So it seems to me that this ideal — regarded as an ideal and without reference to the question of fact, which we could deal with, if necessary, when the time came — testifies to the curious lack of imagination which, in other fields also, people so often display. When we look at it, calmly and searchingly, it fails to work out.

THE FEAR OF DEATH

March 12, [1921.] — Last week, when I was feeling, as ever since I left Cornwall I have felt, singularly firm against assault, Death, in his casual tentative indifferent way, just gave me a torturing prick with his scythe as he passed by, leaving me alive but bleeding. Ever since I lie on my back invalid, for the first time in my active life, and whether he is likely to come again soon there is none to tell me.

Yet, I find, I remain serene, even continuously cheerful. For some years past I have accommodated my arrangements to Death and guided my activities accordingly, even though I may not yet have completed everything I had planned as the minimum — for I am content the maximum should go — of my Day's Work — my Day's Play — in the world. Without rest yet without haste — it is the law of my nature which I have no intention of changing now. My faith has carried me through so far and will accompany me to the end. Death is the final Master and Lord. But Death must await my good pleasure. I command Death because I have no fear of Death, but only love.

WIND IN THE ROCKS [1]

JOHN GALSWORTHY

THOUGH dew-dark when we set forth, there was stealing
into the frozen air an invisible white host of the wan-
winged light — born beyond the mountains, and already,
like a drift of doves, harbouring grey-white high up on
the snowy sky-caves of Monte Cristallo; and within us,
tramping over the valley meadows, was the incredible
elation of those who set out before the sun has risen;
every minute of the precious day before us — we had not
lost one!

At the mouth of that enchanted chine, across which for
a million years the howdahed rock elephant has marched,
but never yet passed from sight, we crossed the stream,
and among the trees began our ascent. Very far away
the first cowbells chimed; and, over the dark heights, we
saw the thin, sinking moon, looking like the white horns
of some devotional beast watching and waiting up there
for the god of light. That god came slowly, stalking
across far over our heads from top to top; then, of a
sudden, his flame-white form was seen standing in a gap of
the valley walls; the trees flung themselves along the
ground before him, and censers of pine gum began swinging in the dark aisles, releasing their perfumed steam.
Throughout these happy ravines where no man lives, he
shows himself naked and unashamed, the colour of pale
honey; on his golden hair such shining as one has not

[1] From *The Inn of Tranquillity*. Copyright, 1912, by Charles Scribner's Sons. By permission of the publishers.

elsewhere seen; his eyes like old wine on fire. And already he had swept his hand across the invisible strings, for there had arisen the music of uncurling leaves and flitting things.

A legend runs, that, driven from land to land by Christians, Apollo hid himself in Lower Austria, but those who aver they saw him there in the thirteenth century were wrong; it was to these enchanted chines, frequented only by the mountain shepherds, that he certainly came.

And as we were lying on the grass of the first alp, with the star gentians — those fallen drops of the sky — and the burnt-brown dandelions, and scattered shrubs of alpen-rose round us, we were visited by one of these very shepherds, passing with his flock — the fiercest-looking man who ever spoke in a gentle voice; six feet high, with an orange cloak, bare knees, burnt as the very dandelions, a beard blacker than black, and eyes more glorious than if sun and night had dived and were lying imprisoned in their depths. He spoke in an unknown tongue, and could certainly not understand any word of ours; but he smelled of the good earth, and only through interminable watches under sun and stars could so great a gentleman have been perfected.

Presently, while we rested outside that Alpine hut which faces the three sphinx-like mountains, there came back, from climbing the smallest and most dangerous of those peaks, one, pale from heat, and trembling with fatigue; a tall man, with long brown hands, and a long, thin, bearded face. And, as he sipped cautiously of red wine and water, he looked at his little conquered mountain. His kindly, screwed-up eyes, his kindly, bearded lips, even his limbs seemed smiling; and not for the world

would we have jarred with words that rapt, smiling man,
enjoying the sacred hour of him who has just proved himself. In silence we watched, in silence left him smiling,
knowing somehow that we should remember him all our
days. For there was in his smile the glamour of adventure just for the sake of danger; all that high instinct
which takes a man out of his chair to brave what he need
not.

Between that hut and the three mountains lies a
saddle — astride of all beauty and all colour, master of a
titanic chaos of deep clefts, tawny heights, red domes, far
snow, and the purple of long shadows; and, standing
there, we comprehended a little of what Earth had been
through in her time, to have made this playground for
most glorious demons. Mother Earth! What travail
undergone, what long heroic throes, had brought on her
face such majesty!

Hereabout edelweiss was clinging to the smoothed-out
rubble; but a little higher, even the everlasting plant was
lost, there was no more life. And presently we lay down
on the mountain side, rather far apart. Up here above
trees and pasture the wind had a strange, bare voice, free
from all outer influence, sweeping along with a cold,
whiffling sound. On the warm stones, in full sunlight,
uplifted over all the beauty of Italy, one felt at first only
delight in space and wild loveliness, in the unknown valleys, and the strength of the sun. It was so good to be
alive; so ineffably good to be living in this most wonderful world, drinking air nectar.

Behind us, from the three mountains, came the frequent thud and scuffle of falling rocks, loosened by rains.
The wind, mist, and winter snow had ground the pow-

dery stones on which we lay to a pleasant bed, but once on a time they, too, had clung up there. And very slowly, one could not say how or when, the sense of joy began changing to a sense of fear. The awful impersonality of those great rock-creatures, the terrible impartiality of that cold, clinging wind which swept by, never an inch lifted above ground! Not one tiny soul, the size of a midge or rock flower, lived here. Not one little "I" breathed here, and loved!

And we, too, some day would no longer love, having become part of this monstrous, lovely earth, of that cold, whiffling air. To be no longer able to love! It seemed incredible, too grim to bear; yet it was true! To become powder, and the wind; no more to feel the sunlight; to be loved no more! To become a whiffling noise, cold, without one's self! To drift on the breath of that noise, homeless! Up here, there were not even those little velvet, grey-white flower-comrades we had plucked. No life! Nothing but the creeping wind, and those great rocky heights, whence came the sound of falling — symbols of that cold, untimely state into which we, too, must pass. Never more to love, nor to be loved! One could but turn to the earth, and press one's face to it, away from the wild loveliness. Of what use loveliness that must be lost; of what use loveliness when one could not love? The earth was warm and firm beneath the palms of the hands; but there still came the sound of the impartial wind, and the careless roar of the stones falling.

Below, in those valleys amongst the living trees and grass, was the comradeship of unnumbered life, so that to pass out into Peace, to step beyond, to die, seemed but a brotherly act, amongst all those others; but up here, where no creature breathed, we saw the heart of the desert that stretches before each little human soul. Up here, it froze the spirit; even Peace seemed mocking — hard as a stone. Yet, to try and hide, to tuck one's head under one's own wing, was not possible in this air so crystal clear, so far above incense and the narcotics of set creeds, and the fevered breath of prayers and protestations. Even to know that between organic and inorganic matter there is no gulf fixed, was of no peculiar comfort. The jealous wind came creeping over the lifeless limestone, removing even the poor solace of its warmth; one turned from it, desperate, to look up at the sky, the blue, burning, wide, ineffable, far sky.

Then slowly, without reason, that icy fear passed into a feeling, not of joy, not of peace, but as if Life and Death were exalted into what was neither life nor death, a strange and motionless vibration, in which one had been merged, and rested, utterly content, equipoised, divested of desire, endowed with life and death.

But since this moment had come before its time, we got up, and, close together, marched on rather silently, in the hot sun.

WALT WHITMAN [1]

EDMUND GOSSE

I

FATIMA was permitted, nay encouraged, to make use of all the rooms, so elegantly and commodiously furnished, in Bluebeard Castle, with one exception. It was in vain that the housemaid and the cook pointed out to her that each of the ladies who had preceded her as a tenant had smuggled herself into that one forbidden chamber and had never come out again. Their sad experience was thrown away upon Fatima, who penetrated the fatal apartment and became an object of melancholy derision. The little room called "Walt Whitman," in the castle of literature, reminds one of that in which the relics of Bluebeard's levity were stored. We all know that discomfort and perplexity await us there, that nobody ever came back from it with an intelligible message, that it is piled with the bones of critics; yet such is the perversity of the analytic mind, that each one of us, sooner or later, finds himself peeping through the keyhole and fumbling at the lock.

As the latest of these imprudent explorers, I stand a moment with the handle in my hand and essay a defence of those whose skeletons will presently be discovered. Was it their fault? Was their failure not rather due to a sort of magic that hangs over the place? To drop metaphor, I am sadly conscious that, after reading what a

[1] From *Critical Kit-Kats* (1896). By permission of William Heinemann, Limited, and Charles Scribner's Sons.

great many people of authority and of assumption have written about Whitman — reading it, too, in a humble spirit — though I have been stimulated and entertained, I have not been at all instructed. Pleasant light, of course, has been thrown on the critics themselves and on their various peculiarities. But upon Whitman, upon the place he holds in literature and life, upon the questions, what he was and why he was, surely very little. To me, at least, after all the oceans of talk, after all the extravagant eulogy, all the mad vituperation, he remains perfectly cryptic and opaque. I find no reason given by these authorities why he should have made his appearance, or what his appearance signifies. I am told that he is abysmal, putrid, glorious, universal and contemptible. I like these excellent adjectives, but I cannot see how to apply them to Whitman. Yet, like a boy at a shooting-gallery, I cannot go home till I, too, have had my six shots at this running-deer.

On the main divisions of literature it seems that a critic should have not merely a firm opinion, but sound argument to back that opinion. It is a pilgarlicky mind that is satisfied with saying, "I like you, Dr. Fell, the reason why I cannot tell." Analysis is the art of telling the reason why. But still more feeble and slovenly is the criticism that has to say, "I liked Dr. Fell yesterday and I don't like him to-day, but I can give no reason." The shrine of Walt Whitman, however, is strewn around with remarks of this kind. Poor Mr. Swinburne has been cruelly laughed at for calling him a "strong-winded soul, with prophetic lips hot with the blood-beats of song," and yet a drunken apple-woman reeling in a gutter. But he is not alone in this inconsistency. Almost every competent writer who has attempted to give an estimate of Whitman has tumbled about in the same extraordinary way. Something mephitic breathes from this strange personality, something that maddens the judgment until the wisest lose their self-control.

Therefore, I propound a theory. It is this, that there is no real Walt Whitman, that is to say, that he cannot be taken as any other figure in literature is taken, as an entity of positive value and defined characteristics, as, for instance, we take the life and writings of Racine, or of Keats, or of Jeremy Taylor, including the style with the substance, the teaching with the idiosyncrasy. In these ordinary cases the worth and specific weight of the man are not greatly affected by our attitude towards him. An atheist or a quaker may contemplate the writings of the Bishop of Dromore without sympathy; that does not prevent the *Holy Dying* from presenting, even to the mind of such an opponent, certain defined features which are unmodified by like or dislike. This is true of any fresh or vivid talent which may have appeared among us yesterday. But I contend that it is not true of Whitman. Whitman is mere *bathybius;* he is literature in the condition of protoplasm — an intellectual organism so simple that it takes the instant impression of whatever mood approaches it. Hence the critic who touches Whitman is immediately confronted with his own image stamped upon that viscid and tenacious surface. He finds, not what Whitman has to give, but what he himself has brought. And when, in quite another mood, he comes again to Whitman, he finds that other self of his own stamped upon the provoking protoplasm.

If this theory is allowed a moment's consideration, it

cannot, I think, but tend to be accepted. It accounts for all the difficulties in the criticism of Whitman. It shows us why Robert Louis Stevenson has found a Stevenson in *Leaves of Grass*, and John Addington Symonds a Symonds. It explains why Emerson considered the book "the most extraordinary piece of wit and wisdom that America has yet [in 1855] produced"; why Thoreau thought all the sermons ever preached not equal to it for divinity; why Italian *dilettanti* and Scandinavian gymnasts, anarchists and parsons and champions of women's rights, the most opposite and incongruous types, have the habit of taking Whitman to their hearts for a little while and then flinging him away from them in abhorrence, and, perhaps, of drawing him to them again with passion. This last, however, I think occurs more rarely. Almost every sensitive and natural person has gone through a period of fierce Whitmanomania; but it is a disease which rarely afflicts the same patient more than once. It is, in fact, a sort of highly-irritated egotism come to a head, and people are almost always better after it.

Unless we adopt some such theory as this, it is difficult to account in any way for the persistent influence of Walt Whitman's writings. They have now lasted about forty years, and show no sign whatever of losing their vitality. Nobody is able to analyse their charm, yet the charm is undeniable. They present no salient features, such as have been observed in all other literature, from Homer and David down to the latest generation. They offer a sort of Plymouth Brethrenism of form, a negation of all the laws and ritual of literature. As a book, to be a living book, must contain a vigorous and appropriate

arrangement of words, this one solitary feature occurs in
Leaves of Grass. I think it is not to be denied by any
candid critic, however inimical, that passages of extreme
verbal felicity are to be found frequently scattered over
the pages of Whitman's rhapsodies. But, this one con-
cession made to form, there is no other. Not merely are
rhythm and metre conspicuously absent, but composition, evolution, vertebration of style, even syntax and the
limits of the English tongue, are disregarded. Every
reader who comes to Whitman starts upon an expedition
to the virgin forest. He must take his conveniences with
him. He will make of the excursion what his own spirit
dictates. There are solitudes, fresh air, rough landscape,
and a well of water, but if he wishes to enjoy the latter he
must bring his own cup with him. When people are still
young and like roughing it, they appreciate a picnic into
Whitman-land, but it is not meant for those who choose to
see their intellectual comforts round them.

II

In the early and middle years of his life, Whitman was
obscure and rarely visited. When he grew old, pilgrims
not unfrequently took scrip and staff, and set out to worship him. Several accounts of his appearance and mode
of address on these occasions have been published, and if
I add one more it must be my excuse that the visit to be
described was not undertaken in the customary spirit.
All other accounts, so far as I know, of interviews with
Whitman have been written by disciples who approached
the shrine adoring and ready to be dazzled. The visitor
whose experience — and it was a very delightful one —
is now to be chronicled, started under what was, perhaps,

the disadvantage of being very unwilling to go; at least, it will be admitted that the tribute — for tribute it has to be — is all the more sincere.

When I was in Boston, in the winter of 1884, I received a note from Whitman asking me not to leave America without coming to see him. My first instinct was promptly to decline the invitation. Camden, New Jersey, was a very long way off. But better counsels prevailed; curiosity and civility combined to draw me, and I wrote to him that I would come. It would be fatuous to mention all this, if it were not that I particularly wish to bring out the peculiar magic of the old man, acting, not on a disciple, but on a stiff-necked and froward unbeliever.

To reach Camden, one must arrive at Philadelphia, where I put up on the 2nd of January, 1885, ready to pass over into New Jersey next morning. I took the hall-porter of the hotel into my confidence, and asked if he had ever heard of Mr. Whitman. Oh, yes, they all knew "Walt," he said; on fine days he used to cross over on the ferry and take the tram into Philadelphia. He liked to stroll about in Chestnut Street and look at the people, and if you smiled at him he would smile back again; everybody knew "Walt." In the North, I had been told that he was almost bedridden, in consequence of an attack of paralysis. This seemed inconsistent with wandering round Philadelphia.

The distance being considerable, I started early on the 3rd, crossed the broad Delaware River, where blocks of ice bumped and crackled around us, and saw the flat shores of New Jersey expanding in front, raked by the broad morning light. I was put ashore in a crude and ap-

parently uninhabited village, grim with that concentrated
ugliness that only an American township in the depth of
winter can display. Nobody to ask the way, or next to
nobody. I wandered aimlessly about, and was just ready
to give all I possessed to be back again in New York,
when I discovered that I was opposite No. 328 Mickle
Street, and that on a minute brass plate was engraved
"W. Whitman." I knocked at this dreary little two-
storey tenement house, and wondered what was going to
happen. A melancholy woman opened the door; it was
too late now to go away. But before I could speak, a
large figure, hobbling down the stairs, called out in a
cheery voice, "Is that my friend?" Suddenly, by I know
not what magnetic charm, all wire-drawn literary reserva-
tions faded out of being, and one's only sensation was of
gratified satisfaction at being the "friend" of this very
nice old gentleman.

There was a good deal of greeting on the stairs, and
then the host, moving actively, though clumsily, and with
a stick, advanced to his own dwelling-room on the first
storey. The opening impression was, as the closing one
would be, of extreme simplicity. A large room, without
carpet on the scrubbed planks, a small bedstead, a little
round stove with a stack-pipe in the middle of the room,
one chair — that was all the furniture. On the walls and
in the fireplace such a miserable wall-paper — tinted,
with a spot — as one sees in the bedrooms of labourers'
cottages; no pictures hung in the room, but pegs and
shelves loaded with objects. Various boxes lay about,
and one huge clamped trunk, and heaps, mountains of
papers in a wild confusion, swept up here and there into
stacks and peaks; but all the room, and the old man him-

self, clean in the highest degree, raised to the nth power of
stainlessness, scoured and scrubbed to such a pitch that
dirt seemed defied for all remaining time. Whitman, in
particular, in his suit of hodden grey and shirt thrown
wide open at the throat, his grey hair and whiter beard
voluminously flowing, seemed positively blanched with
cleanliness; the whole man sand-white with spotlessness,
like a deal table that has grown old under the scrubbing-
brush.

Whitman sat down in the one chair with a small poker
in his hand and spent much of his leisure in feeding and
irritating the stove. I cleared some papers away from
off a box and sat opposite to him. When he was not
actively engaged upon the stove his steady attention was
fixed upon his visitor, and I had a perfect opportunity of
forming a mental picture of him. He sat with a very
curious pose of the head thrown backward, as if resting it
one vertebra lower down the spinal column than other
people do, and thus tilting his face a little upwards. With
his head so poised and the whole man fixed in contemplation of the interlocutor, he seemed to pass into a state of
absolute passivity, waiting for remarks or incidents, the
glassy eyes half closed, the large knotted hands spread out
before him. So he would remain, immovable for a
quarter of an hour at a time, even the action of speech
betraying no movement, the lips hidden under a cascade
of beard. If it be true that all remarkable human beings
resemble animals, then Walt Whitman was like a cat
— a great old grey Angora Tom, alert in repose, serenely
blinking under his combed waves of hair, with eyes
inscrutably dreaming.

His talk was elemental, like his writings. It had none

of the usual ornaments or irritants of conversation. It welled out naturally, or stopped; it was innocent of every species of rhetoric or epigram. It was the perfectly simple utterance of unaffected urbanity. So, I imagine, an Oriental sage would talk, in a low uniform tone, without any excitement or haste, without emphasis, in a land where time and flurry were unknown. Whitman sat there with his great head tilted back, smiling serenely, and he talked about himself. He mentioned his poverty, which was patent, and his paralysis; those were the two burdens beneath which he crouched, like Issachar; he seemed to be quite at home with both of them, and scarcely heeded them. I think I asked leave to move my box, for the light began to pour in at the great uncurtained window; and then Whitman said that some one had promised him a gift of curtains, but he was not eager for them, he thought they "kept out some of the light." Light and air, that was all he wanted; and through the winter he sat there patiently waiting for the air and light of summer, when he would hobble out again and bask his body in a shallow creek he knew "back of Camden." Meanwhile he waited, waited with infinite patience, uncomplaining, thinking about the sand, and the thin hot layer of water over it, in that shy New Jersey creek. And he winked away in silence, while I thought of the Indian poet Valmiki, when, in a trance of voluptuous abstraction, he sat under the fig-tree and was slowly eaten of ants.

In the bareness of Whitman's great double room only two objects suggested art in any way, but each of these was appropriate. One was a print of a Red Indian, given him, he told me, by Catlin; it had inspired the passage about "the red aborigines" in *Starting from Paumanok*.

The other — positively the sole and only thing that re-deemed the bareness of the back-room where Whitman's bound works were stored — was a photograph of a very handsome young man in a boat, sculling. I asked him about this portrait and he said several notable things in consequence. He explained, first of all, that this was one of his greatest friends, a professional oarsman from Can-ada, a well-known sporting character. He continued, that these were the people he liked best, athletes who had a business in the open air; that those were the plainest and most affectionate of men, those who lived in the light and air and had to study to keep their bodies clean and fresh and ruddy; that his soul went out to such people, and that they were strangely drawn to him, so that at the lowest ebb of his fortunes, when the world reviled him and ridiculed him most, fortunate men of this kind, highly prosperous as gymnasts or runners, had sought him out and had been friendly to him. "And now," he went on, "I only wait for the spring, to hobble out with my staff into the woods, and when I can sit all day long close to a set of woodmen at their work, I am perfectly happy, for something of their life mixes with the smell of the chopped timber, and it passes into my veins and I am old and ill no longer." I think these were his precise words, and they struck me more than anything else that he said throughout that long and pleasant day I spent with him.

It might be supposed, and I think that even admirers have said, that Whitman had no humour. But that seemed to me not quite correct. No boisterous humour, truly, but a gentle sort of sly fun, something like Tenny-son's, he certainly showed. For example, he told me of some tribute from India, and added, with a twinkling smile, "You see, I 'sound my barbaric yawp over the roofs of the world.'" But this was rare: mostly he seemed dwelling in a vague pastoral past life, the lovely days when he was young, and went about with "the boys" in the sun. He read me many things; a new "poem," intoning the long irregular lines of it not very distinctly; and a preface to some new edition. All this has left, I confess, a dim impression, swallowed up in the serene self-unconsciousness, the sweet, dignified urbanity, the feline immobility.

As I passed from the little house and stood in dull, deserted Mickle Street once more, my heart was full of affection for this beautiful old man, who had just said in his calm accents, "Good-bye, my friend!" I felt that the experience of the day was embalmed by something that a great poet had written long ago, but I could not find what it was till we started once more to cross the frosty Delaware; then it came to me, and I knew that when Shelley spoke of

> Peace within and calm around,
> And that content, surpassing wealth,
> The sage in meditation found,
> And walk'd with inward glory crown'd,

he had been prophesying of Walt Whitman, nor shall I ever read those lines again without thinking of the old rhapsodist in his empty room, glorified by patience and philosophy.

And so an unbeliever went to see Walt Whitman, and was captivated without being converted.

III

It is related of the great Condé that, at the opening of

his last campaign, sunken in melancholy, half maddened with fatigue and the dog-star heat of summer, having reached at length the cool meadows in front of the Abbey of St. Antoine, he suddenly leaped from his horse, flung away his arms and his clothing, and rolled stark-naked in the grass under a group of trees. Having taken this bath amidst his astonished officers, he rose smiling and calm, permitted himself to be dressed and armed anew. and rode to battle with all his accustomed resolution, The instinct which this anecdote illustrates lies deep down in human nature, and the more we are muffled up in social conventions the more we occasionally long for a whimsical return to nudity. If a writer is strong enough, from one cause or another, to strip the clothing off from civilisation, that writer is sure of a welcome from thousands of over-civilised readers.

Now the central feature of the writings of Walt Whitman is their nakedness. In saying this I do not refer to half-a-dozen phrases, which might with ease be eliminated, that have thrown Mrs. Grundy into fits. No responsible criticism will make a man stand or fall by what are simply examples of the carrying of a theory to excess. But of the theory itself I speak, and it is one of uncompromising openness. It is a defence of bare human nature, stripped, not merely of all its trappings and badges, but even of those garments which are universally held necessary to keep the cold away. In so many of his writings, and particularly, of course, in the *Discours* of 1750, Rousseau undertook the defence of social nudity. He called upon his world, which prided itself so much upon its elegance, to divest the body politic of all its robes. He declared that while Nature has made man happy and virtuous, society it is that renders him miserable and depraved, therefore let him get rid of social conventions and roll naked in the grass under the elm-trees. The invitation, as I have said, is one which never lacks acceptance, and Rousseau was followed into the forest by a multitude.

If Walt Whitman goes further than Rousseau, it merely is that he is more elementary. The temperament of the American is in every direction less complex. He has none of the restless intellectual vivacity, none of the fire, none of the passionate hatred of iniquity which mark the French philosopher. With Walt Whitman a coarse simplicity suffices, a certain blunt and determined negation of artificiality of every kind. He is, roughly speaking, a keenly observant and sentient being, without thought, without selection, without intensity, egged on by his nervous system to a revelation of himself. He records his own sensations one after another, careful only to present them in veracious form, without drapery or rhetoric. His charm for others is precisely this, that he observes so closely, and records so great a multitude of observations, and presents them with so complete an absence of prejudice, that any person who approaches his writings with an unbiassed mind must discover in them a reflection of some part of himself. This I believe to be the secret of the extraordinary attraction which these rhapsodical utterances have for most emotional persons at one crisis or another in their life's development. But I think criticism ought to be able to distinguish between the semi-hysterical pleasure of self-recognition and the sober and legitimate delights of literature.

The works of Walt Whitman cover a great many pages, but the texture of them is anything but subtle. When once the mind perceives what it is that Whitman says, it is found that he repeats himself over and over again, and that all his "gospel" (as the odious modern cant puts it) is capable of being strained into very narrow limits. One "poem" contains at least the germ of all the sheaves and sheaves of writing that Whitman published. There is not one aspect of his nature which is not stated, or more than broadly hinted at, in the single piece which he named after himself, *Walt Whitman*. It was appropriately named, for an unclothing of himself, an invitation to all the world to come and prove that, stripped of his clothes, he was exactly like everybody else, was the essence of his religion, his philosophy, and his poetry.

It is not unfair to concentrate attention on the section of sixty pages which bears the name *Walt Whitman* in the volume of his collected writings. It is very interesting reading. No truly candid person meeting with it for the first time, and not previously prejudiced against it, could but be struck with its felicities of diction and its air of uncontrolled sincerity. A young man of generous impulses could scarcely, I think, read it and not fall under the spell of its sympathetic illusions. It contains unusually many of those happy phrases which are, I contend, the sole purely literary possession of Whitman. It contains dozens of those closely packed lines in each of which Whitman contrives to concentrate a whole picture of some action or condition of Nature. It contains, perhaps, the finest, certainly the most captivating, of all Whitman's natural apostrophes:

Press close, bare-bosom'd night.   Press close, magnetic, nourishing
     night!
Night of south winds! night of the large few stars!

Still, nodding night! mad, naked summer night!
Smile, O voluptuous, cool-breath'd earth!
Earth of the slumbering and liquid trees!
Earth of departed sunset! earth of the mountains, misty-topt!
Earth of the vitreous pour of the full moon, just tinged with blue!
Earth of shine and dark, mottling the tide of the river!
Earth of the limpid grey of clouds, brighter and clearer for my sake!
Far-swooping, elbow'd earth! rich, apple-blossom'd earth!
Smile, for your lover comes!

All this represents the best side of the author; but *Walt Whitman* exhibits his bad sides as well — his brutality, mis-styling itself openness, his toleration of the ugly and the forbidden, his terrible laxity of thought and fatuity of judgment.

If he studies *Walt Whitman* carefully, a reader of middle life will probably come to the conclusion that the best way to classify the wholly anomalous and irregular writer who produced it is to place him by himself as a maker of poems in solution. I am inclined to admit that in Walt Whitman we have just missed receiving from the New World one of the greatest of modern poets, but that we have missed it must at the same time be acknowledged. To be a poet it is not necessary to be a consistent and original thinker, with an elaborately-balanced system of ethics. The absence of intellectual quality, the superabundance of the emotional, the objective, the pictorial, are no reasons for undervaluing Whitman's imagination. But there is one condition which distinguishes art from mere amorphous expression; that condition is the result of a process through which the vague and engaging observations of Whitman never passed. He felt acutely and accurately, his imagination was purged of external impurities, he lay spread abroad in a condition of literary

solution. But there he remained, an expanse of crystal-
lisable substances, waiting for the structural change that
never came; rich above almost all his coevals in the pro-
perties of poetry, and yet, for want of a definite shape and
fixity, doomed to sit for ever apart from the company of
the Poets.

MANDALAY[1]

PHILIP GUEDALLA

THERE is, there was always, a certain remoteness about Mr. Rudyard Kipling. His imagination played perpetually round the ends of the earth. His earliest works were imported in blue-grey paper covers from Allahabad. Even his name came from Staffordshire. He specialised in the outer edges of Mercator's Projection, in Lungtung-pen and Mandalay and those miraculous regions east of Suez where Queen Victoria's writ ran a trifle uncertainly. He even went so far afield (it was an incredible achievement in the heyday of Mrs. Humphry Ward) as to have an American public. In a generation which regarded stories of Scottish life as travellers' tales from the far North, he extended the public imagination to broad and distant horizons; and, taking whole degrees of latitude in his stride, he jerked a familiar thumb over his shoulder in the direction of the Equator, a Pole or so, and all the uncomfortable wonders of the world which lie outside the Temperate Zone. It became his mission to convince his fellow-subjects that the British Empire was an ideal and not merely an accident, and that the oddly dressed equestrians with dark faces, who rode in the cavalcade of Queen Victoria's second Jubilee, possessed a significance beyond that normally attributed to them by the proprietors of circuses. It was a high theme, which took

[1] From *A Gallery* (1924). By permission of Hodder & Stoughton, Limited, and G. P. Putnam's Sons.

him up and down the map, and even into agreement with Mr. Joseph Chamberlain.

But his remoteness in place was more than equalled by his remoteness, as one looks at him now, in point of time. The Dinosaurus, one feels, can give points in modernity to Mr. Kipling. After all, it is on speaking terms with Mr. H. G. Wells. But the author of *Soldiers Three* seems to belong to an age of almost fabulous antiquity. His flag, his Queen, his soldiers are the vague figures of a mythology that is rapidly fading into folklore. His political message has a dim interest for research students. And patient excavation will, no doubt, confirm many of the statements that are to be found in his text. The old, flamboyant Anglo-Saxon challenge to the inferior peoples of the earth went under, long before Mr. Kipling had a grey hair, in the dreary watches of the South African War. It was seen in that dismal winter of 1899 that the dashing subaltern of his dreams was not even an infallible master of his own profession. It was feared that the British soldier was even capable of fighting on the wrong side. And when the South African Constitution handsomely admitted as much, there was no place in Mr. Kipling's scheme for Louis Botha and Jan Smuts. The Imperial ideal wilted through the long years between the Peace of Vereeniging and the outbreak in 1914 of a life-sized war. The White Man grew more interested in his own highly complicated affairs than in his Burden; and gradually British opinion came to regard a Labour leader as a more important person than a retired proconsul. It was, for Lord Curzon, Lord Milner, and Lord Cromer as well as for Mr. Kipling, an embittering interlude. Then, as they say in novels when the author feels an acute need for a change of scene, the war came; and when it went, it left behind a dismal world groping for some cohesion among the broken pieces, snatching hungrily at any fragment of common organisation, but profoundly unfriendly to the old, self-seeking gesture which had painted the map red· Perhaps the map seemed quite red enough after the war. Three Empires had been hissed off the stage, and there was a sharp drop in Imperial quotations on the world market. The old ideals were looking a little guilty, even when they spoke perfect English; and there was an uneasy suspicion that the gleam which Mr. Kipling had followed was the silver gleam of an eagle perched on an old man's helmet among the trees at Doorn.

But as one turns the page and passes into Mr. Kipling's kingdom, one is centuries away from the pale uncertainties, the dingy, poor-spirited doubts of the world we live in. The Queen is on her throne again at Windsor; her sentries pace up and down the world; and the secrets of the universe fall open at the command of a cocksure young man in spectacles with a large moustache, "a strangely clever youth," as a startled commentator observed him, "who has stolen the formidable mask of maturity and rushes about making people jump with the deep sounds, the sportive exaggerations of tone, that issue from its painted lips." There is something which must remind one of Gulliver among the largest and most majestic of his hosts in the spectacle of Mr. Henry James turning that solemn microscope on Mr. Kipling. Yet the criticism (it is in a forgotten preface of an obscure American volume) contains the wisest enumeration of Mr. Kipling's qualities.

His extreme youth is indeed what I may call his window-bar

— the support on which he somewhat rowdily leans while he
looks down at the human scene with his pipe in his teeth; just
as his other conditions (to mention only some of them) are his
prodigious facility, which is only less remarkable than his stiff
selection; his unabashed temperament, his flexible talent, his
smoking-room manner, his familiar friendship with India —
established so rapidly, and so completely under his control;
his delight in battle, his "cheek" about women — and indeed
about men and about everything; his determination not to be
duped, his "imperial" fibre, his love of the inside view, the
private soldier, and the primitive man.

The whole of Mr. Kipling is to be found somewhere
along the branches of that ramifying sentence. It has
been written more than thirty years; and in the interval
his familiarity with India has taken in another continent
or so; the flexible talent has been bent to verse, to pro-
phecy, to ancient history, to the elusive pursuit of English
landscape; and the prodigious facility, alas! has run dry.
But the smoking-room manner, the love of the inside
view, remained constant; and criticism, through the
mouth of Mr. Henry James in 1891, had said its last word
on Mr. Kipling.

Technically, of course, his achievement has been astounding. He handled the foils in the short story with
unparalleled skill; and as a stylist he enlarged the limits
of the English language with all the gusto of an Empire-
builder planting the flag in undiscovered regions. But
not all his conquests (one has noticed the same weakness
among Empire-builders) were of equal value. His contribution to the poetic vocabulary seemed principally
to consist in scraps of Hindustani, the simple litany of the
blaspheming soldier, and the deeper tone of the Author-
ised Version (O. T.). By persons unfamiliar with the

original, Mr. Kipling is frequently admired for qualities which should be attributed with greater accuracy to the Jacobean translator of the Book of Psalms. But one feels that as a poet he found the English language marble and left it stucco. The new building material is at once cheaper to get and easier to handle; and his introduction of it on the market has brought poetic composition within the means of persons who should never have been able to afford a Rhyming Dictionary. Perhaps his imitators are the gravest wrong which Mr. Kipling has inflicted upon his country's literature.

But his contribution to English prose is more serious. That instrument, since English falls naturally into poetry just as French falls into prose and German into ballads, is perhaps the most difficult to play upon in the whole range of language. Mr. Kipling played on his instrument with queer, *staccato* jerks and sudden discords. There were new notes in it which shocked the old concert-goers; and to some hearers the music seems sometimes to degenerate into mere noise. But his touch was astonishingly sure, and he played on the English language an air which had never been heard before. One may say that under his hand the instrument of prose lost some of its deeper notes, grew shriller, often trailed away into discord. But it rendered strange airs which could never have come over the old strings, and Mr. Kipling left it the richer and the better for his innovations.

It is easy enough to find his stale politics ridiculous, or to see, with Mr. Beerbohm, an ineluctable vulgarity in the perpetual knowingness of his unchanging wink. But Mr. Kipling, in his true perspective, is something more than a warning to young poets or a monument of late-

Victorian Imperialism. He sharpened the English language to a knife-edge, and with it he has cut brilliant patterns on the surface of our prose literature. At least two of the best stories in the world are somewhere behind that line of red book-backs; and scattered up and down inside the books are scores of vivid little etchings, fit for a place in any portfolio — blazing sunlight, some seascapes of the North Atlantic, frontier fighting, a dozen men, some women, and one doleful little boy. He has made his contribution to letters; and one day, when the new voices are less insistent and through a silence we can catch his strange, halting tones, it will be remembered.

THE KAABAH OF ANGLERS[1]

STEPHEN GWYNN

It is very difficult for a person who is keenly interested in
life at first hand to enter into the joys of a collector.
What is new, what is in the making, what holds in it perhaps the seeds of the future, has little attraction for the
picker-up of rarities: he dredges for the wreckage of the
past. And yet, by an odd inconsistency, he is most vividly alert to capture something that shall make the past
seem present — some piece of flotsam which, instead of
suffering the common fate, has lingered in a back eddy,
and now passes, belated, on its way to that annihilation
of all material objects, from which his dragnet can give
it a short or a long reprieve. My metaphor, which is none
of the newest, demands a bank to the stream of time, on
which may be carefully reposited and lifted out of the
flux of things such articles as the world or fate decides
shall be not altogether transitory. The collector, as I
conceive him, has a double function. Sometimes he
brings up out of the flood objects whose real beauty en-
titles them to the reprieve — things of intrinsic value.
But, more often, his choicest spoils are such as in themselves have no claim to be rescued from the general doom,
yet, for the sake of some man or some event whose memory has been preserved, inherit a worthy place in our regard. We are grateful to the collectors, almost as to the
historians, yet I cannot but wonder at them. There are
hundreds of highly intelligent men who would have paid

[1] From *Fishing Holidays* (1900). By permission of the author.

high for Lord Edward Fitzgerald's snuffbox, but would
not have crossed the street to see Parnell. Now indeed,
now that the uncrowned king is fairly under ground, and
on his way to become a legend, they will prick their ears
at the mention of his name: but they follow the precept
in Aristotle, and will always wait to see the end.

In presence of these votaries of the past I feel myself
rebuked for crudity. The present with its stirring life
is, after all, so obvious, so intrusive; it has not the settled
dignity of what comes down. And if I do not envy, I admire the more, their latest acquisition, the authentic
treasure-trove. Yet my friends, the well-turned legs of
whose Chippendale I praise heart-whole — *teretesque
suras integer laudo* — whose first editions I handle with
discreet enthusiasm—whose portfolio-guarded prints I
care for perhaps as much as they do, yet without the desire of possession — would rather, I know, see the ill-
repressed twinge of jealousy in a rival hunter's face, or
detect in his voice the light inflection of spleen. The
charmed circle which I never enter is a circle of their
dearest enemies.

Still, from the outside, I distinguish sharply between
collector and collector. The stamp-hunter has no place
in my regard; he yields basely to the lust of acquisitive-
ness, anxious only to have what some one else has not. It
is a competition over counters, meaningless save for the
competition; and counters whose value is decidedly their
market-price. With all collectors who deserve the name
the mere fact of rarity must weigh; and no man need be
reckoned seriously in the list who does not pride himself
upon a bargain. But there are men who collect not less
for beauty than for rarity, or for that skill of workman-

ship which is almost beauty, and who value the historic and the human interest far beyond any consideration of a selling price. In a word, there are the collectors who have the artist's instinct and the scholar's; there are those who have only the passion of the miser for his hoard. And high in the most honourable class would rank the friend whose singular good fortune I have the honour to relate, and whom (after the bygone fashion) I will call simply by his appropriate adjective, Virtuoso.

Virtuoso, then, is a collector born and bred; but not of the tragic variety. He need not deny himself life's comforts, nor scrimp his stomach to fulfil the desire of his eyes. The bragging purchase of some world's wonder in the crowded auction-room is not for him; but neither does he need to pass a treasure for the lack of some few pounds. He has no narrow limitations of taste; whatever is rare and fine, whether it come from east or west, from two thousand years back or from the day of our grandfathers, has its interest for him. And for a final perfection — perhaps the most important for the collector's own felicity — Virtuoso has no wife. Was there ever yet a woman who saw with contentment, and with that entire sympathy which an enthusiast must inevitably exact, money transforming itself daily into objects, many of which are expensive, and all of which gather dust?

Virtuoso, then, this model of his kind, had occasion to take his way from a point in the south-western district to the City. The day was unattractive, and he debated in his mind the question of a bus, but decided for the advantages of a constitutional. Observe the finger of Providence. His way took him through a street in Westminster, quite out of his habitual beat, and in that street was a shop, which you or I would have passed unregarding. Not so the collector, whose well-trained eye detected from across the road a brown leather object in the window with a label attached to it, "Izaak Walton's Fishing-Bag." Well, of course, on the face of it, no collector was going to believe that! If you saw advertised for sale in a casual window Shakespeare's pen, Nelson's spy-glass, Sir Joshua's palette, would you attach any importance to the label? Still less would a collector, who knows by long experience the wicked ways of dealers. And, in sober earnest, neither Shakespeare's pen nor Nelson's spy-glass, could they be proved genuine, would excite a much keener emulation among collectors than Izaak Walton's fishing-bag.

Fame is an odd thing. Here was a little London linen-draper, a man of parts, no doubt, distinguished by his friends, distinguished by the trust reposed in him, but still a linen-draper living in a very quiet way, who in the evening of his life published a little book about his favourite recreation. And to-day, for the English-speaking race, there is one Abraham, one Jacob, one Rachel, one Rebecca, and so on, but there are two Izaacs. The draper disputes the patriarch's monopoly: one is thankful to him at times for having adopted a different spelling of the name. Is this hyperbole? I hardly think so. But at all events consider the case of Dr. Donne. Donne was Dean of Saint Paul's (in itself no small position), a Dean famous for his eloquence, for his subtlety, and also all-famous for his conversion; marked with that romantic halo which distinguishes the saint who once has enjoyed a very different reputation. For this dean was the author of poems, as we all know, which he suppressed indeed, but

which none the less circulated, until, with his good will or
without it, Donne occupied to Ben Jonson much the same
relation as Browning bore to Tennyson in the estimation
of contemporaries. Donne's poetry survives, I know; it
is read by the handful of literary persons who really read,
and who read poetry, but of this illustrious figure, poet,
orator, divine, dignitary, what does the world know?
Why, that Walton wrote his life. Or take again Sir
Henry Wotton, a great courtier, a great diplomatist, a
fine poet, courteous and affable, one who unbent so far
as to fish with the accomplished little Fleet Street trader.
To-day there are forty thousand men who know Walton's
name for one who has heard of Wotton. It might seem,
indeed, that this were impossible, for are not the two
names indissolubly united by Walton's frequent mention
of his distinguished friend and quotation of his writings?
But the immortal Izaak has risen far beyond the repute
that goes with first-hand knowledge; he survives as a
personality, like Johnson, vaguely familiar to thousands
who never read a line that came from his pen. He is
more a genius than a man — the patron saint of his
craft.

And now Virtuoso was being asked to believe that he
saw before him Izaak Walton's fishing-bag. It was too
much for credulity. For generations, men had rum-
maged archives to discuss every little detail of the man's
life; and here before him, there cropped up what purported
to be, not some indifferent relic, a book with his auto-
graph, a piece of his furniture, but the very sign and symbol of his own peculiar mystery — the one thing of all
others that a collector could most desire.

It may be said, perhaps, that I attach an undue impor-

tance to the relic. The bag is not essential to the angler;
the rod is. Granted. And still, if one of the two was
miraculously destined to re-emerge, to slip out of its long
stay in the back eddy of things — for of course I have to
explain that this treasure was no other than the real article — I am glad it was the creel. The rod would have
been a disillusionment. It would have brought home to
us relentlessly the fact which so many gloze over to their
imagination, or only whisper to their own souls — that
after all Izaak was by the essence and temperament of
him addicted to the baser branches of the sport. Let us
say it and chance the consequences. He preferred the
natural fly to the artificial, and the worm to either. And
I greatly fear that if we were confronted with his rod, it
would be too apparently of the kind that is naturally left
on the bank to fish by itself while the owner sits under a
sycamore tree and rhapsodises about the sweet smells of
earth and meadow-grass after summer rain.

But the bag — that tells no tales but such as one would
gladly hear; and if it is not essential to the act of angling,
it is certainly indispensable in more ways than one to the
angler's comfort and pleasure. Changes of fashion,
modern improvements, have detracted no whit from its
respectability; there it is to-day, as sound, strong, and
serviceable as it was two hundred and fifty years ago
when the Londoner strapped it on his back. That is
why Virtuoso bought it.

The bag was a rarity, for one seldom sees a wallet of
such a shape; and it was a model of good workmanship.
Three pieces of the stoutest leather — such leather as
makes the very best portmanteaux — composed the
fabric: a flat piece to lie against the back; a large rounded

piece, admirably cut and moulded, to make the belly of
the bag; another small flat piece for the lid, fastened to
the back piece by three brass hinges, and pierced of course
with a hole so that fish could be dropped in without opening the lid. The whole shape of the thing as it bellied
out was satisfying to the eye, and spoke of a time when
craftsmanship was not far removed from art. The
colour had darkened with time to that of a much-used
football, but the leather was as smooth, and as hard, as
polished wood. On the back piece was applied a strong
strip of leather, through which the strap might run, and
the face of this was neatly decorated with an incised pattern. Underneath it was cut with a knife the following
inscription:

J. D. ANDERSON
FROM MY FRIEND IZAAK WALTON
1646

Virtuoso paid little attention to the inscription, the
work, he presumed, of some ingenious person anxious to
give his possession a fictitious value; but at least it detracted nothing from the bag, which he bought and took
home as a fine specimen of seventeenth-century leather
work. If there lingered in his mind some faint hope that
after all the thing might be what it professed itself, that
was a human weakness which he did not unduly encour-
age. It was only after three weeks that the discovery
was made. Some word of the relic had got abroad, and
a paragraph appeared in an evening paper, stating that
Walton's fishing-bag was to be seen at a curiosity shop in
Westminster. Virtuoso, like a good collector, cut out the
paragraph — chuckling to himself over the fact that the

bag was in other keeping than a dealer's — and pasted it on to the object. Observe again the Providence. He fixed it, of course, on the inner side of the lid. The whole interior of the leather had been originally painted with a white enamel, so as to admit of the bag being thoroughly cleansed of all scaliness; and this enamel had cracked in every direction with time. Virtuoso was opening the lid to show this to a friend — not the first friend, by many, to whom the trophy had been displayed — and also to call his attention to the paragraph. The friend read the paragraph and said to the astonished Virtuoso: "It's all right; there is the man's name!"

And sure enough — oh, rapture! on the inside of the lid, one on either side of the hole, were branded the consecrated letters, "I. W." It was possible to miss them owing to the cracks of the enamel — impossible to mistake them once they were pointed out.

Here, indeed, was confirmation. The bag had no pedigree. Either it was genuine or it was not. Against the belief that it was genuine stood the antecedent improbability — hardly to be overstated — that such a relic should so long have survived unnoticed. But the improbable is always happening. Moreover, the lettering of the exterior inscription looked like a modern hand. But, *per contra*, against the theory of forgery stood almost insuperable objections. First, was it possible to give to the initials *inside* the cover that extraordinary appearance of old age? Secondly, if the thing had been forged, was it conceivable that the very point and essence of the forgery should come to be so completely overlooked that a dealer could sell the bag in absolute ignorance that the initials existed? Those two arguments alone seemed to dispose of the idea. Others presented themselves on further thought. Was it likely that any forger should bestow upon the supposed recipient a name not to be traced in Waltoniana (so far as my investigation of elaborate indices has gone)? Or was it at all probable that the date would be one prior and not subsequent to the publication of the *Compleat Angler*? In 1646 seven years had yet to run before the immortal work saw the light.

So far the proof is negative, and merely shows the improbability of forgery. But one can get a step farther. What was Walton doing in 1646? Is there any reason assignable why he should part from a cherished possession? There is. Anthony Wood states that in 1643 Walton, whose friends and sympathies were Royalist, left the troubled and unfriendly atmosphere of London for a country retreat at Stafford. But it has since been shown (by Nicolas) that Wood's date is wrong. In December 1645 Walton was in London. It is known, of course, that he was in Stafford, and after the battle of Worcester the King's George, saved from the enemy, was committed to no other person than Walton to hand over to Colonel Blagne for safe custody. I suggest, then, that the date of his departure from London was in 1646, and that in making a clearance of his effects, and in seeking for mementoes to bestow on valued friends, he was led to make this gift to J. D. Anderson. That Walton used a bag is happily beyond dispute, and used it, like many another man, to carry more things than fish.

Listen to Piscator. "My honest scholar, it is now past five of the clock; we will fish till nine and then go to breakfast. Go you to yonder sycamore tree and hide your

bottle of drink under the hollow root of it; for about that
time and in that place we will make a brave breakfast
with a piece of powdered beef, and a radish or two, that
I have in my fish-bag."

Yet the bag was not universal, for Cotton in a very
similar passage of the Second Part mentions his "fish-
pannier." Another fact may have some bearing on the
matter — that about 1646 Walton married for the second
time, and heaven knows what far-reaching revolution
that may have worked in his personal furniture.

I do not think further argument is needed; the thing is,
to a plain man's intelligence, beyond dispute. Virtuoso
possesses a most enviable relic; we fishermen are a devout
folk, we cherish the literature of our pastime; Cobbett's
cricket guides are not better known than the classics of
the angle. And surely to anglers this belonging of the
patron of our craft should be a thing hardly less venerable than the sacred Kaabah towards which the Mahome-
dan would look in his devotions. Virtuoso does well to
suppress his name, or the steps of his house had like to
become a highway of pilgrimage.

Yet, I confess, one thing is wanting to complete satisfaction. There is the bag, with fair round belly, not im-
moderate, and yet ample to contain your "great logger-
headed chub," or such a trout as that Piscator showed to
his disciple for the first-fruits of his skill with the nobler
fish: a fish that was warranted "to fill six reasonable
bellies"; that was twenty-two inches long when it was
taken, and "the belly looked some part of it as yellow as
a marigold, and part of it as white as a lily" — and "yet
methinks looks better in this good sauce," says Piscator.
In that description the fish survives; the bag is here to

testify; but who was J. D. Anderson? The boon that
fortune may still have in store for Virtuoso is the discovery, first of some further connecting evidence between
Walton and a person of that name, and then — but that
I fear is impossible — the demonstration that the man
to whom the angler, leaving London, consigned the bag
that had so often swung from his shoulders as he stretched
his legs up Tottenham Hill on the way to Ware and the
banks of the Lea, was no other than his honest disciple,
Piscator of the book.

MEMORIES OF RICHARD WAGNER[1]

FRANK HARRIS

IT was in 1878 or '79, I think, that I was studying in Munich, and one evening at the opera Heinrich Vogl, the great singer, told me that Wagner had come to town. People no longer treated him, as Berlioz said, as "a scamp and impostor or idiot," but I was often amazed to find that nine out of ten capable musicians were inclined to question his greatness and usually spoke disdainfully of "the Music of the Future" and Wagner's theatrical innovations!

The journalists I met took a still lower view, and talked of him with shrugs and jeers as the parasite and chamber-musician of the profligate young King, and did not scruple to hint at viler reasons for what they regarded as the peculiar alliance of age with youth.

The ordinary citizen, or so-called man in the street, was even more venomous. He would talk wildly of the sums lavished upon Wagner by the King, and declare that the monarch must be mad to indulge in such extravagance: "It's our money, you know, and we shall have to pay for this new-fangled theatre. We Muenchener folk have no reason to like this renegade Socialist who now lives off the fat of the land and does nothing for it — mad King, bad favourite!"

In spite of the King's favour — or because of it — Wagner was more than once compelled to leave Munich.

[1] From *Contemporary Essays, Fourth Series.* Copyright, 1923, by Brentano's. By permission of the author and the publishers.

In 1865 he had answered continuous newspaper calumnies in a quiet, dignified letter, but it availed him nothing. The police assured the King that Wagner's life was in danger, and the King himself asked him to leave Munich for a time, in order that the people might come to their senses. Another proof may be given of the low estimate of Wagner cherished in German musical centres, even in the latter years of his life.

The King wanted to build Wagner a theatre in Munich, but the Town Council would not hear of it. They vetoed the proposal, and in consequence the house and theatre were built at Bayreuth.

Wagner's unpopularity filled me with absolute amazement, for at that time I had no faintest notion of how universally greatness is disliked and persecuted, and I knew enough about Wagner to feel sure he deserved admiration and a certain reverence.

While a student at Heidelberg a year before, I had met a Jew named Louis Waldstein, brother of the Charles Waldstein who has since come to some honour as a Cambridge professor; and Louis Waldstein really understood Wagner. I had gone to the theatre at Mannheim with him and heard *Der Fliegende Hollaender* and *Lohengrin* and *Tannhaeuser* time and again; I had sat up nights while Waldstein explained to me the leading motives of these dramas and played them over on the piano.

So when I heard that Wagner was in Munich, I was on fire to meet him.

"Where's he living?" I asked, and Vogl told me that he was staying near the Englischer Garten, in the house of a Fräulein Schmidt, who let rooms and kept boarders.

Next morning I went to call on Fräulein Schmidt. She

told me that she could only let three rooms at a time, but her price was so much below what I was paying at the Vierjahreszeiten Hotel that I transferred my belongings to her house that same afternoon.

After a day or so I brought Fräulein Schmidt some flowers and gave her some theatre tickets, which pleased her very much, and hinted that I should like to meet Wagner. Her face changed immediately, and she had a very expressive face. She was a woman, at that time, of perhaps thirty-five or thirty-six years of age, tall, with a good figure, nice-looking, but a little staid.

"Oh my," she cried doubtfully, "I'd have to ask him first; he's sometimes very irritable. I introduced him once to a Herr Professor — and he told me never to do it again; said the professor was a fool, and he couldn't stand fools. He is sometimes very cross. If you meet him, you'll have to be very careful; you will be, won't you?"

"Of course I will," I replied. "Besides, I have a great admiration for him, and I would like to tell him how much his music means to me."

"That will please him," she said. "He likes praise — a good deal of praise. I'll find an opportunity and ask him, but you must not blame me if he refuses."

"Of course I shan't," I smiled. "It is very kind indeed of you to try."

But in spite of my flowers and little presents in the shape of tickets for the opera, etc., a fortnight elapsed and I had not seen Wagner except once, when I met him by chance at the door of the house. His appearance surprised me. He was below middle height, and broad, though rather thin; he wore glasses; his eyes were greyish-blue; his nose Jewish-long and rather heavy. The feature of his face, however, was his chin — a hard, bony, prominent chin, with which as a ploughshare he drove to the front everywhere. I noticed he was irritably quick and abrupt in his movements. As I passed him in the doorway I bowed, smiling; he just nodded, as if he wanted nothing to do with me. The chance meeting revived my desire to know him, and I approached Fräulein Schmidt again.

"Why not let us meet at dinner?" I proposed. "Try and arrange it."

A day or so later she said to me: "It is for Tuesday, but he only said he would see you after I told him you were an American and a great admirer of his. Take great care, won't you? He's very crotchetty!"

I reassured her, for indeed I was grateful to her.

On the Tuesday we all met at dinner. Fräulein Schmidt had invited another lady, who spoke with bated breath to the *Meister*, and I took my tone a little from her and scored my first success by telling him how we used to form knots of ten or twenty students and go across from Heidelberg to Mannheim to hear his operas, and on our return spend the night playing over the *Leit-Motiven* of the different scores.

He listened, but to my astonishment said a little curtly:

"That's not my music; *Der Fliegende Hollaender* and even *Tannhaeuser* and *Lohengrin* are merely German music, a continuation of the *Freischuetz* of Weber. If I had never been born that would have got itself written, or something like it about as good."

I felt snubbed, but saw he hadn't meant any rebuff. I wondered afterwards what he would have said twenty years before to any one who treated *Tannhaeuser* and *Lohengrin* as negligible.

I did not agree with him, but it was not my cue to contradict; so while still praising the early operas, I confessed that "my favourite of all operas was *Die Meistersinger*, though the second act of *Tristan* was a miracle and even dearer to me."

Then I saw his eyes change. The pupils seemed to dilate, the eyes to grow deeper in colour, and his whole face was transfigured, the true Wagner — genial and impassioned — coming into sight.

"That is nearer the true faith," he said, smiling happily.

And then I let myself go, and told him how the passion in *Tristan and Isolde's* magnificent love duet moved me, and the victory that was a perpetual encouragement and inspiration in the *Meistersinger;* the whole music lifting higher and higher in great waves of harmony to a supreme triumph.

"It must have been due to some great success in your own life?" I questioned. "Was it not? Perhaps some early triumph."

"I had no early triumphs," he replied shortly, and the light died out of his face. "My success with *Rienzi* in Dresden in 1842, or with *Lohengrin* in Vienna twenty years later, may have had something to do with it. That *Lohengrin* celebration was a great event coming after the blank misery and defeat in Paris. But I am sure patriotic feeling or some nonsense of that sort was at the bottom of it. Paris wouldn't have *Tannhaeuser* even when the Emperor wanted it. Vienna cheered *Lohengrin*, but would not have my *Tristan and Isolde!* . . ."

A gloomy bitterness seemed to emanate from him, and

then came the great word: "I was over thirty years in the wilderness before reaching the promised land, and that's too long, much too long for any man. . . ."

He moved me profoundly: everything in him, I thought — bitterness, enthusiasm, and the insight that enabled him to understand that his success in Vienna was mere patriotic revolt. He had only got just enough success to call out the very best in him continually — and the triumph came when the work had all been done. Perhaps the reflection came that he was fortunate in his misfortunes, for, at least, he had completed his work.

This first disjointed talk showed me that Richard Wagner was a really great man. And what words he found! That "thirty years in the wilderness" proved the man's quality!

I noticed this first evening that he was very careful in what he ate and drank: he broke up the party early, excusing himself briefly, and going away after shaking hands with me and bowing to the ladies.

In the days that followed he became the chief subject of our conversations. Fräulein Schmidt, womanlike, told me of his love of gorgeous silk dressing-gowns and silk underclothes, too, of the finest. This rather astonished me, because, except in summer, silk is not good for underclothing in Munich. The proximity of the Bavarian Alps makes it a dangerous town to live in; there are frequent cold winds, even in summer, a treacherous climate like that of Madrid.

Then she explained that Wagner had some form of skin irritation or disease — erysipelas, or something of that sort — and that silk prevented the itching.

I noticed, as I have said, that he was careful about what

he ate, and Fräulein Schmidt told me that he suffered
very badly from indigestion and had to take great care.

"I have to fetch him hot water," she added, "very
often," and suddenly she astonished me by a word of insight. "There is more spirit than strength in him," she
concluded.

It was true; one could see that the spirit was wearing
out the flesh covering, wearing it thin, threadbare even.
His hair was already sparse and grey, and the hair round
his neck and under his jaws was quite grey too, and thin;
yet he was only sixty-five or sixty-six, though he looked
like an old, old man.

We met again, I remember, one evening at the entrance
to the house, and the moon was out, though the sunlight
still lingered in the sky. I said something about watching for the "*holder Abendstern*," and repeated the line:

> "*Oh, du mein holder Abendstern.*"

He smiled pleasantly, and said a few words of no importance.

I told him that *Fidelio* was about to be given in the
opera house and that the Vogls were going to sing, and
how I admired the overture and the aria in the prison:
"*Sie fuehrt mich zur Freiheit in's himmlische Reich.*"

He smiled again. "Might one ask," I began, "what
you are working on, *Meister?*"

"Come up some afternoon and we'll talk about it," he
said pleasantly, and passed before me through the door.

I went once or twice, and heard about *Parsifal*, and not
only the music of the future, about which I knew a good
deal, but, strange to say, about the religion of the future,
which seemed to me very like Christianity Bayswatered

down to practicable strength. At that time I was very much opposed to Christianity, and regarded it as a sort of disease, so I did not care much for what Wagner had to say about the religion of the future, but I pretended admiration and excited interest, and so won bit by bit to greater intimacy.

At that time he seemed to think *Parsifal* his greatest work: "That's where I give my whole soul," he said to me once; but if you praised *Parsifal* over long, he would recall the *Ring* or the *Meistersinger*.

I spoke to him once about his silk underclothes, and he told me the whole story quite frankly:

"I think it was the privations in Paris in those dreadful years, '41 and '42, that gave me first indigestion. Then after '48, when I was driven from Dresden to Zurich, I got this sort of skin rash — some doctors call it erysipelas, because they don't know what it is — but it plagued me for years. I used to scratch myself till I bled.

"I found out that silk prevented a good deal of the irritation, and I told Frau von Wesendonck, who was very good to me, and she sent me a dressmaker who undertook to make silk underclothes for me, and silk dressing-gowns. I gave her a large order. She was astonished, but evidently Frau von Wesendonck had told her that I was a king of art, so she went off and did the work and sent me the things, and I was able to go on with my work much more comfortably.

"At the end of about a month the dressmaker came wanting to be paid. I told her I had no money. She said: 'But you must have money; you could not order so many suits without money.' I said to her, 'The simple truth is that if I had ordered one dressing-gown and three suits, you would have wanted the money immediately, but the order was so big that you deceived yourself into thinking I was very rich, and gave me credit. Now you will have to wait, my good lady.'

"I knew quite well," he added, "that the frontier was only an hour away, and if I were bothered I could go across."

"But you paid her later?" I asked.

"Oh, of course," he shouted; "of course. I hated to be in debt, and the very first money I got a little later from King Ludwig, the first two hundred thousand gulden I spent in paying my debts. I paid her threefold. I was very grateful to her."

I think this story probably true, because when, just before her death, his first wife heard that he was accused of having treated her badly and left her in destitution, she wrote to the papers to say that nothing could be further from the truth; that as soon as Wagner had money, he gave it royally, and more than she even needed or expected.

Wagner went on: "The idiots say if the artist wants this or that, let him pay for it like an ordinary man. The artist often wants luxuries to better his art, to increase his gift to men. I've won through and done all my work, and that's the proof I was right. Success is the crown of an artist's work: no one now denies it to me. What men call luxuries are sometimes more necessary to us than bread. We artists don't live by bread alone."

I nodded; I understood that even then, and I admired him for taking what men would not give, though I'd have admired him more if he had not needed to take.

In spite of my ever-growing sympathy and admiration

for him, one day I nearly spoiled myself for ever with him.

There had appeared in some paper a bitter criticism of him and his work. The critic declared that he was a mere favourite of the King, a chamber-musician without genius, and with a very imperfect knowledge of music.

Half out of *Schadenfreude* and half from an American youth's eagerness to see what would happen, I took him the article and showed it to him. He read it through, then jumped up and threw the sheet on the floor.

"You oughtn't to have shown me that," he exclaimed, "it can do nothing but harm. The man is a liar and slanderer."

"Oh, I am sorry," I cried, and indeed his intense, angry excitement showed me how foolish I had been.

"I don't blame the journalist for not understanding my genius," he went on passionately. "No man on a daily paper is required to understand genius; he cannot be expected to know anything about it. It takes genius to recognize genius; when a journalist says I have none, it doesn't matter; it merely means he is a journalist. But this writer is a musician. When he speaks of music, he knows what he is talking about. There and there," he cried, pointing to the article, "he shows musical knowledge. When he tells his readers that I am not a musician, he lies, and knows that he is lying. I was a great conductor before I was twenty, and for years earned my living as an operatic conductor; I have enlarged the orchestra, too, out of all recognition. That's why you should not have shown the lying screed to me. Mere slanderous lies do no one any good; they do genius a great deal of harm, unluckily!"

"You have no idea how sorry I am," I said, and indeed

I felt a certain contrition; I had no notion he would take the foolish attack so to heart.

But he went on thundering against the critics for more than an hour.

"It's all envy and malice," he barked. "Nine mediocrities out of ten are base and vile; they hate you because you have climbed the heights. One gives of one's best, and the mediocrities loathe you for it. . . . One of these days they'll know who I am, and the name of Wagner will stand high above their calumnies. . . ."

When we were parting, he said to me: "Please don't show me such slanders again; they hurt and don't help. I've been annoyed with such calumnies ten thousand times."

I assured him warmly I would never offend again in that way, and I quoted the sacred words:

"Forgive them, for they know not what they do."

He looked at me earnestly, and the anger died out of his face; his eyes showed a sort of despair, an abyss of tearless misery; and he began in an utterly different tone: *"Mein guter Junge!* You, too, may learn in time what a dreadful task is the artist's, to create a new world as perfect as possible, eternally dissatisfied with what you have done, always hoping for some diviner achievement, and, as if it was not enough to be thus spurred and harassed and driven by your own *daimon*, the crowd mock at you, and those who should help stand aside and sneer, till you almost doubt your own soul; no life so hard as ours — none."

I bowed in silence; the sadness in his face and voice were testimony enough to the dark hours he had passed through, and the bitter waters.

Other talks I remember that may, too, be recorded:

"*Meister*," I began one day, "you told me once that I could know all about music if I gave time and study to it. Why do I like Mozart so excessively?"

"Mozart is beloved by all of us," he said, "musicians and the rest, for the sheer beauty in him — his lovely melodies."

"His characterisation is what strikes me as so fine," I pursued. "Cherubino, for instance, is revealed in *voi che sapete* and the great lady in her arias — characterisation like Shakespeare's, or de Musset's."

"True," replied Wagner, thoughtfully, "those are the things you say that show an original mind and promise more — perhaps in poetry — eh?"

To change the talk, I cried: "O, *Meister*, please tell me about the greatest musicians and how you would rank them!"

He shrugged his shoulders: "Mozart and Beethoven, of course, and Bach; then Handel and Weber. Handel was a high priest of our art. His oratorios are like cathedrals —"

"But you, *Meister?*" I persisted. "You are the greatest of them all, aren't you?"

"In opera, yes, I think so," he said, in cool appraisement.

"You may yet hear it said," he went on, "that in orchestral harmonies the step from Bach to Beethoven is hardly longer than the step from Beethoven to Wagner."

This extravagant self-estimate, as it seemed to me, emboldened me to ask him about his life and the sources of his inspiration. I had heard (it was, indeed, the common talk among musicians) that his liaison with Madame von

Wesendonck, with whom he had lived in Switzerland, had given Wagner the passion-music of the *Tristan*. "Was she, in fact, the Isolde of that astonishing second act?" was the question always in my heart, if not on my tongue.

Time and again, whenever indeed I got him in a good humour, I came to the burning point, and once he answered me with some directness: "The artist can only give what he has felt," he said, "but it is unlikely that he will get all from any one person."

On another similar occasion, he combated the idea that English women were nearly always cold: "Just as they are sometimes astoundingly beautiful," he said, "so they are sometimes rarely endowed," and then he spoke of one English woman he met and followed to the south of France, to Bordeaux, who was a wonder of passionate feeling; he had admired her intensely, and had won her love I believe.

On another occasion: "The strongest passion in a man," he said, "usually comes between thirty-five and forty-five," and then he added, with a smile: "it's earlier in women, isn't it? But then," he added, with a shrug, "who can tell what women feel, or when they feel most — *verschlossene Geschoepfe, raethselhaft!*" (reticent creatures, riddles almost unreadable).

In spite of constant thought and many efforts, I could not get much more out of him: I was diffident, in spite of my admiration, and it was only occasionally that he would speak at all on such intimate personal subjects; the difference of age between us was a barrier which I regret the more, because he and Goethe and Heine live with Shakespeare in my thought as the greatest and most passion-vexed of mortals.

He resented criticism always with peculiar, singular acerbity; at that time I had the foolish idea that there was some approach to truth in every honest opinion; but he wouldn't hear of it; all criticism of his work was mere "blind envy and hate," was his favourite phrase; "men find fault with their betters because of their own limitations," was his settled conviction. Only once did I ever hear any self-questionings from his lips.

"They all find fault and reject me," he said one day, as if speaking to himself, "just as they all found fault with Heine; was it — "; and he broke off abruptly. "Is there perhaps too much theatre in me, too much searching after stage pictures and scenic effects? . . .

"I don't think so; but I wish I knew certainly." He went on still in self-communing:

"There's nothing harder on this earth than to see the limitations of one's own genius. I see that I followed Weber inevitably; but who will follow me in that same sense, and supply some unforeseen shortcoming of mine? . . .

"We cannot know. We are prisoned in our own limitations and in our lifetime. The future is shut to us; no inspiration takes us across the gulf." And then a new vein of thought, that was evidently habitual: "No one was ever attacked with such malignancy as I have been; when I was poor, they all sneered; now successful, they all slander. Fancy Berlioz vilifying me!"

"Berlioz?" I exclaimed in surprise. "Where? When?"

"In some Paris paper, *The Musical Gazette*, I think it was called. I've been attacked more persistently and ferociously than any one at any time."

"Jesus?" I suggested.

He smiled and nodded, flattered, I could see.

"In *Parsifal* I hope to show the *Religion of the Future* as well as I've shown the Art of the Future in the *Meistersinger* and the *Ring*."

The words stuck in my gizzard: "The step from Bach to Beethoven is not so great as the step from Beethoven to Wagner." The summit of all conceit, I thought it.

Yet twenty years later Wagner's prediction was fulfilled. Arnold Dolmetsch, the Belgian musician, said one evening in London: "In dramatic music Wagner is as much above Beethoven as Beethoven is above Bach."

Why are we so slow to recognise living greatness? Why does it take so long for genius to come into its kingdom?

Wagner always took a nap after the midday meal about two o'clock till three or so. Then I could usually see him and he'd go for a walk in the Englischer Garten. But he often suffered from indigestion and had to keep lying down. He was then rather irritable, rude even sometimes. I attributed much of this to indigestion but I was wrong; it was chiefly spiritual.

One phrase I remember he used often: "*The burden is too heavy; the stupid people too numerous!*"

He had not to endure the torment much longer. Like Shakespeare, he had scarcely finished his creative work when death took him!

In 1882 rehearsals of *Parsifal* began at Bayreuth. The first performance was given on July 26. The solemn story created a profound impression; critics who had found little to please them in the *Ring* admitted that *Parsifal* was a great work. But the exertion told severely on the great composer's health. He fainted after one rehearsal and on recovering exclaimed: "Once more I have beaten death."

But the weakness of his heart had made dangerous progress. After the *Parsifal* performance he went back with his family to Venice and lived in the Vendramin Palace on the Grand Canal. Liszt came in the middle of September and spent a couple of months with them, and at Christmas Wagner conducted his juvenile symphony in honour of his wife, Cosima, whose birthday was December 25. Wagner did not overrate his boyish composition but he puts on record that the symphony "really seemed to please the audience." At the end of the performance he laid down his *bâton* declaring that he would never conduct again.

On January 13 Liszt left and Wagner began to discuss with great eagerness the preparations for the Bayreuth festival of the summer.

On February 13, 1883, he stayed in bed all the morning. At noon he called the maid and ordered luncheon. After luncheon she heard Wagner cry out and running into the room, found him in agony. "Call my wife and the doctor," he gasped. His wife reached his side while he was still alive, but when the doctor came Wagner had passed away.

King Ludwig sent Adolph Gross, a Bayreuth banker who had long been a supporter of Wagner, to Venice as his representative. Venice offered a public funeral, but the widow declined it. Silently through the canals on February 16 went a gondola draped in black. A special mourning car carried the remains to Bayreuth and Wagner was laid to rest in Wahnfried.

The *Parsifal* performances in Bayreuth were given in

the summer but without the presence of the widow, who would not even see Liszt, her father. But the following year Cosima took up the work of continuing the festivals and almost to our own day has dedicated herself to the task of producing her husband's masterpieces — a great woman and noble helpmate!

And now, June, 1923, I read in the paper that Cosima wishes to inaugurate a yearly festival at Bayreuth in Wagner's honour. I had thought she was dead: but it seems I was mistaken: she is alive and still eager to immortalise her husband's memory. But why bind Wagner to Bayreuth: he lives in the heart of the German people for ever, and indeed is lord of an ever-widening circle, of all those who have been moved by his music and inspired by his genius.

THE DEATH OF SOCIETY [1]

MAURICE HEWLETT

I AM not proposing to review Miss Romer Wilson's *Siegmund-and-Sieglinde* idyll [*The Death of Society*] at the moment, but have made bold to lift the title she has given it to what I think a more appropriate place, and that is a short consideration of the manners and customs reflected in Miss Rose Macaulay's recent study of a section of society. Miss Wilson's book could have done with an apter name. No kind of Society is going to die because youthful mouth seeks youthful mouth. That has been going on ever since there was a society to live or die, and long before that. By way of parenthesis, however, I might stay to remark that when youthful mouth seeks two youthful mouths of the other sex for its satisfaction, and those of mother and daughter at that, such society as it represents, though not likely to die, lacks tone, and had better see a doctor. That is by the way.

I regard Miss Macaulay's study of her world as more indicative of a moribund society. *Dangerous Ages*, she calls it; and as she selects sixty-three, forty-three, and twenty for diagnosis, it will be seen that, according to her, society is pretty generally sick. It is true that her field is limited. She only deals with the maladies of women, and of a particular class of women — those who live in London and the suburbs, and used to be called the Idle Rich

[1] From *Extemporary Essays.* By permission of the publisher, the Oxford University Press, and of Mr. Robin Richards, executor of the estate of Maurice Hewlett.

a few years ago. But London is a very large place, which
seems larger still when you live in it. Miss Macaulay
makes it reach to Guildford on one side and Saint Marga-
ret's Bay on another. And so it does; and to Brighton on
another, and Hitchin on another. It is also the fact that
it holds a great many of those women, and of the para-
sites of both sexes and no sexes who live upon them. I
doubt myself whether they are worth the ability and
subtlety she has bestowed. I prefer Miss Macaulay when
she is doing burlesque. Serious novel-writing demands
a more serious subject, a something of the universal, a
something of the abiding element in life. Her people are
perverts or neurotics: *libido*, as she thinks, money and
idleness have made them what they are, a thing not permanent. They are infertile, and in the struggle which is
hard upon us must go down before the fertile classes.
That is a certainty, because child-bearing and child-rear-
ing women must and will be fed, whatever happens.

I have lived almost wholly in the country for several
years, and my visits to London have been fitful and as
short as possible. I don't pretend that I have furrowed
very deeply into life as it is lived up there now; but I have
been struck by a little thing or two which seem to me
significant. Most of the young men I have met with belong to the Labour Party, a Platonic attachment which
does not seem to involve them in labour, at least; and
practically all the young women walk about half-clad.
The symptoms correlate. The undressing of the mind of
man has always involved that of the body of woman.
Supply follows demand. Until that relationship can be
corrected female suffrage is not going to be much advantage to the female sex. But most people knew that

before. The peculiar mental twist which the symptoms indicate is not, with all respect to Miss Macaulay and her psycho-analysts, properly towards *libido*. There is more involved than appetite and curiosity. *Libido, le plaisir*, has lost itself now in *talento*. *Il talento*, according to the Italians who first observed the thing and made the phrase to suit it, is that mixture of desire and opportunity to gratify which can raise itself, like a bed of nettles in a croft, the moment the moral forces are let down. Cæsar Borgia is the common example of *il talento*. Shakespeare, who knew everything without learning anything, put up Iago, who cannot be bettered. The fences were markedly down, and *il talento* gadded like a weed, in the Italian Renaissance; so here from 1660 onwards until the Revolution; so in France when Louis XIV's hand was taken off; and now it is all over Europe. "Who fills the butchers' shops with large blue flies?" What keeps Europe as a butcher's shop? *Il talento*. It urged D'Annunzio into Fiume; it was behind Korfanty in Silesia. It is the ferment in the blood of De Valera. It inspires young men to murder their sweethearts for a pound note or two, to hold up post-office assistants while the till is cleared, to club chauffeurs from behind and steal their motor-cars. Men fear neither God nor the policeman. In its own smaller way the class which Miss Macaulay has been studying is similarly affected, though not moved to deeds of blood or to rapes: we are dealing with a community of talkers. Here is one of her subjects, bored with an unsuccessful love-chase in Cornwall:

"At Newlyn Nan stopped. She said she was going to supper with some one there and would come on later. She was, in fact, tired of them. She dropped into Stephen

Lumley's studio, which was, as usual after painting hours, full of his friends, talking and smoking. That was the only way to spend the evening, thought Nan, talking and smoking and laughing, and never pausing."

London is full of such Nans. The sanctions are down, and the darnels thrive. The end of it all will be, broadly speaking, the end of the nettle-bed. It will seed and gad until it becomes a nuisance or an offence. When the real party — I mean the people who labour and don't talk — labour has reached the appointed term, whether it be the point of starvation or the limit of irritability, it will take to the scythe. After the scythe the plow. And then, no doubt, the whole thing will begin over again. It sounds like a *mauvaise plaisanterie;* but Nature works like that.

Although nobody might be so surprised to know it as Miss Macaulay's young Bolsheviks and Russian Ballet ladies, there *is* a labour party, not yet a Labour Party, which works, and says nothing, observes much, and knows all about it. It is a silent but uncompromising critic. It has standards of its own based upon tradition incredibly ancient, rigidly observed — standards which have scarcely shifted since the neolithic age, which sometimes conflict with the political or social law of the day, but never with the laws of being. A society which still works, still breeds, and still believes in love, not as an aberration but as a function of sex; one also which confesses to a moral law, needs but little more to be formidable. I think it is in the way to obtain it. If it has learned anything out of modern life it is the right of private judgment of which a long servitude had until lately deprived it. If it has gained anything out of mechanical development it is facility of communication.

These two advantages taken together make it now possible for an inexpressive host to become self-conscious, and class-conscious; and those are the first steps, always, to revolution. Here they will be prelude to a revolution which must indeed prove incidentally the death of Society. Neither strikes, nor red flags, nor Bolshevism, will so surely procure it. Nor can a parliament prevent it. Parliament, if it ever hold up its head again, which many doubt, will do little more than wag it. Irritation, flaming into sudden passion, will make an end of the Society so acutely observed by Miss Macaulay. The people who obey the laws of being will take what they need under pressure of those laws, and the others, who neither work, nor love, nor breed, will disappear. The logic of things will see to it, aided by economic pressure. The bubbles of talk in their envelope of cigarette smoke will break and merge in the atmosphere. Poverty will make Britain a small country again, and very soon. But a very jolly country! Imagine it — a place inhabited only by people who do their jobs!

THE DECEASED [1]

ROBERT CORTES HOLLIDAY

I THINK it was William Hazlitt's brother who remarked that "no young man thinks he will ever die." Whoever it was he was a mysterious person who lives for us now in that one enduring observation. That is his "literary remains," his "complete works." And many a man has written a good deal more and said a good deal less than that concerning that "animal, man" (in Swift's phrase), who, as Sir Thomas Browne observes, "begins to die when he begins to live."

No young man, I should say, reads obituary notices. They are hardly "live news" to him. Most of us, I fancy, regard these "items" more or less as "dead matter" which papers for some reason or other are obliged to carry. But old people, I have noticed, those whose days are numbered, whose autumnal friends are fast falling, as if leaf by leaf from the creaking tree, those regularly turn to the obituary column, which, doubtless, is filled with what are "personals" for them.

And yet, if all but knew it, there is not in the press any reading so improving as the "obits" (to use the newspaper term), none of so softening and refining a nature, none so calculated to inspire one with the Christian feelings of pity and charity, with the sentiment of malice toward none, to bring anon a smile of tender regard for one's fellow mortals, to teach that man is an admirable creature, full of courage and faith withal, constantly striving for the light, interesting beyond measure, that his destiny is divinely inscrutable, that dust unto dust all men are brothers, and that he, man, is (in the words of *Urn Burial*) "a noble animal, splendid in ashes and pompous in the tomb." I doubt very much indeed whether any one could read obituaries every day for a year and remain a bad man or woman.

In many respects, the best obituaries are to be found in country papers. There, in country papers, none ever dies. It may be because, as it is said, the country is nearer to God than the town. But so it is that there, in country papers, in the fulness of time, or by the fell clutch of chance, one "enters into his final rest," or "passes from his earth life," or one "on Wed. last peacefully accepted the summons to Eternity," or "on Thurs." (it may be) "passed to his eternal reward." "Died" is indeed a hard word. It has never found admittance to hearts that love and esteem. Whitman (was it not?) when he heard that Carlyle was dead went out in the night and looked up at the stars and said that he did not believe it. Even so, are not all who take their passing "highly esteemed" in country papers? In small places, doubtless, death wears for the community a more tragic mien than in cities, where it is more frequent and where we knew not him that lies on his bier next door but one away. In the country places this man who is now no longer upright and quick was a neighbour to all. And the provincial writer of obituaries follows a high authority, another rustic poet, deathless and known throughout the world, who sang of his Hoosier friend "he is not dead but just away."

214

When one enters upon his last rôle in this world, which all fill in their turn, he becomes in rural journals that personage known throughout the countryside as "the deceased." It might be argued that, alas! the only thing you can do with one deceased is to bury him. It might be held that you cannot educate him. That he, the deceased, cannot enter upon the first steps of his career as a bookkeeper. That he cannot marry the daughter of the Governor of the State. That whatever happened to him, whatever he accomplished, enjoyed, endured, in his pilgrimage through this world he experienced before he became, as it is said, deceased. That, in short, he is now dead. And that it should be said of him, as we say in the Metropolitan press, as a young man Mr. Doe did this and later that. But in places simpler, and so more eloquent, than the Metropolis the final fact of one's existence colours all the former things of his career. In country obituaries all that has been done was done by the deceased. In this association of ideas between the prime and the close of life is to be felt a sentiment which knits together each scene. This Mr. Some One did not merely apprentice himself to a printer at fourteen (as city papers say it) and marry at twenty-one. But he that is now deceased was once full of hope and strength (at fourteen), and in the brave days of twenty-one did he, that is now struck down, plight his troth. So, doubtless, runs the thought in that intimate phrase so dear to the country papers, "the deceased."

And there are no funerals in the country. That is a word, funeral, of too forbidding, ominous, a sound to be under the broad and open sky. There where the neighbours gather, all those who knew and loved the departed from a boy, the "last sad rites are read," and the "mortuary services are performed." Then from the fruitful valley where he dwelt after his fathers, and their fathers, he mounts again the old red hill, bird enchanted.

He is not buried, though he rests in the warm clasp of the caressing earth. Buried has an inhuman sound, as though a man were a bone. The deceased is always "interred," or he may be "laid to rest," or his "interment takes place."

Now, it is in these biographical annals of small places that one finds the justest estimates of life. There folks are valued for what they are as well as for what they do. Inner worth is held in regard equally with the flash and glitter of what the great world calls success. I was reading just the other day of a late gentleman, "aged 61," whose principal concern appeared to be devotion to his family. His filial feeling was indeed remarkable. It was told that "after the death of his parents, three years ago, he had resided with his sister." After his attachment to his own people, his chief interest, apparently, was in the things of the mind, in literature. He had "never engaged in business," it was said, but he "was a great reader," he could "talk intelligently on many topics which interested him," and in the circles which he frequented he was admired, that is, it was thought that he was "quite a bright man." Who would not feel in this sympathetic record of his goodly span something of the charm of the modest nature of this man? Again, there was the recent intelligence concerning William Jackson, "a coloured gentleman employed as a deck hand on a pleasure craft in this harbour," who "met his demise" in an untimely manner. Clothes do not make the man, nor doth occupation decree the bearing. This is a great and fundamental truth very clearly grasped by the country obituary, and much obscured elsewhere.

On the other hand, positively nowhere else does the heart to dare and the power to do find such generous recognition as in the obituaries of country papers. The "prominence" of blacksmiths, general store keepers, undertakers, notaries public, and other townspeople bright in local fame has been made a jest by urban persons of a humorous inclination, who take scorn of merit because it is not vast merit. Pleasing to contemplate in contrast to this waspish spirit is the noble nature of the country obituary, inspiration to humanism. Here was a man, to the seeing eye, of sterling stamp: "He attended public grammar school where he profited by his opportunities in obtaining as good an education as possible, etc." Later in life, he became "well and favourably known for his conservative and sane business methods," and was esteemed by his associates, it is said, "fraternally and otherwise." He was "mourned," by those who "survived" him, as people are not mourned in cities, that is, frankly, in a manner undisguised. Country obituaries are not afraid to be themselves. In this is their appeal to the human heart.

They are the same in spirit, identical in turn of phrase, from Maine to California, from the Gulf to the Upper Provinces. That is one of the remarkable things about them. You might expect to come across, here or there, a writer of country paper obituaries out of step, as it were, with his fellow mutes, so to put it, one raising his voice in a slightly off, or different key, a trace, in short, of the hand of some student of the modes of thought of the world beyond his bosky dell or rolling plain. But it is not so in any paper truly of the countryside. And, perhaps, that is well.

A type of obituary which very likely is read rather generally in cities is that of slow growth and released from the newspaper-office "morgue" as occasion calls. One such timely and capable biographical account is waiting for each of us that is a Vice-President, King, lord of great dominions, high commander of armed forces, intellectual immortal of any kind, recognised superman in this or that, Big Chief anywhere, or beloved popular idol, nicely proportioned according to our space value. Of course, if we are a very great Mogul indeed we get a display head on the first page upon the dramatic occasion of our exit. But, generally speaking, this type of matter would run somewhere between the seventh and the thirteenth or fifteenth page, according to the number of pages of the issue of the paper coinciding with the date of the ending of our day's work. There, if we are pretty important, we should lead the column, and take a two line head, with a pendant "comb." This, altogether, would announce to the passing eye that we went out (as the poet, Edwin Arlington Robinson, puts it) in such or such a year of our age, that pneumonia, or what not, "took" us, that we were a member of one of the city's oldest families, that a family breach was healed at the death of our sister, or the general points of whatever it is that makes us interesting to the paper's circulation. We are likely to have a date line and a brief despatch from Rome, or Savannah, or wherever we happen to be when we shuffle off, stating that we have done so. This to be followed by a "shirt-tail dash." Then begins a beautifully dispassionate and highly dignified recital of the salient facts connected with our career, which may run to a couple of sticks, or, even, did our activities command it, turn the column.

Or, suppose for the sake of our discussion that your achievements have not been quite of the first rank. You get a one-line head, a subhead, and a couple of paragraphs. Somebody has exclaimed concerning how much life it takes to make a little art. Just so. How much life it takes to make a very little obituary in the great city! Early and late, day in and day out, week in and week out, month in and month out, in the sun's hot eye of summer, through the winter's blizzard, year after year for thirty-six years you have been a busy practising physician. You have lived in the thick of births and life and death for thousands of hours. What you know, and have lived and have seen would fill rows of volumes. You are a distinguished member of many learned societies, widely known as an educator. You are good for about a hundred and fifty words.

Perhaps not. Perhaps you were a person of rather minor importance. You are, that is, you were, we will say, an astronomer, or you were a mineralogist, or a former Alderman, or something like that. So you call for a paragraph, with a head. Your virtues (and your vices) have been many. You were three times married. As Mr. Bennett says of another of like momentous history, the love of life was in you, three times you rose triumphant over death. Goodness! what a novel you would make. You call for a paragraph, with a head. All your clubs are given.

You are doing pretty well. Many of us, just some-bodies but nobodies in especial particular, do not have a separate head at all but go in a group into the feature "Obituary Notes." Our names are set in "caps," and we have a brisk paragraph apiece, admirable pieces of composition, pellucid, compact, nervous. Our stories are contained in these dry-point-like portraits stript of all that was occasional, accidental, ephemeral, leaving alone the essential facts, such as, for instance, that we were, say, a civil engineer. I think it would be well for each of us occasionally to visualise his obituary "note." This should have the effect of clarifying our outlook. Amid the welter of existence what is it that we are above all to do? To thine own self be true. You are a husband, a father, and a civil engineer. That is all that matters in the end.

But after all, all obituaries in a great city are for the elect. The great majority of us have none at all, in print. What we were is, indeed, graven on the hearts that knew us, and told in the places where we have been. But in the written word we go into the feature headed "Died," a department similar in design to that on the literary page headed "Books Received." We are arranged alphabetically according to the first letter of our surnames. We are set in small type with lines following the name line indented. It is difficult for me to tell with certainty from the printed page but I think we are set without leads. Here again, frequently, the reader comes upon the breath of affection, the hand of some one near to the one that is gone: "Beloved husband of ——." And he is touched by the realisation that even in the rushing city, somewhere unseen amid the hard glitter and the gay scene, to-day warm hearts are torn, and that simple grief throbs in and makes perennially poignant a bromidian phrase.

As this column lengthens the paragraphs shorten, until is reached what seems to me the most moving obituary of all, that most eloquent of the destiny of men. "ROE. — Richard. 1272 West 96th St., Dec. 30, aged 54." It is like to the most moving line, perhaps, in modern literature. For nowhere else, I think, is there one of such simplicity and grandeur as this from *The Old Wives' Tale:* "He had once been young, and he had grown old, and was now dead."

ON RE–READING *CANDIDE*[1]

ALDOUS HUXLEY

THE furniture vans had unloaded their freight in the new
house. We were installed, or, at least, we were left to
make the best of an unbearable life in the dirt and the
confusion. One of the Pre-Raphaelites, I forget at the
moment which, once painted a picture called "The Last
Day in the Old Home." A touching subject. But it
would need a grimmer, harder brush to depict the horrors
of "The First Day in the New Home." I had sat down
in despair among the tumbled movables when I noticed
— with what a thrill of pleased recognition — the top of
a little leather-bound book protruding from among a
mass of bulkier volumes in an uncovered case. It was
Candide, my treasured little first edition of 1759, with its
discreetly ridiculous title-page, "*Candide ou l'Optimisme*,
Traduit de l'Allemand de Mr. le Docteur Ralph."

Optimism — I had need of a little at the moment, and
as Mr. le Docteur Ralph is notoriously one of the preach-
ers most capable of inspiring it, I took up the volume and
began to read: "Il y avait en Westphalie, dans le Château de Mr. le Baron de Thunder-ten-tronckh. . . ."
I did not put down the volume till I had reached the final:
"Il faut cultiver notre jardin." I felt the wiser and the
more cheerful for Doctor Ralph's ministrations.

But the remarkable thing about re-reading *Candide* is
not that the book amuses one, not that it delights and

[1] From *On the Margin*. Published, 1923, by Chatto and Windus. By
permission of the author.

astonishes with its brillance; that is only to be expected. No, it evokes a new and, for me at least, an unanticipated emotion. In the good old days, before the Flood, the history of Candide's adventures seemed to us quiet, sheltered, middle-class people only a delightful phantasy, or at best a high-spirited exaggeration of conditions which we knew, vaguely and theoretically, to exist, to have existed, a long way off in space and time. But read the book to-day; you feel yourself entirely at home in its pages. It is like reading a record of the facts and opinions of 1922; nothing was ever more applicable, more completely to the point. The world in which we live is recognizably the world of Candide and Cunegonde, of Martin and the Old Woman who was a Pope's daughter and the betrothed of the sovereign Prince of Massa-Carrara. The only difference is that the horrors crowd rather more thickly on the world of 1922 than they did on Candide's world. The manœuvrings of Bulgare and Abare, the intestine strife in Morocco, the earthquake and *auto-da-fé* are but pale poor things compared with the Great War, the Russian Famine, the Black and Tans, the Fascisti, and all the other horrors of which we can proudly boast. "Quand Sa Hautesse envoye un vaisseau en Egypte," remarked the Dervish, "s'embarrasse-t-elle si les souris qui sont dans le vaisseau sont à leur aise ou non?" No; but there are moments when Sa Hautesse, absent-mindedly no doubt, lets fall into the hold of the vessel a few dozen of hungry cats; the present seems to be one of them.

Cats in the hold? There is nothing in that to be surprised at. The wisdom of Martin and the Old Woman who was once betrothed to the Prince of Massa-Carrara has

become the everyday wisdom of all the world since 1914.
In the happy Victorian and Edwardian past, Western
Europe, like Candide, was surprised at everything. It
was amazed by the frightful conduct of King Bomba,
amazed by the Turks, amazed by the political chicanery
and loose morals of the Second Empire — (what is all
Zola but a prolonged exclamation of astonishment at the
goings-on of his contemporaries?). After that we were
amazed at the disgusting behaviour of the Boers, while
the rest of Europe was amazed at ours. There followed
the widespread astonishment that in this, the so-called
twentieth century, black men should be treated as they
were being treated on the Congo and the Amazon. Then
came the war: a great outburst of indignant astonishment, and afterwards an acquiescence as complete, as
calmly cynical as Martin's. For we have discovered, in
the course of the somewhat excessively prolonged *histoire
à la Candide* of the last seven years, that astonishment is
a supererogatory emotion. All things are possible, not
merely for Providence, whose ways we had always known,
albeit for some time rather theoretically, to be strange,
but also for men.

Men, we thought, had grown up from the brutal and
rampageous hobbledehoyism of earlier ages and were now
as polite and genteel as Gibbon himself. We now know
better. Create a hobbledehoy environment and you will
have hobbledehoy behaviour; create a Gibbonish environment and every one will be, more or less, genteel.
It seems obvious, now. And now that we are living in a
hobbledehoy world, we have learnt Martin's lesson so
well that we can look on almost unmoved at the most ap-
palling natural catastrophes and at exhibitions of human

stupidity and wickedness which would have aroused us in the past to surprise and indignation. Indeed, we have left Martin behind and are become, with regard to many things, Pococurante.

And what is the remedy? Mr. le Docteur Ralph would have us believe that it consists in the patient cultivation of our gardens. He is probably right. The only trouble is that the gardens of some of us seem hardly worth cultivating. The garden of the bank clerk and the factory hand, the shop-girl's garden, the garden of the civil servant and the politician — can one cultivate them with much enthusiasm? Or, again, there is my garden, the garden of literary journalism. In this little plot I dig and delve, plant, prune, and finally reap — sparsely enough, goodness knows! — from one year's end to another. And to what purpose, to whom for a good, as the Latin Grammar would say? Ah, there you have me.

There is a passage in one of Tchekov's letters which all literary journalists should inscribe in letters of gold upon their writing desks. "I send you," says Tchekov to his correspondent, "Mihailovsky's article on Tolstoy. . . . It's a good article, but it's strange: one might write a thousand such articles and things would not be one step forwarder, and it would still remain unintelligible why such articles are written."

Il faut cultiver notre jardin. Yes, but suppose one begins to wonder why?

FIRES [1]

E. V. LUCAS

Oh, pile a bright fire!

Edward FitzGerald

A FRIEND of mine making a list of the things needed for
the cottage that he had taken, put at the head "bellows."
Then he thought for some minutes, and was found merely
to have added "tongs" and "poker." Then he asked
someone to finish it. A fire, indeed, furnishes. Nothing
else, not even a chair, is absolutely necessary; and it is
difficult for a fire to be too large. Some of the grates put
into modern houses by the jerry-builders would move an
Elizabethan to tears, so petty and mean are they, and so
incapable of radiation. We English people would suffer
no loss in kindliness and tolerance were the ingle-nook
restored to our homes. The ingle humanises.

Although the father of the family no longer, as in ancient Greece, performs on the hearth religious rites, yet it
is still a sacred spot. Lovers whisper there, and there
friends exchange confidences. Husband and wife face
the fire hand in hand. The table is for wit and good
humour, the hearth is for something deeper and more
personal. The wisest counsels are offered beside the
fire, the most loving sympathy and comprehension are
there made explicit. It is the scene of the best dual

[1] From *Fireside and Sunshine*, by E. V. Lucas; but there "reprinted
almost *verbatim* from *Domesticities* (Smith, Elder, 1900)." By permission of the publishers, E. P. Dutton and Company, and Methuen and
Company.

companionship. The fire itself is a friend, having the prime attribute — warmth. One of the most human passages of that most human poem, *The Deserted Village*, tells how the wanderer was now and again taken by the memory of the hearth of his distant home:

> I still had hopes my latest hours to crown,
> Amidst these humble bowers to lay me down. . . .
> Around my fire an evening group to draw,
> And tell of all I felt, and all I saw. . . .

Only by the fireside could a man so unbosom himself. A good fire extracts one's best; it will not be resisted. Fitz-Gerald's *Meadows in Spring* contains some of the best fireside stanzas:

> Then with an old friend
>   I talk of our youth —
> How 'twas gladsome, but often
>   Foolish, forsooth:
>   But gladsome, gladsome!
>
> Or to get merry
>   We sing some old rhyme,
> That made the wood ring again
>   In summer time —
>   Sweet summer time!
>
> Then we go to drinking,
>   Silent and snug;
> Nothing passes between us
>   Save a brown jug —
>   Sometimes!
>
> And sometimes a tear
>   Will rise in each eye,
> Seeing the two old friends
>   So merrily —
>   So merrily!

The hearth also is for ghost stories; indeed, a ghost story demands a fire. If England were warmed wholly by hot-water pipes or gas stoves, the Society for Psychical Research would be dissolved. Gas stoves are poor comforters. They heat the room, it is true, but they do so after a manner of their own, and there they stop. For encouragement, for inspiration, you seek the gas stove in vain. Who could be witty, who could be humane, before a gas stove? It does so little for the eye and nothing for the imagination; its flame is so artificial and restricted a thing, its glowing heart so shallow and ungenerous. It has no voice, no personality, no surprises; it submits to the control of a gas company, which, in its turn, is controlled by Parliament. Now, a fire proper has nothing to do with Parliament. A fire proper has whims, ambitions, and impulses unknown to gas-burners, undreamed of by asbestos. Yet even the gas stove has advantages and merits when compared with hot-water pipes. The gas stove at least offers a focus for the eye, unworthy though it be; and you can make a semicircle of good people before it. But with hot-water pipes not even that is possible. From the security of ambush they merely heat, and heat whose source is invisible is hardly to be coveted at all. Moreover, the heat of hot-water pipes is but one remove from stuffiness.

Coals are a perpetual surprise, for no two consignments burn exactly alike. There is one variety that does not burn — it explodes. This kind comes mainly from the slate quarries, and, we must believe, reaches the coal merchant by accident. Few accidents, however, occur so frequently. Another variety, found in its greatest perfection in railway waiting-rooms, does everything but emit heat. A third variety jumps and burns the hearth-rug. One can predicate nothing definite concerning a new load of coal at any time, least of all if the consignment was ordered to be "exactly like the last."

A true luxury is a fire in the bedroom. This is fire at its most fanciful and mysterious. One lies in bed watching drowsily the play of the flames, the flicker of the shadows. The light leaps up and hides again, the room gradually becomes peopled with fantasies. Now and then a coal drops and accentuates the silence. Movement with silence is one of the curious influences that come to us: hence, perhaps, part of the fascination of the cinematoscope, wherein trains rush into stations, and streets are seen filled with hurrying people and bustling vehicles, and yet there is no sound save the clicking of the mechanism. With a fire in one's bedroom sleep comes witchingly.

Another luxury is reading by firelight, but this is less to the credit of the fire than the book. An author must have us in no uncertain grip when he can induce us to read him by a light so impermanent as that of the elfish coal. Nearer and nearer to the page grows the bended head, and nearer and nearer to the fire moves the book. Boys and girls love to read lying full length on the hearthrug.

Some people maintain a fire from January to December; and, indeed, the days on which a ruddy grate offends are very few. According to Mortimer Collins, out of the three hundred and sixty-five days that make up the year only on the odd five is a fire quite dispensable. A perennial fire is, perhaps, luxury writ large. The very fact that sunbeams falling on the coals dispirit them to greyness and ineffectual pallor seems to prove that when the sun rides high it is time to have done with fuel except in the kitchen or in the open air.

The fire in the open air is indeed joy perpetual, and there is no surer way of renewing one's youth than by kindling and tending it, whether it be a rubbish fire for potatoes, or an aromatic offering of pine spindles and fir cones, or the scientific structure of the gipsy to heat a tripod-swung kettle. The gipsy's fire is a work of art. "Two short sticks were stuck in the ground, and a third across to them like a triangle. Against this frame a number of the smallest and driest sticks were leaned, so that they made a tiny hut. Outside these there was a second layer of longer sticks, all standing, or rather leaning, against the first. If a stick is placed across, lying horizontally, supposing it catches fire, it just burns through the middle and that is all, the ends go out. If it is stood nearly upright, the flame draws up to it; it is certain to catch, burns longer, and leaves a good ember." So wrote one who knew — Richard Jeffries, in *Bevis*, that epic of boyhood. Having built the fire, the next thing is to light it. An old gipsy woman can light a fire in a gale, just as a sailor can always light his pipe, even in the cave of Æolus; but the amateur is less dexterous. The smoke of the open-air fire is charged with memory. One whiff of it, and for a swift moment we are in sympathy with our remotest ancestors, and all that is elemental and primitive in us is awakened.

An American poet, R. H. Messinger, wrote:

> Old wood to burn! —
> Ay, bring the hillside beech
> From where the owlets meet and screech,

And ravens croak;
The crackling pine, and cedar sweet;
Bring, too, a clump of fragrant peat,
  Dug 'neath the fern;
  The knotted oak,
  A faggot, too, perhaps,
Whose bright flame, dancing, winking,
Shall light us at our drinking;
  While the oozing sap
Shall make sweet music to our thinking.

There is no fire of coals, not even the blacksmith's, that can compare with the blazing fire of wood. The wood fire is primeval. Centuries before coals were dreamed of, our rude forefathers were cooking their meat and gaining warmth from burning logs.

Coal is modern, decadent. Look at this passage concerning fuel from an old Irish poem: "O man," begins the lay, "that for Fergus of the feasts does kindle fire, whether afloat or ashore never burn the king of woods. . . . The pliant woodbine, if thou burn, wailings for misfortunes will abound; dire extremity at weapons' points or drowning in great waves will come after thee. Burn not the precious apple tree." The minstrel goes on to name wood after wood that may or may not be burned. This is the crowning passage: "Fiercest heat-giver of all timber is green oak, from him none may escape unhurt; by partiality for him the head is set on aching, and by his acrid embers the eye is made sore. Alder, very battle-witch of all woods, tree that is hottest in the fight — undoubtedly burn at thy discretion both the alder and the white thorn. Holly, burn it green; holly, burn it dry; of all trees whatsoever the critically best is holly." Could any one write with this enthusiasm and poetic feeling about Derby Brights and Silkstone — even the best Silkstone and the best Derby Brights?

The care of a wood fire is, in itself, daily work for a man; for far more so than with coal is progress continuous. Something is always taking place and demanding vigilance — hence the superiority of a wood fire as a beguiling influence. The bellows must always be near at hand, the tongs not out of reach; both of them more sensible implements than those that usually appertain to coals. The tongs have no pretensions to brightness and gentility; the bellows, quite apart from their function in life, are a thing of beauty; the fire-dogs, on whose backs the logs repose, are fine upstanding fellows; and the bricks on which the fire is laid have warmth and simplicity and a hospitable air to which decorative tiles can never attain. Again, there is about the logs something cleanly, in charming contrast to the dirt of coal. The wood hails from the neighboring coppice. You have watched it grow: your interest in it is personal, and its interest in you is personal. It is as keen to warm you as you are to be warmed. Now there is nothing so impersonal as a piece of coal. Moreover, this wood was cut down and brought to the door by some good-humoured countryman of your acquaintance, whereas coal is obtained by miners — bad-tempered, truculent fellows that strike. Who ever heard of a strike among coppicers? And the smoke from a wood fire! — clean and sweet and pungent, and, against dark foliage, exquisite in colour as the breast of a dove. The delicacy of its grey-blue is not to be matched.

Whittier's *Snow-Bound* is the epic of the wood-piled hearth. Throughout we hear the crackling of the brush, the hissing of the sap. The texture of the fire was "the oaken log, green, huge, and thick," and "rugged brush":

> Hovering near,
> We watched the first red blaze appear,
> Heard the sharp crackle, caught the gleam
> On whitewashed wall and sagging beam,
> Until the old, rude-furnished room
> *Burst flower-like into rosy bloom.*

That italicised line — my own italics — is good. For the best fire (as for the best celery) — the fire most hearty, most inspired, and inspiring — frost is needed. When old Jack is abroad and there is a breath from the east in the air, then the sparks fly and the coals glow. In moist and mild weather the fire only burns, it has no enthusiasm for combustion. Whittier gives us a snowstorm:

> Shut in from all the world without,
> We sat the clean-winged hearth about,
> Content to let the north wind roar
> In baffled rage at pane and door,
> While the red logs before us beat
> The frost line back with tropic heat;
> And ever, when a louder blast
> Shook beam and rafter as it passed,
> The merrier up its roaring draught
> *The great throat of the chimney laughed.*

But the wood fire is not for all. In London it is impracticable; the builder has set his canon against it. Let us, then — those of us who are able to — build our coal fires the higher, and flourish in their kindly light. Whether one is alone or in company, the fire is potent to cheer. Indeed, a fire *is* company. No one need fear to be alone if the grate but glows. Faces in the fire will smile at him, mock him, frown at him, call and repulse; or, if there be no faces, the smoke will take a thousand shapes and lead his thoughts by delightful paths to the land of reverie; or he may watch the innermost heart of the fire burn blue (especially if there is frost in the air); or, poker in hand, he may coax a coal into increased vivacity. This is an agreeable diversion, suggesting the mediæval idea of the Devil in his domain.

PREFACE TO A CALENDAR [1]

DON MARQUIS

In a former preface we had something to say about the shape of the universe. We established the fact, we believe, that it is spherical. Having thus said all that it is essential to say about Space, let us take up Time in a serious way and see what can be made of it.

We will deal more particularly with Future Time. It is difficult to discuss the Present, because it will not hold still long enough. As for the Past, great portions of it lie open to the view of all men; they see it differently, and anything we might say about it would be sure to start an argument. It is not our purpose, in these prefaces, to argue with our readers; we merely intend to shout things at them and run on.

The most interesting question with regard to the Future is whether it exists already, or whether it has not yet been created. Our own opinion is that a great deal of the Future exists already, and that it has not yet caught up with us.

Or, to put it another way, Past, Present and Future exist simultaneously in different parts of the same solar system.

Let us say that it takes eight thousand years for a ray of sunlight to travel from the sun to this earth.

We do not know exactly how long it does take. We wish we did, for we like to be accurate even in these

[1] From *Prefaces* (1919). By permission of the publishers, D. Appleton and Company.

trivial details. There is a book in the house that might tell us. But we have just moved. And some confounded sliding arrangement at the side of the baby's crib was broken in the move. That side of the crib is now propped off the floor with twenty or thirty books. The book that tells exactly the distance from the sun to the earth and the length of time it takes a ray of light working union hours to go that distance is one of those particular books. We would rather (great as is our passion for exactitude) never know the facts than risk waking the baby by trying to get the book.* Even in neighborhoods where we are known it has been whispered about that no child would cry like that unless his parents deliberately tortured him throughout the night. And in a new neighborhood. . . .

Let us say that it takes eight thousand years for a ray of light to travel from the sun to the earth. The light that makes this day *to-day* left the sun centuries before dog-faced Agamemnon launched his Grecian barks or Hector was a pup at Troy. A million days that we know not yet are already in existence and on their way to us, carrying with them their light and heat and the germs of their events, since all life is from the sun. A day that is four thousand years within our Future is four thousand years within the sun's Past; the sun got rid of it, threw it at us, that many years ago; halfway between the sun and the earth that day speeds merrily along, making a brief Present wherever it passes, but we will not be here when it arrives. By the sun's time you and we, and the infant phenomenon across the hall reposing in such blessed un-

---

* We have since found the book and learned that our figures are astonishingly incorrect. But the principle remains the same.

sophistication above two dozen second hand volumes of encyclopedia full of entirely immaterial knowledge, have been dead nearly eight thousand years.

One may have been dead that long, of course, and still feel young and strong occasionally; there is some comfort in that. And always, to remember that one has been dead that long, is a salutary check upon human vanity. It should give us — (we always try to get some moral reflection into these prefaces) — it should give us a more kindly fellow feeling for such dusty celebrities as the Mummy of Rameses, the Piltdown Skull and Senator La Follette. If it discourages ambition, it also discourages discouragement. Since the sun threw off our death day nearly eight thousand years ago, it is scarcely worth while worrying about a future event that is so far in the past; we will be sticking around somewhere when said death day reaches us, but no one need be expected to act as if he found any news in it when it gets here.

This Future that rushes upon us, cries presently and confusingly in our ears and is gone before we can collect our wits to answer — where does it go to then? The day existed; it overtook us; it went by; does it still exist somewhere? It came to earth; it left earth; perhaps it took something as it went by — and is it now, with what it took, traversing the next planet to the west as you steer toward the cosmic jumping-off place? Does the day, with what we gave the day, await us? And may we overtake it by a sudden acceleration of speed, such as a soul must manifest when it pops hot and light and eager out of a body? — and may we live in the warm middle and tingling presence of that day again? It seems altogether possible to us that when we shill through the pearly gates we may find some of these days sitting up with the lights all turned on waiting for us, like commuters' wives.

Now and then we have the feeling that a certain action has been performed before; we are arrested in mid-gesture with the consciousness that the situation is not new to us; it comes over us with a sudden eeriness that we are repeating a particular rôle; many persons are very subject to such uncanny seizures. Perhaps these strange moments are stray bits of days that our souls have lived through previously; bits that have been broken off somehow and are left lying about loose; they went by us and then they lagged, and now we have caught up with them again.

There isn't, really, any such thing as Time. If there were there couldn't be eternity. Past, Present and Future are all alike, all one. There is no time. There are only imperishable events, in the midst of which we flutter and change to something else and flutter on again. The Cosmos -- (poor thing!) -- didn't begin and it can't end.

Which is one advantage a preface has over the cosmos.

EXEUNT OMNES[1]

H. L. MENCKEN

One of the hardest jobs that faces an American magazine editor in this, the one-hundred-and-forty-fifth year of the Republic, is that of keeping the minnesingers of the land from filling his magazine with lugubrious dithyrambs to, on and against somatic death. Of spiritual death, of course, not many of them ever sing. Most of them, in fact, deny its existence in plain terms; they are all sure of the immortality of the soul, and in particular they are absolutely sure of the immortality of their own souls, and of those of their best girls. In this department the most they ever allow to the materialism of the herds that lie bogged in prose is such a benefit of the half doubt as one finds in Christina Rossetti's *When I am Dead*. But when it comes to somatic death, the plain brutal death of coroners' inquests and vital statistics, their optimism vanishes, and, try as they may, they can't get around the harsh fact that on such and such a day, often appallingly near, each and every one of us will heave a last sigh, roll his eyes despairingly, turn his face to the wall and then suddenly change from a proud and highly complex mammal, made in the image of God, to a mere inert aggregate of disintegrating colloids, made in the image of a stale cabbage.

[1] Reprinted from *Prejudices: Second Series* (1921), by H. L. Mencken, by kind permission of and special arrangement with Alfred A. Knopf, Inc., authorized publisher.

The inevitability of it seems to fascinate them. They write about it more than they write about anything else save love. Every day my editorial desk is burdened with their manuscripts — poems in which the poet serves notice that, when his time comes, he will die bravely and even a bit insolently; poems in which he warns his mistress that he will wait for her on the roof of the cosmos and keep his harp in tune; poems in which he asks her grandly to forget him, and, above all, to avoid torturing herself by vain repining at his grave; poems in which he directs his heirs and assigns to bury him in some lonely, romantic spot, where the whippoorwills sing; poems in which he hints that he will not rest easily if Philistines are permitted to begaud his last anchorage with *couronnes des perles;* poems in which he speaks jauntily of making a rendezvous with death, as if death were a wench; poems in which —

But there is no need to rehearse the varieties. If you read the strophes that are strung along the bottoms of magazine pages you are familiar with all of them; even in the great moral periodical that I help to edit, despite my own excessive watchfulness and Dr. Nathan's general theory that both death and poetry are nuisances and in bad taste, they have appeared multitudinously, no doubt to the disgust of the *intelligentsia.* As I say, it is almost impossible to keep the minnesingers off the subject. When my negro flops the morning bale of poetry manuscripts upon my desk and I pull up my chair to have at them, I always make a bet with myself that, of the first dozen, at least seven will deal with death — and it is so long since I lost that I don't remember it. Periodically I send out a circular to all the recognized poets of the land, begging them in the name of God to be less mortuary, but it never does any good. More, I doubt that it ever will — or any other sort of appeal. Take away death and love and you would rob poets of both their liver and their lights; what would remain would be little more than a feeble gurgle in an illimitable void. For the business of poetry, remember, is to set up a sweet denial of the harsh facts that confront all of us — to sooth us in our agonies with emollient words — in brief, to lie sonorously and reassuringly. Well, what is the worst curse of life? Answer: the abominable magnetism that draws unlikes and incompatibles into delirious and intolerable conjunction — the kinetic over-stimulation called love. And what is the next worse? Answer: the fear of death. No wonder the poets give so much attention to both! No other foe of human peace and happiness is one-half so potent, and hence none other offers such opportunities to poetry, and, in fact, to all art. A sonnet designed to ease the dread of bankruptcy, even if done by a great master, would be banal, for that dread is itself banal, and so is bankruptcy. The same may be said of the old fear of hell, now no more. There was a day when this latter raged in the breast of nearly every man — and in that day the poets produced antidotes that were very fine poems. But to-day only the elect and anointed of God fear hell, and so there is no more production of sound poetry in that department.

As I have hinted, I tire of reading so much necrotic verse in manuscript, and wish heartily that the poets would cease to assault me with it. In prose, curiously enough, one observes a corresponding shortage. True enough, the short story of commerce shows a good many murders and suicides, and not less than eight times a day

I am made privy to the agonies of a widower or widow who, on searching the papers of his wife or her husband immediately after her or his death, discovers that she or he had a lover or a mistress. But I speak of serious prose: not of trade balderdash. Go to any public library and look under "Death: Human" in the card index, and you will be surprised to find how few books there are on the subject. Worse, nearly all the few are by psychical researchers who regard death as a mere removal from one world to another or by New Thoughters who appear to believe that it is little more than a sort of illusion. Once, seeking to find out what death was physiologically — that is, to find out just what happened when a man died — I put in a solid week without result. There seemed to be nothing whatever on the subject even in the medical libraries. Finally, after much weariness, I found what I was looking for in Dr. George W. Crile's *Man: An Adaptive Mechanism* — incidentally, a very solid and original work, much less heard of than it ought to be. Crile said that death was acidosis — that it was caused by the failure of the organism to maintain the alkalinity necessary to its normal functioning — and in the absence of any proofs or even arguments to the contrary I accepted his notion forthwith and have held to it ever since. I thus think of death as a sort of deleterious fermentation, like that which goes on in a bottle of Château Margaux when it becomes corked. Life is a struggle, not against sin, not against the Money Power, not against malicious animal magnetism, but against hydrogen ions. The healthy man is one in whom those ions, as they are dissociated by cellular activity, are immediately fixed by alkaline bases. The sick man is one in whom the process has begun to lag, with the hydrogen ions getting ahead. The dying man is one in whom it is all over save the charges of fraud.

But here I get into chemical physics, and not only run afoul of revelation but also reveal, perhaps, a degree of ignorance verging upon intellectual coma. The thing I started out to do was to call attention to the only full-length and first-rate treatise on death that I have ever encountered or heard of, to wit, *Aspects of Death and Correlated Aspects of Life*, by Dr. F. Parkes Weber, a fat, hefty and extremely interesting tome, the fruit of truly stupendous erudition. What Dr. Weber has attempted is to bring together in one volume all that has been said or thought about death since the time of the first human records, not only by poets, priests and philosophers, but also by painters, engravers, soldiers, monarchs and the populace generally. The author, I take it, is primarily a numismatist, and he apparently began his work with a collection of inscriptions on coins and medals. But as it stands it covers a vastly wider area. One traces, in chapter after chapter, the ebb and flow of human ideas upon the subject, of the human attitude to the last and greatest mystery of them all — the notion of it as a mere transition to a higher plane of life, the notion of it as a benign panacea for all human suffering, the notion of it as an incentive to this or that way of living, the notion of it as an impenetrable enigma, inevitable and inexplicable. Few of us quite realize how much the contemplation of death has colored human thought throughout the ages. There have been times when it almost shut out all other concerns; there has never been a time when it has not bulked enormously in the racial consciousness. Well, what Dr. Weber does in his book is to detach and set forth the salient ideas that have emerged from all that consideration and discussion — to isolate the chief theories of death, ancient and modern, pagan and Christian, scientific and mystical, sound and absurd.

The material thus digested is appallingly copious. If the learned author had confined himself to printed books alone, he would have faced a labor fit for a new Hercules. But in addition to books he has given his attention to prints, to medals, to paintings, to engraved gems and to monumental inscriptions. His authorities range from Saint John on what is to happen at the Day of Judgment to Sir William Osler on what happens upon the normal human death-bed, and from Socrates on the relation of death to philosophy to Havelock Ellis on the effects of Christian ideas of death upon the mediæval temperament. The one field that Dr. Weber has overlooked is that of music, a somewhat serious omission. It is hard to think of a great composer who never wrote a funeral march, or a requiem, or at least a sad song to some departed love. Even old Papa Haydn had moments when he ceased to be merry, and let his thought turn stealthily upon the doom ahead. To me, at all events, the slow movement of the *Military Symphony* is the saddest of music — an elegy, I take it, on some young fellow who went out in the incomprehensible wars of those times and got himself horribly killed in a far place. The trumpet blasts towards the end fling themselves over his hasty grave in a remote cabbage field; one hears, before and after them, the honest weeping of his comrades into their wine-pots. In truth, the shadow of death hangs over all the music of Haydn, despite its lightheartedness. Life was gay in those last days of the Holy Roman Empire,

but it was also precarious. If the Turks were not at the
gate, then there was a peasant rising somewhere in the
hinterland, or a pestilence swept the land. Beethoven,
a generation later, growled at death surlily, but Haydn
faced it like a gentleman. The romantic movement
brought a sentimentalization of the tragedy; it became a
sort of orgy. Whenever Wagner dealt with death he
treated it as if it were some sort of gaudy tournament —
a thing less dreadful than ecstatic. Consider, for example,
the *Char-Freitag* music in *Parsifal* — death music for the
most memorable death in the history of the world.
Surely no one hearing it for the first time, without previous warning, would guess that it had to do with anything
so gruesome as a crucifixion.

But if Dr. Weber thus neglects music, he at least gives
full measure in all other departments. His book, in fact,
is encyclopædic; he almost exhausts the subject. One
idea, however, I do not find in it: the conception of death
as the last and worst of all the practical jokes played upon
poor mortals by the gods. That idea apparently never
occurred to the Greeks, who thought of almost everything, but nevertheless it has an ingratiating plausibility.
The hardest thing about death is not that men die tragi-
cally, but that most of them die ridiculously. If it were
possible for all of us to make our exits at great moments,
swiftly, cleanly, decorously, and in fine attitudes, then
the experience would be something to face heroically and
with high and beautiful words. But we commonly go
off in no such gorgeous, poetical way. Instead, we die in
raucous prose — of arterio-sclerosis, of diabetes, of tox-
emia, of a noisome perforation in the ileo-cæcal region, of
carcinoma of the liver. The abominable acidosis of

Dr. Crile sneaks upon us, gradually paralyzing the adrenals, flabbergasting the thyroid, crippling the poor old liver, and throwing its fog upon the brain. Thus the ontogenetic process is recapitulated in reverse order, and we pass into the mental obscurity of infancy, and then into the blank unconsciousness of the prenatal state, and finally into the condition of undifferentiated protoplasm. A man does not die quickly and brilliantly, like a lightning stroke; he passes out by inches, hesitatingly and, one may almost add, gingerly. It is hard to say just when he is fully dead. Long after his heart has ceased to beat and his lungs have ceased to swell him up with the vanity of his species, there are remote and obscure parts of him that still live on, quite unconcerned about the central catastrophe. Dr. Alexis Carrel has cut them out and kept them alive for months. The hair keeps on growing for a long while. Every time another one of the corpses of Barbarossa or King James I is examined, it is found that the hair is longer than it was the last time. No doubt there are many parts of the body, and perhaps even whole organs, which wonder what it is all about when they find that they are on the way to the crematory. Burn a man's mortal remains, and you inevitably burn a good portion of him alive, and no doubt that portion sends alarmed messages to the unconscious brain, like dissected tissue under anæsthesia, and the resultant shock brings the deceased before the hierarchy of heaven in a state of collapse, with his face white, sweat bespangling his forehead and a great thirst upon him. It would not be pulling the nose of reason to argue that many a cremated Sunday-School superintendent thus confronting the ultimate tribunal in the aspect of a man

taken with the goods, has been put down as suffering
from an uneasy conscience when what actually ailed him
was simply surgical shock. The cosmic process is not
only incurably idiotic; it is also indecently unjust.

But here I become medico-legal. What I had in mind
when I began was this: that the human tendency to make
death dramatic and heroic has little excuse in the facts.
No doubt you remember the scene in the last act of
Hedda Gabler, in which Dr. Brack comes in with the news
of Lövborg's suicide. Hedda immediately thinks of him
putting the pistol to his temple and dying instantly and
magnificently. The picture fills her with romantic delight. When Brack tells her that the shot was actually
through the breast, she is disappointed, but soon begins
to romanticise even *that*. "The breast," she says, "is
also a good place.... There is something beautiful in
this!" A bit later she recurs to the charming theme,
"In the breast — ah!" Then Brack tells her the plain
truth — in the original, thus: "*Nej — det traf ham i
underlivet!*" ... Edmund Gosse, in his first English translation of the play, made the sentence: "No — it struck
him in the abdomen." In the last edition William
Archer makes it "No — in the bowels!" Abdomen is
nearer to *underlivet* than bowels, but belly would probably render the meaning better than either. What
Brack wants to convey to Hedda is the news that Lövborg's death was not romantic in the least — that he
went to a brothel, shot himself, not through the cerebrum
or the heart, but through the duodenum or perhaps the
jejunum, and is at the moment of report awaiting au-
topsy at the Christiania *Allgemeinekrankenhaus*. The
shock floors her, but it is a shock that all of us must learn

to bear. Men upon whom we lavish our veneration reduce it to an absurdity at the end by dying of chronic cystitis, or by choking upon marshmallows or dill pickles, or as the result of getting cut by dirty barbers. Women whom we place upon pedestals worthy of the holy saints come down at last with mastoid abscesses or die obscenely of hiccoughs. And we ourselves? Let us not have too much hope. The chances are that, if we go to war, eager to leap superbly at the cannon's mouth, we'll be finished on the way by an ingrowing toenail or by being run over by an army truck driven by a former Greek bus-boy and loaded with imitation Swiss cheeses made in Oneida, New York. And that if we die in our beds, it will be of measles or albuminuria.

The aforesaid Crile, in one of his smaller books, *A Mechanistic View of War and Peace*, has a good deal to say about death in war, and in particular, about the disparity between the glorious and inspiring passing imagined by the young soldier and the messy finish that is normally in store for him. He shows two pictures of war, the one ideal and the other real. The former is the familiar print, "The Spirit of '76," with the three patriots springing grandly to the attack, one of them with a neat and romantic bandage around his head — apparently, to judge by his liveliness, to cover a wound no worse than an average bee-sting. The latter picture is what the movie folks call a close-up of a French soldier who was struck just below the mouth by a German one-pounder shell — a soldier suddenly converted into the hideous simulacrum of a cruller. What one notices especially is the curious expression upon what remains of his face — an expression of the utmost surprise and indignation. No doubt he

marched off to the front firmly convinced that, if he died
at all, it would be at the climax of some heroic charge,
up to his knees in blood and with his bayonet run
clear through a Bavarian at least four feet in diameter.
He imagined the clean bullet through the heart, the
stately last gesture, the final words: "Thérèse! Sophie!
Olympe! Marie! Suzette! Odette! Dénise! Julie!
... France!" Go to the book and see what he got. ...
Dr. Crile, whose experience of war has soured him
against it, argues that the best way to abolish it would be
to prohibit such romantic prints as "The Spirit of '76"
and substitute therefor a series of actual photographs of
dead and wounded men. The plan is plainly of merit.
But it would be expensive. Imagine a war getting on its
legs before the conversion of the populace had become
complete. Think of the huge herds of spy-chasers, letter-
openers, pacifist-hounds, burlesons and other such oper-
ators that it would take to track down and confiscate all
those pictures! ...

Even so, the vulgar horror of death would remain, for,
as Ellen La Motte well says in her little book, *The Back-
wash of War*, the finish of a civilian in a luxurious hospital, with trained nurses fluttering over him and his
pastor whooping and heaving for him at the foot of his
bed, is often quite as terrible as any form of exitus witnessed in war. It is, in fact, always an unpleasant business. Let the poets disguise it all they may and the
theologians obscure the issue with promises of *post-
mortem* felicity, the plain truth remains that it gives one
pause to reflect that, on some day not far away, one must
yield supinely to acidosis, sink into the mental darkness
of an idiot, and so suffer a withdrawal from these en-

gaging scenes. "No. 8," says the nurse in faded pink, tripping down the corridor with a hooch of rye for the diabetic in No. 2, "has just passed out." "Which is No. 8?" asks the new nurse. "The one whose wife wore that awful hat this afternoon?" ... But all the authorities, it is pleasant to know, report that the final scene is placid enough. Dr. Weber quotes many of them. The dying man doesn't struggle much and he isn't much afraid. As his alkalies give out he succumbs to a blest stupidity. His mind fogs. His will power vanishes. He submits decently. He scarcely gives a damn.

MRS. JOHNSON [1]

ALICE MEYNELL

THIS paper shall not be headed "Tetty." What may be
a graceful enough freedom with the wives of other men
shall be prohibited in the case of Johnson's, she with
whose name no writer until now has scrupled to take free-
doms whereto all graces were lacking. "Tetty" it should
not be, if for no other reason, for this — that the chance
of writing "Tetty" as a title is a kind of facile literary
opportunity; it shall be denied. The Essay owes thus
much amends of deliberate care to Dr. Johnson's wife.
But, indeed, the reason is graver. What wish would he
have had but that the language in the making whereof he
took no ignoble part should somewhere, at some time,
treat his only friend with ordinary honour?

Men who would trust Dr. Johnson with their orthodoxy, with their vocabulary, and with the most intimate
vanity of their human wishes, refuse, with every mark of
insolence, to trust him in regard to his wife. On that one
point no reverence is paid to him, no deference, no respect, not so much as the credit due to our common sanity. Yet he is not reviled on account of his Thrale —
nor, indeed, is his Thrale now seriously reproached for her
Piozzi. It is true that Macaulay, preparing himself and
his reader "in his well-known way" (as a rustic of
Mr. Hardy's might have it) for the recital of her second
marriage, says that it would have been well if she had
been laid beside the kind and generous Thrale when, in

[1] From *Essays* (1914). By permission of Mr. Wilfrid Meynell.

the prime of her life, he died. But Macaulay has not left us heirs to his indignation. His well-known way was to exhaust those possibilities of effect in which the commonplace is so rich. And he was permitted to point his paragraphs as he would, not only by calling Mrs. Thrale's attachment to her second husband "a degrading passion," but by summoning a chorus of "all London" to the same purpose. She fled, he tells us, from the laughter and hisses of her countrymen and countrywomen to a land where she was unknown. Thus when Macaulay chastises Mrs. Elizabeth Porter for marrying Johnson, he is not inconsistent, for he pursues Mrs. Thrale with equal rigour for her audacity in keeping gaiety and grace in her mind and manners longer than Macaulay liked to see such ornaments added to the charm of twice-"married brows."

It is not so with succeeding essayists. One of these minor biographers is so gentle as to call the attachment of Mrs. Thrale and Piozzi "a mutual affection." He adds, "No one who has had some experience of life will be inclined to condemn Mrs. Thrale." But there is no such courtesy, even from him, for Mrs. Johnson. Neither to him nor to any other writer has it yet occurred that if England loves her great Englishman's memory, she owes not only courtesy, but gratitude, to the only woman who loved him while there was yet time.

Not a thought of that debt has stayed the alacrity with which a caricature has been acclaimed as the only possible portrait of Mrs. Johnson. Garrick's school reminiscences would probably have made a much more charming woman grotesque. Garrick is welcome to his remembrances; we may even reserve for ourselves the liberty of envying those who heard him. But honest laughter should not fall into that tone of common antithesis which seems to say, "See what are the absurdities of the great! Such is life! On this one point we, even we, are wiser than Dr. Johnson — we know how grotesque was his wife. We know something of the privacies of her toilet-table. We are able to compare her figure with the figures we, unlike him in his youth, have had the opportunity of admiring — the figures of the well-bred and well-dressed." It is a sorry success to be able to say so much.

But in fact such a triumph belongs to no man. When Samuel Johnson, at twenty-six, married his wife, he gave the dull an advantage over himself which none but the dullest will take. He chose, for love, a woman who had the wit to admire him at first meeting, and in spite of first sight. "That," she said to her daughter, "is the most sensible man I ever met." He was penniless. She had what was no mean portion for those times and those conditions; and, granted that she was affected, and provincial, and short, and all the rest with which she is charged, she was probably not without suitors; nor do her defects or faults seem to have been those of an unadmired or neglected woman. Next, let us remember what was the aspect of Johnson's form and face, even in his twenties, and how little he could have touched the senses of a widow fond of externals. This one loved him, accepted him, made him happy, gave to one of the noblest of all English hearts the one love of its sombre life. And English literature has had no better phrase for her than Macaulay's — "She accepted, with a readiness which did her little honour, the addresses of a suitor who might have been her son."

Her readiness did her incalculable honour. But it is at

last worth remembering that Johnson had first done her incalculable honour. No one has given to man or woman the right to judge as to the worthiness of her who received it. The meanest man is generally allowed his own counsel as to his own wife; one of the greatest of men has been denied it. "The lover," says Macaulay, "continued to be under the illusions of the wedding day till the lady died." What is so graciously said is not enough. He was under those "illusions" until he too died, when he had long passed her latest age, and was therefore able to set right that balance of years which has so much irritated the impertinent. Johnson passed from this life twelve years older than she, and so for twelve years his constant eyes had to turn backwards to dwell upon her. Time gave him a younger wife.

And here I will put into Mrs. Johnson's mouth, that mouth to which no one else has ever attributed any beautiful sayings, the words of Marceline Desbordes-Valmore to the young husband she loved: "Older than thou! Let me never see thou knowest it. Forget it! I will remember it, to die before thy death."

Macaulay, in his unerring effectiveness, uses Johnson's short sight for an added affront to Mrs. Johnson. The bridegroom was too weak of eyesight "to distinguish ceruse from natural bloom." Nevertheless, he saw well enough, when he was old, to distinguish Mrs. Thrale's dresses. He reproved her for wearing a dark dress; it was unsuitable, he said, for her size; a little creature should show gay colours, "like an insect." We are not called upon to admire his wife; why, then, our taste being thus compromised, do we not suffer him to admire her? It is the most gratuitous kind of intrusion. Moreover, the biographers are eager to permit that touch of romance and grace in his relations to Mrs. Thrale, which they officially deny in the case of Mrs. Johnson. But the difference is all on the other side. He would not have bidden his wife dress like an insect. Mrs. Thrale was to him "the first of womankind" only because his wife was dead.

Beauclerc, we learn, was wont to cap Garrick's mimicry of Johnson's love-making by repeating the words of Johnson himself in after-years — "It was a love-match on both sides." And obviously he was as strange a lover as they said. Who doubted it? Was there any other woman in England to give such a suitor the opportunity of an eternal love? "A life radically wretched," was the life of this master of Letters; but she, who has received nothing in return except ignominy from these unthankful Letters, had been alone to make it otherwise. Well for him that he married so young as to earn the ridicule of all the biographers in England; for by doing so he, most happily, possessed his wife for nearly twenty years. I have called her his only friend. So indeed she was, though he had followers, disciples, rivals, competitors, and companions, many degrees of admirers, a biographer, a patron, and a public. He had also the houseful of sad old women who quarrelled under his beneficent protection. But what friend had he? He was "solitary" from the day she died.

Let us consider under what solemn conditions and in what immortal phrase the word "solitary" stands. He wrote it, all Englishmen know where. He wrote it in the hour of that melancholy triumph when he had been at last set free from the dependence upon hope. He hoped no more, and he needed not to hope. The "notice" of

Lord Chesterfield had been too long deferred; it was granted at last, when it was a flattery which Johnson's court of friends would applaud. But not for their sake was it welcome. To no living ear would he bring it and report it with delight.

He was indifferent, he was known. The sensitiveness to pleasure was gone, and the sensitiveness to pain, slights, and neglect would thenceforth be suffered to rest; no man in England would put that to proof again. No man in England, did I say? But, indeed, that is not so. No slight to him, to his person, or to his fame could have had power to cause him pain more sensibly than the customary, habitual, ready-made ridicule that has been cast by posterity upon her whom he loved for twenty years, prayed for during thirty-two years more, who satisfied one of the saddest human hearts, but to whom the world, assiduous to admire him, hardly accords human dignity. He wrote praises of her manners and of her person for her tomb. But her epitaph, that does not name her, is in the greatest of English prose. What was favour to him? "I am indifferent. . . . I am known. . . . I am solitary, and cannot impart it."

AUTUMN TINTS IN CHIVALRY [1]

C. E. MONTAGUE

I

In either of two opposite tempers you may carry on war. In one of the two you will want to rate your enemy, all round, as high as you can. You may pursue him down a trench, or he you; but in neither case do you care to have him described by somebody far, far away as a fat little short-sighted scrub. Better let him pass for a paladin. This may at bottom be vanity, sentimentality, all sorts of contemptible things. Let him who knows the heart of man be dogmatic about it. Anyhow, this temper comes, as they would say in Ireland, of decent people. It spoke in Porsena of Clusium's whimsical prayer that Horatius might swim the Tiber safely; it animates Velasquez' knightly *Surrender of Breda;* it prompted Lord Roberts's first words to Cronje when Paardeberg fell — "Sir, you have made a very gallant defence"; it is avowed in a popular descant of Newbolt's

> To honour, while you strike him down,
> The foe who comes with eager eyes.

The other temper has its niche in letters, too. There was the man that "wore his dagger in his mouth." And there was Little Flanigan, the bailiff's man in Goldsmith's play. During one of our old wars with France he was always "damning the French, the parle-vous, and all that belonged to them." "What," he would ask the

---

[1] From *Disenchantment*. Published, 1922, by Chatto and Windus. By permission of the author.

company, "makes the bread rising? The parle-vous that devour us. What makes the mutton fivepence a pound? The parle-vous that eat it up. What makes the beer threepence-halfpenny a pot?"

Well, your first aim in war is to hit your enemy hard, and the question may well be quite open — in which of these tempers can he be hit hardest? If, as we hear, a man's strength be "as the strength of ten because his heart is pure," possibly it may add a few foot-pounds to his momentum in an attack if he has kept a clean tongue in his head. And yet the production of heavy woollens in the West Riding, for War Office use, may, for all that we know, have been accelerated by yarns about crucified Canadians and naked bodies of women found in German trenches. There is always so much, so bewilderingly much, to be said on both sides. All I can tell is that during the war the Newbolt spirit seemed, on the whole, to have its chief seat in and near our front line, and thence to die down westward all the way to London. There Little Flanigan was enthroned, and, like Montrose, would bear no rival near his throne, so that a man on leave from our trench system stood in some danger of being regarded as little better than one of the wicked. Anyhow, he was a kind of provincial. Not his will, but that of Flanigan, had to be done. For Flanigan was at the centre of things; he had leisure, or else volubility was his trade; and he had got hold of the megaphones.

II

In the first months of the war there was any amount of good sportsmanship going; most, of course, among men who had seen already the whites of enemy eyes. I remember the potent emetic effect of Flaniganism upon a little blond Regular subaltern maimed at the first battle of Ypres. "Pretty measly sample of the sin against the Holy Ghost!" the one-legged child grunted savagely, showing a London paper's comic sketch of a corpulent German running away. The first words I ever heard uttered in palliation of German misdoings in Belgium came from a Regular N.C.O., a Dragoon Guards sergeant, holding forth to a sergeants' mess behind our line. "We'd have done every damn thing they did," he averred, "if it had been we." I thought him rather extravagant, then. Later on, when the long row of hut hospitals, jammed between the Calais-Paris Railway at Etaples and the great reinforcement camp on the sandhills above it, was badly bombed from the air, even the wrath of the R.A.M.C. against those who had wedged in its wounded and nurses between two staple targets scarcely exceeded that of our Royal Air Force against war correspondents who said the enemy must have done it on purpose.

Airmen, no doubt, or some of them, went to much greater lengths in the chivalrous line than the rest of us. Many things helped them to do it. Combatant flying was still new enough to be almost wholly an officer's job; the knight took the knocks, and the squire stayed behind and looked after his gear. Air-fighting came to be pretty well the old duel, or else the mediæval mêlée between little picked teams. The clean element, too, may have counted — it always looked a clean job from below, where your airy notions got mixed with trench mud, while the airmen seemed like Sylvia in the song, who so excelled "each mortal thing upon the dull earth dwelling." Whatever the cause, he excelled in his bearing towards enemies, dead or alive. The funeral that he gave to Richthofen in France was one of the few handsome gestures exchanged in the war. And whenever Little Flanigan at home began squealing aloud that we ought to take some of our airmen off fighting and make them bomb German women and children instead, our airmen's scorn for these ethics of the dirt helped to keep up the flickering hope that the post-war world might not be ignoble.

Even on the dull earth it takes time and pains to get a clean-run boy or young man into a mean frame of mind. A fine N.C.O. of the Grenadier Guards was killed near Laventie — no one knows how — while going over to shake hands with the Germans on Christmas morning. "What! not shake on Christmas Day?" He would have thought it poor, sulky fighting. Near Armentières at the Christmas of 1914 an incident happened which seemed quite the natural thing to most soldiers then. On Christmas Eve the Germans lit up their front line with Chinese lanterns. Two British officers thereupon walked some way across No Man's Land, hailed the enemy's sentries, and asked for an officer. The German sentries said, "Go back, or we shall have to shoot." The Englishmen said, "Not likely!" advanced to the German wire, and asked again for an officer. The sentries held their fire and sent for an officer. With him the Englishmen made a one-day truce, and on Christmas Day the two sides exchanged cigarettes and played football together. The English intended the truce to end with the day, as agreed, but decided not to shoot next day till the enemy did. Next morning the Germans were still to be seen washing and breakfasting outside their wire; so our men, too, got out of the trench and sat about in the open. One of them, cleaning his rifle, loosed a shot by accident, and an English subaltern went to tell the Germans it had not been fired to kill. The ones he spoke to understood, but as he was walking back a German somewhere wide on a flank fired and hit him in the knee, and he has walked lame ever since. Our men took it that some German sentry had misunderstood our fluke shot. They did not impute dishonour. The air in such places was strangely clean in those distant days. During one of the very few months of open warfare a cavalry private of ours brought in a captive, a gorgeous specimen of the terrific Prussian Uhlan of tradition. "But why didn't you put your sword through him?" an officer asked, who belonged to the school of Froissart less obviously than the private. "Well, sir," the captor replied, "the gentleman wasn't looking."

III

At no seat of war will you find it quite easy to live up to Flanigan's standards of hatred towards an enemy. Reaching a front, you find that all you want is just to win the war. Soon you are so taken up with the pursuit of this aim that you are always forgetting to burn with the gem-like flame of pure fury that fires the lion-hearted publicist at home.

A soldier might have had the Athanasian ecstasy all right till he reached the firing line. Every individual German had sunk the Lusitania; there was none righteous, none. And yet at a front the holy passion began to ooze out at the ends of his fingers. The bottom trouble is that you cannot fight a man in a physical way without somehow touching him. The relation of actual combatants is a personal one — no doubt, a rude, primitive one, but still quite advanced as compared with that between a learned man at Berlin who keeps on saying *Delenda est Britannia!* at the top of his voice and a learned man in London who keeps on saying that every German must have a black heart because Cæsar did not conquer Germany as he did Gaul and Britain. Just let the round head of a German appear for a passing second, at long intervals, above a hummock of clay in the middle distance. Before you had made half a dozen sincere efforts to shoot him the fatal germ of human relationship had begun to find a nidus again: he had acquired in your mind the rudiments of a personal individuality. You would go on trying to shoot him with zest — indeed, with a diminished likelihood of missing, for mere hatred is a flustering emotion. And yet the hatred business had started crumbling. There had begun the insidious change that was to send you home, on your first leave, talking unguardedly of "old Fritz" or of "the good old Boche" to the pain of your friends, as if he were a stout dog fox or a real stag of a hare.

The deadliest solvent of your exalted hatreds is laughter. And you can never wholly suppress laughter between two crowds of millions of men standing within earshot of each other along a line of hundreds of miles. There was, in the Loos salient in 1916, a German who, after his meals, would halloo across to an English unit taunts about certain accidents of its birth. None of his British hearers could help laughing at his mistakes, his knowledge, and his English. Nor could the least humorous priest of ill-will have kept his countenance at a relief when the enemy shouted: "We know you are re-

lieving," "No good hiding it," "Good-bye, Ox and
Bucks," "Who's coming in?" and some humorist in the
obscure English battalion relieving shouted back, with a
terrific assumption of accent, "Furrst Black Watch!" or
"Th' Oirish Gyards!" and a hush fell at the sound of these
great names. Comedy, expelled with a fork by the dignified figure of Quenchless Hate, had begun to steal back
of herself.

At home that tragedy queen might do very well; she did
not have these tenpenny nails scattered about on her road
to puncture the nobly inflated tyres of her chariot. The
heroes who spoke up for shooing all the old German gov-
ernesses into the barbed wire compounds were not exposed to the moral danger of actually hustling, *propria
persona*, these formidable ancients. But while Hamilcar
at home was swearing Hannibal and all the other little
Hamilcars to undying hatred of the foe, an enemy dog
might be trotting across to the British front line to sample
its rats, and its owner be losing in some British company's
eyes his proper quality as an incarnation of all the Satan-
ism of Potsdam and becoming simply "him that lost the
dog."

If you took his trench it might be no better; perhaps
Incarnate Evil had left its bit of food half-cooked, and
the muddy straw, where it lay last, was pressed into a
hollow by Incarnate Evil's back as by a cat's. Incarnate
Evil should not do these things that other people in
trenches do. It ought to be more strange and beastly
and keep on making *beaux gestes* with its talons and tail,
like the proper dragon slain by Saint George. Perhaps
Incarnate Evil was extinct and you went over its pockets.
They never contained the right things — no poison to

put in our wells, no practical hints for crucifying Canadians; only the usual stuffing of all soldiers' pockets — photographs and tobacco and bits of string and the wife's letters, all about how tramps were always stealing potatoes out of the garden, and how the baby was worse, and was his leave never coming? No good to look at such things.

IV

With this guilty weakness gaining upon them our troops drove the Germans from Albert to Mons. There were scandalous scenes on the way. Imagine two hundred German prisoners grinning inside a wire cage while a little Cockney corporal chaffs them in half the dialects of Germany! His father, he says, was a slop tailor in Whitechapel; most of his journeymen came from somewhere or other in Germany — "Ah! and my dad sweated 'em proper," he says proudly; so the boy learnt all their kinds of talk. He convulses Bavarians now with his flow of Silesian. He fraternizes grossly and jubilantly. Other British soldiers laugh when one of the Germans sings, in return for favours received, the British ballad "Knocked 'em in the Ol' Kent Road." By the time our men had marched to the Rhine there was little hatred left in them. How can you hate the small boy who stands at the farm door visibly torn between dread of the invader and deep delight in all soldiers, as soldiers? How shall a man not offer a drink to the first disbanded German soldier who sits next to him in a public house at Cologne, and try to find out if he was ever in the line at the Brickstacks or near the Big Crater? Why, that might have been his dog!

The billeted soldier's immemorial claim on "a place by the fire" carried on the fell work. It is hopelessly bad for your grand Byronic hates if you sit through whole winter evenings in the abhorred foe's kitchen and the abhorred foe grants you the uncovenanted mercy of hot coffee and discusses without rancour the relative daily yields of the British and the German milch cow. And then comes into play the British soldier's incorrigible propensity, wherever he be, to form virtuous attachments. "Love, unfoiled in the war," as Sophocles says. The broad road has a terribly easy gradient. When all the great and wise at Paris were making peace, as somebody said, with a vengeance, our command on the Rhine had to send a wire to say that unless something was done to feed the Germans starving in the slums it could not answer for discipline in its army; the men were giving their rations away, and no orders would stop them. Rank "Pro-Germanism," you see — the heresy of Edith Cavell; "Patriotism is not enough; I must have no hatred or bitterness in my heart." While these men fought on, year after year, they had mostly been growing more void of mere spite all the time, feeling always more and more sure that the average German was just a decent poor devil like everyone else. One trembles to think what the really first-class haters at home would have said of our army if they had known at the time.

v

Even at places less distant than home the survival of old English standards of fighting had given some scandal. In that autumn of the war when our generalship seemed to have explored all its own talents and found only the means to stage in an orderly way the greatest possible number of combats of pure attrition, the crying up of unknightliness became a kind of fashion among a good many Staff Officers of the higher grades. "I fancy our fellows were not taking many prisoners this morning," a Corps Commander would say with a complacent grin, on the evening after a battle. Jocose stories of comic things said by privates when getting rid of undesired captives became current in messes far in the rear. The other day I saw in a history of one of the most gallant of all British divisions an illustration given by the officer who wrote it of what he believed to be the true martial spirit. It was the case of a wounded Highlander who had received with a bomb a German Red Cross orderly who was coming to help him. A General of some consequence during part of the war gave a lecture, towards its end, to a body of officers and others on what he called "the fighting spirit." He told with enthusiasm an anecdote of a captured trench in which some of our men had been killing off German appellants for quarter. Another German appearing and putting his hands up, one of our men — so the story went — called out, "'Ere! Where's 'Arry? 'E ain't 'ad one yet." Probably some one had pulled the good general's leg, and the thing never happened. But he believed it, and deeply approved the "blooding" of 'Arry. That, he explained, was the "fighting spirit." Men more versed than he in the actual hand-to-hand business of fighting this war knew that he was mistaken, and that the spirit of trial by combat and that of pork-butchery are distinct. But that is of course. The notable thing was that such things should be said by anyone wearing our uniform. Twenty years before, if it had been rumoured, you would, without waiting, have called the rumour a lie invented by some detractor of England or of her army. Now it passed quite unhissed. It was the latter-day wisdom. Scrofulous minds at home had long been itching, publicly and in print, to bomb German women and children from aeroplanes, and to "take it out of" German prisoners of war. Now the disease had even affected some parts of the non-combatant Staff of our army.

VI

You know the most often quoted of all passages of Burke. Indeed, it is only through quotations of it that most of us know Burke at all —

"But the age of chivalry is gone . . . the unbought grace of life, the cheap defence of nations, the nurse of manly sentiment and heroic enterprise is gone! It is gone, that sensibility of principle, that chastity of honour, which felt a stain like a wound, which inspired courage whilst it mitigated ferocity, which ennobled whatever it touched, and under which vice itself lost half its evil by losing all its grossness."

Burke would never say a thing by halves. And as truth goes by halves, and declines to be sweeping like rhetoric, Burke made sure of being wrong to the tune of some fifty per cent. The French Revolution did not, as his beautiful language implies, confine mankind for the rest of its days to the procreation of curs. And yet his words do give you, in their own lush, Corinthian way, a notion of something that probably did happen, a certain limited shifting of the centre of gravity of West European morals or manners.

267

One would be talking like Burke — talking, perhaps you might say, through Burke's hat — if one were to say that the war found chivalry alive and left it dead. Chivalry is about as likely to perish as brown eyes or the moon. Yet something did happen, during the war, to which these wild words would have some sort of relation. We were not all Bayards in 1914; even then a great part of our Press could not tell indignation from spite, nor uphold the best cause in the world without turpitude. Nor were we all, after the Armistice, rods of the houses of Thersites and Cleon; Haig was still alive, and so were Gough and Hamilton and thousands of Arthurian subalterns and privates and of like-minded civilians, though it is harder for a civilian not to lose generosity during a war. But something had happened; the chivalrous temper had had a set-back; it was no longer the mode; the latest wear was a fine robust shabbiness. All through the war there had been a bear movement in Newbolts and Burkes, and, corresponding to this, a bull movement in stocks of the Little Flanigan group.

THOMAS BAILEY ALDRICH [1]

PAUL ELMER MORE

ANYBODY to-day into whose hands a few documents have
fallen can write a biography, forgetful in his haste that
"easy writing's curst hard reading." Indeed, one cannot
follow the tide of Lives turned out by the press without
feeling that now in earnest the Philistines be upon us, and,
with the memory fresh in mind of certain recent biographies, one shudders to think of what might have happened
to Mr. Aldrich. Here, above all, delicacy and reticence
(not concealment, for there is little or nothing to conceal)
were necessary, and, by good fortune, these are eminently the qualities that Mr. Greenslet has brought to
his task,[2] together with a skill in words that reproduces
something of the charm of one who made refinement the
end of all his labour. Mr. Greenslet knows when to stop.
He tells just enough of the child's surroundings at Ports-
mouth; he finds the right note of emphasis for the half-
hearted association of the clerk and youthful editor in
New York with that sad Bohemian band before the war,
out of which Poe escaped by wine and opium, and from
which Whitman was saved only by his phlegmatic egotism; he follows the man sympathetically through his
Boston years of prosperous toil and golden ease, to the
honoured close. He does not forget to point out the
happy influence upon his peculiar temperament of that

[1] From *Shelburne Essays, Seventh Series*. Copyright, 1910, by Paul
Elmer More. By permission of the author and of the publishers,
Houghton Mifflin Company.
[2] *The Life of Thomas Bailey Aldrich*. By Ferris Greenslet. Boston:
Houghton Mifflin Company, 1908.

mingling of the literary traditions of Boston and New York, which gave to his work at once a touch of ethical seriousness and of easy urbanity.

If Mr. Greenslet fails to satisfy us anywhere, it is in the last chapter, in which he sums up his criticism of Aldrich's writings. What he says is good and sound, but somehow it is not quite sufficient; it lacks the last transmuting touch. He quotes, but does not entirely take to heart his author's command:

> To the sea-shell's spiral round
> 'Tis your heart that brings the sound:
> The soft sea-murmurs that you hear
> Within, are captured from your ear.
>
> You do poets and their song
> A grievous wrong,
> If your own soul does not bring
> To their high imagining
> As much beauty as they sing.

That is more than should be asked of any reader, no doubt; but at least one may demand of the critic a fuller use of his own high imaginative right by which he lifts the melody of the poet out of its isolation and gives it a place in the music of time.

How much more might be said, which Mr. Greenslet could say so delightfully, about that little volume of *Songs and Sonnets*,[1] selected by Mr. Aldrich himself from the body of his work and published in honour of his seventieth birthday. These catches of "short-breathed music, dying on the tongue," we call *vers de société*, per-

[1] *A Book of Songs and Sonnets*. Selected from the Poems of Thomas Bailey Aldrich. Boston: The Riverside Press, 1906. Only 430 copies of this book, exquisite in form and contents, were printed. It will be a prize for future collectors.

haps, having no better name for them. There is, in fact, something in that phrase that reminds one rather of the glittering, tableau verses of Mr. Austin Dobson than of Mr. Aldrich's shy insinuation, and I could almost wish we had adopted the phrase "Gentle Verse" suggested by Miss Carolyn Wells in her *Anthology*, using the word gentle as Coleridge and Lionel Johnson applied it to Charles Lamb, or as signifying that which is "innately fine, polished by the experience and sophistication of truly good society."

But by whatever name we call them, we should not suppose that these fragile verses of Mr. Aldrich's were mated carelessly or without thought of the destinies of a beautiful accomplishment:

> Enamoured architect of airy rhyme,
> Build as thou wilt, heed not what each man says:
> Good souls, but innocent of dreamers' ways,
> Will come, and marvel why thou wastest time;
> Others beholding how thy turrets climb
> 'Twixt theirs and heaven, will hate thee all thy days;
> But most beware of those who come to praise.
> O Wondersmith, O worker in sublime
> And heaven-sent dreams, let art be all in all;
> Build as thou wilt, unspoiled by praise or blame,
> Build as thou wilt, and as thy light is given;
> Then, if at last the airy structure fall,
> Dissolve, and vanish — take thyself no shame.
> They fail, and they alone, who have not striven.

This art in miniature, of which Mr. Aldrich's *Songs and Sonnets* are so fine a flower, is not, in fact, an easy thing to be thrown off by any untaught hand; beside the tradition of the larger art it has its own long and sacred history. From the time when some monk, it may be, in the decline of Greek letters, gave to his swallow-like trochaics of love and wine the magic name of Anacreon this new muse of wanton wisdom has had a place with the graver sisters of the nine. Perhaps there is too much of wantonness and too little of wisdom in the *Anacreontica* to afford the model we are seeking; they lack the background of seriousness that is always felt in the perfect *vers de société*. Yet the picture of this old man, crowned with flowers and crying the pains and pleasures of youth, took a strange hold of the fancy of later poets, and his mischievous boy Eros has had a sly knack of slipping into the minds of passionate singers who should have invoked only the sterner god, known and worshipped by the ancient true Anacreon.

There is seriousness and to spare in the Greek *Anthology*, if we open its heart, and here, if anywhere, has been the inexhaustible source from which our rhymers have drawn their hippocrene. But still the tone is not tempered to just the mood for our present purpose. Somewhat too insistently the might and tragic glory of Greece weigh on the mind as we read these deliberate efforts to hide its grave under flowers; whether by a trick of fancy or not, too poignantly almost we feel that the end of that world is near at hand. These brief epigrams, as they are called, were written to pass from mouth to mouth during the banquet hour, or, at least, took their mode from that norm. Into the heart that began to doubt of wine and love they were designed to bring the Epicurean zest that comes with the intruding thought of universal transience. Some trace of that shadow may always, no doubt, be detected in the eyes of our *Musa philommeides*, even when she visits the far New England clime:

Ho, eglantine and cresses
  For her tresses! —
Let Care, the beggar, wait
  Outside the gate.

Tears if you will — but after
  Mirth and laughter;
Then, folded hands on breast
  And endless rest.

That is also in the *Anthology*, that and something more. It is not only the Egyptian death-masque among the feasters to crown their pleasure, but, sitting with them, one seems to hear, amid the pauses of their singing, from afar off, muffled by the windings of many streets, the engines of the enemy beating at the city gates. The banquet hall is in a beleaguered town, the barbarians are beneath the walls, and the guests cling to one another in friendship, and to "the fair things of Hellas," their inheritance now about to be scattered and trodden under foot. It is the consummation of Greece one sings in the epigram best known to us in its Latin version, *Spes et Fortuna valete:*

To Hope, farewell, and Fortune; having found the port
  I leave you; others now shall be your sport.

The Romans also had their votaries of this Muse, greater names in this kind than Greece could count. Catullus, the lover of Lesbia, has, indeed, accomplished all that is possible in bestowing upon passion a high-bred ease. No one has surpassed his song of the kisses, the *basia mille, deinde centum, dein mille altera*, with its solemn reminder:

So may we live and love, till life be our,
  And let the greybeards wag and flout.

Yon failing sun shall rise another morn,
  And the thin moon round out her horn;
But we, when once we lose our waning light, —
  Ah, Love, the long unbroken night!

Or, if this seem too directly pathetic for our class, there is the inimitable song to Lesbia's sparrow, which so many poets have so bravely tried to imitate.

And yet withal Catullus was too swift and too energetic to belong wholly, or even primarily, within the circle we are trying to draw. He who walked in the terrible company of Cæsar and Mamurra, of Clodius and his sister the *quadrantaria*, may have dallied with the day; but under his fine linen might be felt the surface of steel, and in his hand he carried a dagger, and not a lily.

Despite his inferiority as a poet, perhaps in part because of his lesser force, Martial is really nearer at times to our model than Catullus. Here is the consciousness of a lesser art contrasted with the great tradition, and with it the refuge from failure in ambiguous nonchalance. Here, too, is the note of tenderness for little, broken things, for young children whom neither their loveliness nor their prattling eloquence could save from death:

Soft lie the sod above her; lightly rest,
  O earth, on one who lightly touched thy breast.

But, again, we are deterred from accepting this later singer as our type, if only for the filth and sordidness that choke his pages. His rarer notes of beauty are like iridescent bubbles floating on a foul stream; we fear to touch them lest they burst and soil our hands.

Nevertheless, in these poets are the sources of the kind we are trying to distinguish. Their influence extends to England with the Renaissance, and is never forgotten.

The Caroline poets, Suckling and Carew and the others, knew it; Herrick felt it, and wrote his *Hesperides* under the spell. But somehow these Cavaliers failed to put the shadows in their pictures as well as the lights, or, rather, they left out the moral element too completely; they belong too much to the school of the *Anacreontica* and too little to that of the *Anthology*. The real *vers de société* — they can scarcely here be called Gentle Verse — came in with the wits of Queen Anne; and for the better part of a century Prior's lines to Chloe and Clorinda and the other nymphs of London, and Pope's *Rape of the Lock*, were admired as the very mirror of a society in which good taste was finally codified. Well, it may be unjust, but I, for one, cannot read the lightest and prettiest of those verses without remembering the satyrlike advice of Rochester to his Cælias and Corinnas, or the brutal coarseness of Swift's Strephon and Chloe. The background of that graceful diversion is not the kindly illusion we are seeking, but an undeceived cynicism; the drop of bitter is hatred and not regret.

If any one in that age caught the tone of Gentle Verse, it was the learned, awkward, absent-minded, pious usher of Westminster school, Vincent Bourne, whose Latin poems Cowper placed above those of Tibullus, Propertius, and Ausonius, and not below those of Ovid. Perhaps it is his very use of Latin that makes him so perfect a master in the kind. There is in that union of ancient words with modern ideas, in that wedding of the speech of the schools with the politeness of the man of the world (for, pen in hand, Bourne was one of the wits, not a pedagogue), a something that tantalises the reader like a half-seen, half-vanishing face. One feels this here and there in the lines which Bourne has turned into Latin from Prior and the other singers of Chloe; one feels it still more strongly in the translations of his own poems into English. Cowper, if any one, was fitted to catch the charm of his fables, but *The Jackdaw* and *The Cricket* miss just the piquant meeting of gravity and levity that mark the *Cornicula* and *Ad Grillum*. Lamb, too, has tried his hand and almost succeeded. In the *Epitaph on a Dog* especially he was able to match Vincent with his own experience of the humours and pathos of the London streets; but his verses still lack the Virgilian echo that sighs through the *Epitaphium*. Read the close of the two poems together:

> These were my manners, this my way of life,
> Till age and slow disease me overtook,
> And sever'd from my sightless master's side.
> But lest the grace of so good deeds should die,
> Through tract of years in mute oblivion lost,
> This slender tomb of turf hath Irus rear'd. . . .

> Hi mores, haec vita fuit, dum fata sinebant,
> Dum neque languebam morbis, nec inerte senecta,
> Quae tandem obrepsit, veterique satellite caecum
> Orbavit dominum: prisci sed gratia facti
> Ne tota intereat, longos deleta per annos,
> Exiguum hunc Irus tumulum de cespite fecit. . . .

The very essence of Gentle Verse is in that Virgilian *dum fata sinebant* applied to a blind beggar and his dog; and Lamb has omitted it.

But to write out the full history of this verse would be like laying a burden on the back of a moth. And, indeed, there is not room here even for the names of the poets of the later nineteenth century, Austin Dobson, Andrew Lang, Frederick Locker-Lampson, and a host of others,

Englishmen and Americans, who have written in this vein.
As a rule, their work has just missed the mark, because
their intention was too evident.   One seems to hear them
say: Come, now, we will sit down and compose *vers de société*.   And almost always they use the modes of the past
as a kind of masquerade, so that their scenes may fall
into neat artificial tableaux.   From these, however, and
from the earlier poets one begins to see the limitations and
possibilities of the kind.   Its essence lies in irony — not
the grim sort we know from the tragedians and satirists,
but a self-deprecating irony that is half a confession of
weakness and half a deliberate veiling of strength in
gentleness.   Reticence, suggestion, and accepted little-
ness are its indispensable qualities.   The regret of an
idealised past will linger in it, but its themes are of the
immediate present.   It must have its root in deep emotion, but its manner is rather of one who sees passion in
another than of one who himself feels.   It is touched by
the tragic brevity and insufficiency of life, but has no
grief more clamorous than a sigh.   It sees the incongruity
of human pretensions, but indulges in no mirth more
boisterous than a smile.   It knows the deception of the
world, but harbours pity and not cynicism.   It employs
the most elaborate polish of art, but affects a careless
spontaneity.   It is at once urbane and bashful, the voice
of a lady of the world on the lips of Ariel.

And these are the marks that distinguish the little book
of *Songs and Sonnets* as, in its own field, one of the precious things in English.   Aldrich wrote a good deal in the
course of his life — novels, which have the thin-blooded
amateurishness of the older New England fiction; other
prose, like the *Ponkapog Papers*, too finely woven to

endure harsh handling; long poems and plays, conscientiously devised but lacking in substantial human nature. His chief title to genius is the inerrant taste with which he has after many trials beaten out these few lyrics into perfect form, and set them apart from the rest of his work. Their veil of humility is their beauty. To read them is as if one sat alone in a city park, when the mist of twilight was falling, and beheld a company of fair women pass homeward — magically fair in the glimmering dusk. So, in his verse, the atmosphere is that which divides the day and the night, and the two worlds, meeting together, create an illusion of impalpable loveliness:

> Forever am I conscious, moving here,
> That should I step a little space aside
> I pass the boundary of some glorified
> Invisible domain — it lies so near.

He deals with the old themes in the old way, but with his own delicacy of touch — grave antiquity colouring a whimsical sentiment of the present, as in the *Intaglio Head of Minerva;* death hovering between terror and whimsical fancy, as in *Identity;* the mockery of human fates turned into pity and wonder, as in *Destiny;* and nature —

> These winter nights, against my window-pane
> Nature with busy pencil draws designs
> Of ferns and blossoms and fine spray of pines,
> Oak-leaf and acorn and fantastic vines,
> Which she will shape, when summer comes again —
> Quaint arabesques in argent, flat and cold,
> Like curious Chinese etchings. . . . By and by
> (I in my leafy garden as of old)
> These frosty fantasies shall charm my eye
> In azure, damask, emerald, and gold.

Perhaps, if one had to name a single poem as typical

of Gentle Verse as Aldrich practised the art, it would be
the lines called *Latakia*, in which the gorgeous ex-
travagances of the Orient are held in fee to a smoker's
lazy dream:

I

When all the panes are hung with frost,
Wild wizard-work of silver lace,
I draw my sofa on the rug
Before the ancient chimney-place.
Upon the painted tiles are mosques
And minarets, and here and there
A blind muezzin lifts his hands
And calls the faithful unto prayer.
Folded in idle, twilight dreams,
I hear the hemlock chirp and sing
As if within its ruddy core
It held the happy heart of Spring.
Ferdousi never sang like that,
Nor Saadi grave, nor Hafiz gay:
I lounge, and blow white rings of smoke,
And watch them rise and float away.

II

The curling wreaths like turbans seem
Of silent slaves that come and go —
Of Viziers, packed with craft and crime,
Whom I behead from time to time,
With pipe-stem, at a single blow.
And now and then a lingering cloud
Takes gracious form at my desire,
And at my side my lady stands,
Unwinds her veil with snowy hands —
A shadowy shape, a breath of fire!

O Love, if you were only here
Beside me in this mellow light,
Though all the bitter winds should blow,
Though all the ways be choked with snow,
'Twould be a true Arabian night!

It is a part of the convention thus to touch the reality of a lifelong devotion (for so it was in Aldrich) with the lightness of a passing fancy. And like love, even beauty itself, which poets are fond of magnifying as a great and awful power pervading the world, she will reduce by the delicate wand of irony to the least and most ephemeral form:

> My mind lets go a thousand things,
> Like dates of wars and deaths of kings,
> And yet recalls the very hour —
> 'Twas noon by yonder village tower,
> And on the last blue moon in May —
> The wind came briskly up this way,
> Crisping the brook beside the road;
> Then, pausing here, set down its load
> Of pine-scents, and shook listlessly
> Two petals from that wild-rose tree.

In that exquisite and pathetic diminution, I take it, lies the secret of what is called *vers de société* or Gentle Verse. Mr. Greenslet quotes from a letter in which Whittier speaks of the pleasure given by these lines, "a pleasure that is very near pain in its intensity"; and he tells how the Quaker poet, then old and approaching death, would ask every evening to have certain of Aldrich's poems read to him, closing invariably with the request: "Now thee knows without my saying so that I want *Memory*," and always, with his wonderful far-off gaze, repeating after the reader:

> Two petals from that wild-rose tree.

And many a lesser lover of that Muse will hold in memory the falling petals of the *Songs and Sonnets* long after he has forgotten more ambitious things.

THOUGHTS ON CIDER [1]

CHRISTOPHER MORLEY

OUR friend Dove Dulcet, the poet, came into our kennel
and found us arm in arm with a deep demijohn of Chester
County cider. We poured him out a beaker of the cloudy
amber juice. It was just in prime condition, sharpened
with a blithe tingle, beaded with a pleasing bubble of
froth. Dove looked upon it with a kindled eye. His arm
raised the tumbler in a manner that showed this gesture
to be one that he had compassed before. The orchard
nectar began to sluice down his throat.

Dove is one who has faced many and grievous woes.
His Celtic soul peers from behind cloudy curtains of alarm.
Old unhappy far-off things and battles long ago fume in
the smoke of his pipe. His girded spirit sees agrarian unrest in the daffodil and industrial riot in a tin of preserved
prunes. He sees the world moving on the brink of horror
and despair. Sweet dalliance with a baked bloater on a
restaurant platter moves him to grief over the hard lot of
the Newfoundland fishing fleet. Six cups of tea warm him
to anguish over the peonage of Sir Thomas Lipton's
coolies in Ceylon. Souls in perplexity cluster round him
like Canadian dimes in a cash register in Plattsburgh,
New York. He is a human sympathy trust. When we
are on our deathbed we shall send for him. The perfection of his gentle sorrow will send us roaring out into

[1] From *Pipefuls*, by Christopher Morley; copyright, 1920, by Doubleday, Page and Company. By permission.

the dark, and will set a valuable example to the members of our family.

But it is the rack of clouds that makes the sunset lovely. The bosomy vapours of Dove's soul are the palette upon which the decumbent sun of his spirit casts its vivid orange and scarlet colours. His joy is the more perfect to behold because it bursts goldenly through the pangs of his tender heart. His soul is like the infant Moses, cradled among dark and prickly bullrushes; but anon it floats out upon the river and drifts merrily downward on a sparkling spate.

It has nothing to do with Dove, but we will here interject the remark that a pessimist overtaken by liquor is the cheeriest sight in the world. Who is so extravagantly, gloriously, and irresponsibly gay?

Dove's eyes beaconed as the cider went its way. The sweet lingering tang filled the arch of his palate with a soft mellow cheer. His gaze fell upon us as his head tilted gently backward. We wish there had been a painter there — some one like F. Walter Taylor — to rush onto canvas the gorgeous benignity of his aspect. It would have been a portrait of the rich Flemish school. Dove's eyes were full of a tender emotion, mingled with a charmed and wistful surprise. It was as though the poet was saying he had not realized there was anything so good left on earth. His bearing was devout, religious, mystical. In one moment of revelation (so it appeared to us as we watched) Dove looked upon all the profiles and aspects of life, and found them of noble outline. Not since the grandest of Grand Old Parties went out of power has Dove looked less as though he felt the world were on the verge of an abyss. For several moments revolution and anarchy receded, profiteers were tamed, capital and labour purred together on a mattress of catnip, and the cosmos became a free verse poem. He did not even utter the customary and ungracious remark of those to whom cider potations are given: "That'll be at its best in about a week." We apologized for the cider being a little warmish from standing (discreetly hidden) under our desk. Douce man, he said: "I think cider, like ale, ought not to be drunk too cold. I like it just this way." He stood for a moment, filled with theology and metaphysics. "By gracious," he said, "it makes all the other stuff taste like poison." Still he stood for a brief instant, transfixed with complete bliss. It was apparent to us that his mind was busy with apple orchards and autumn sunshine. Perhaps he was wondering whether he could make a poem out of it. Then he turned softly and went back to his job in a life insurance office.

As for ourself, we then poured out another tumbler, lit a corncob pipe, and meditated. Falstaff once said that he had forgotten what the inside of a church looked like. There will come a time when many of us will perhaps have forgotten what the inside of a saloon looked like, but there will still be the consolation of the cider jug. Like the smell of roasting chestnuts and the comfortable equatorial warmth of an oyster stew, it is a consolation hard to put into words. It calls irresistibly for tobacco; in fact the true cider toper always pulls a long puff at his pipe before each drink, and blows some of the smoke into the glass so that he gulps down some of the blue reek with his draught. Just why this should be, we know not. Also some enthusiasts insist on having small sugared cookies with their cider; others cry loudly for Reading pretzels. Some have ingenious theories about letting the jug stand, either tightly stoppered or else unstoppered, until it becomes "hard." In our experience hard cider is distressingly like drinking vinegar. We prefer it soft, with all its sweetness and the transfusing savour of the fruit animating it. At the peak of its deliciousness it has a small, airy sparkle against the roof of the mouth, a delicate tactile sensation like the feet of dancing flies. This, we presume, is the four and one half to seven per cent of sin with which fermented cider is credited by works of reference. There are pedants and bigots who insist that the jug must be stoppered with a corncob. For our own part, the stopper does not stay in the neck long enough after the demijohn reaches us to make it worth while worrying about this matter. Yet a nice attention to detail may prove that the cob has some secret affinity with cider, for a Missouri meerschaum never tastes so well as after three glasses of this rustic elixir.

That ingenious student of social niceties, John Mistletoe, in his famous *Dictionary of Deplorable Facts* — a book which we heartily commend to the curious, for he includes a long and most informing article on cider, tracing its etymology from the old Hebrew word *shaker* meaning "to quaff deeply" — maintains that cider should only be drunk beside an open fire of applewood logs: "And preferably on an evening of storm and wetness, when the swish and sudden pattering of rain against the panes lend an added agreeable snugness to the cheerful scene within, where master and dame sit by the rosy hearth frying sausages in a pan laid on the embers."

This reminds one of the anecdote related by ex-Senator Beveridge in his *Life of John Marshall*. Justice Story told his wife that the justices of the Supreme Court were of a self-denying habit, never taking wine except in wet weather. "But it does sometimes happen that the Chief Justice will say to me, when the cloth is removed, 'Brother Story, step to the window and see if it does not look like rain.' And if I tell him that the sun is shining brightly, Judge Marshall will sometimes reply, 'All the better, for our jurisdiction extends over so large a territory that the doctrine of chances makes it certain that it must be raining somewhere.'"

Our own theory about cider is that the time to drink it is when it reaches you; and if it hails from Chester County, so much the better.

We remember with gusto a little soliloquy on cider delivered by another friend of ours, as we both stood in a decent ordinary on Fulton Street, going through all the motions of jocularity and cheer. Cider (he said) is our refuge and strength. Cider, he insisted, drawing from his pocket a clipping much tarnished with age, is a drink for men of reason and genteel nurture; a drink for such as desire to drink pleasantly, amiably, healthily, and with perseverance and yet retain the command and superintendence of their faculties. I have here (he continued) a clipping sent me by an eminent architect in the great city of Philadelphia (a city which it is a pleasure for me to contemplate by reason of the beauty and virtue of its women, the infinite vivacity and good temper of its men, the rectitudinal disposition of its highways) — I have here (he exclaimed) a clipping sent me by an architect of fame, charming parts, and infinite cellarage, explaining the virtues of cider. Cider, this clipping asserts, produces a clearness of the complexion. It brightens the eye, particularly in women, conducing to the composition of generous compliment and all the social suavity that endears the intercourse of the sexes. Longevity, this extract maintains, is the result of application to good cider. The Reverend Martin Johnson, vicar of Dilwyn, in Herefordshire, from 1651 to 1698 (he read from his clipping), wrote:

This parish, wherin sider is plentifull, hath many people that do enjoy this blessing of long life; neither are the aged bed-ridden or decrepit as elsewhere; next to God, wee ascribe it to our flourishing orchards, first that the bloomed trees in spring do not only sweeten but purify the ambient air; next, that they yield us plenty of rich and winy liquors, which do conduce very much to the constant health of our inhabitants. Their ordinary course is to breakfast and sup with toast and sider through the whole Lent; which heightens their appetites and creates in them durable strength to labour.

There was a pause, and our friend (he is a man of girth and with a brow bearing all the candor of a life of intense thought) leaned against the mahogany counter.

That is very fine, we said, draining our chalice, and feeling brightness of eye, length of years, and durable strength to labour added to our person. In the meantime (we said) why do you not drink the rich and winy liquor which your vessel contains?

He folded up his clipping and put it away with a sigh.

I always have to read that first, he said, to make the damned stuff palatable. It will be ten years, he said, before the friend who sent me that clipping will have to drink any cider.

HAWTHORNE AT NORTH ADAMS [1]

BLISS PERRY

THE westward-bound passenger on the Fitchburg Railroad, emerging from the long roar of the Hoosac Tunnel, sees the smoke-blurred electric lamps quenched in sudden daylight, shuts his watch, and finds himself in North Adams. The commercial travelers leave the car, and a boy comes in with the Troy papers. A grimy station hides the close-built town, though upon the left one can see row above row of boarding-houses clinging to the face of a rocky foothill of Greylock, and further to the south a bit of meadow land not yet covered with railroad sidings. Then the train moves on, and in a moment plunges into another tunnel, and so out of the Tunnel City.

Thirty years ago, the traveler's first glimpse of North Adams was more picturesque. The big six-horse coaches, starting from Rice's, away over in the winding valley of the Deerfield, and climbing Hoosac Mountain, used to swing at full gallop along the two or three miles of table-land on the summit of the range, past the queer old houses of Florida, the highest township in Massachusetts, and pull up for a moment where the road turned sharply down the western slope. On the right were the last reluctant spurs of the Green Mountains; directly in front, over the broad Williamstown Valley, stretched the clear-cut Taconics; at the left rose the massive lines of Greylock. At one's feet, far below, were two or three church spires,

[1] From *The Amateur Spirit.* Copyright, 1904, by Houghton Mifflin Company. By permission of the publishers.

and the smoke of factories. Tiny houses were already perching here and there on the steep sides of the mill streams; for North Adams has no site whatever, and from the beginning has had to climb for its life. Completely enfolded by hills as the village seemed, one could yet catch a glimpse, as the driver gathered up his reins for the long descent, of a valley extending southward, between Ragged Mountain and the Hoosac Range, toward the towns of lower Berkshire.

It was up this valley, more than half a century ago, that the Pittsfield stage brought Hawthorne to North Adams. He was taking, in rather aimless fashion, one of those summer outings, which gave him more pleasure, he said, than other people had in the whole year beside. Nothing drew him to northern Berkshire, apparently, except the mere chance of travel; but he found the place congenial, and there are facts connected with his stay there that throw a clear light upon Hawthorne, at a period critical both for himself and his art. There are persons still living who well remember his sojourn in North Adams. His favorite companions were men prominent in the little community, and of such marked personal qualities that story and legend are busy with them to this hour; so that even if the graphic delineations of the *American Note-Books* were not at hand, one might still form a fairly accurate picture of the North Adams of 1838.

Halfway down the straggling main street, upon the site of the present Wilson House, was a noted inn, called either after its proprietor, Smith's Tavern, or according to its politics, the Whig Tavern, or else, and more pretentiously, the North Adams House. Those were the days of Martin Van Buren, and the Democratic, or Water-

man Tavern, was across the way, on the corner now occupied by the Richmond House. But Hawthorne though
on the very eve of becoming a Democratic office-holder,
weakly yielded to the attractions of the Whig Tavern,
being doubtless lured by the reputation of Orrin Smith
as a hotel-keeper. Up to the many-pillared piazza of
Smith's Tavern drove the stages from Greenfield and
Pittsfield, from Troy and Albany. The broad stoop was
the favorite loafing-place of the village characters. Here
sat mild-mannered Captain Carter, with butternut meats
and maple sugar for sale in little tin measures, which Hawthorne has described with curious precision; and which
descended, by the way, after the captain's death, to a
well-known vagrant in the adjoining village of Williamstown. Hither hobbled "Uncle John" Sheldon, the
Revolutionary pensioner. Here was to be found the one-
armed soap-maker, Daniel Haynes, nicknamed "Black
Hawk," who had once been a lawyer, and had been ruined
by drink, though there was still "a trace of the gentleman
and man of intellect" in him. And here, accompanied by
his Newfoundland dog, was the brandy-possessed "Doctor Bob" Robinson, a sort of fearless and savage Falstaff,
the fame of whose single combats and evil ways and
miraculous gifts of healing lingers even yet in the Tunnel
City.

Along the piazza, or within the hospitable bar-room,
sat village worthies of a higher grade: Otis Hodge the mill-
wright, Orrin Witherell the blacksmith, Squire Putnam
and Squire Drury and the rest, filling their broad-bot-
tomed chairs with the dignity acquired by years of habi-
tude. Jovial old fellows were these patrons of the Whig
Tavern — Rhode Island Baptists, most of them — hard-

handed and level-headed, with hearty laughs and strongly flavored stories, with coarse appetites for meat and drink, and "a tendency to obesity." Doubtless they scrutinized each new arrival, drew shrewd inferences as to his occupation and character, and decided whether he was worthy of their intimacy. We do not know their first impressions of the young man who stepped out of the Pittsfield stage on the 26th of July, but there is every evidence that he was strongly attracted to these broad-backed tavern-haunters, and was promptly initiated into their circle. Curiously enough, their new friend was the most delicately imaginative genius this country has yet produced; gifted with such elusive qualities, such swift, bright, fairy-like fancies, that his college mates had nicknamed him "Oberon"; so shy and solitary that for years he had scarcely gone upon the streets of his native town except at night; so modest that he concealed his identity as a story-writer under a dozen different signatures; with a personal reserve so absolute and insistent that no liberty was ever taken with him; beautiful in face and form, fresh-hearted and pure-souled. A strange associate, indeed, for Orrin Witherell and Otis Hodge, Orrin Smith and "Doctor Bob" Robinson! Ragged, one-armed "Black Hawk," soap-boiler and phrenologist, stopped in his "wild and ruined and desperate talk" to look at the new guest. "My study is man," he said. "I do not know your name, but there is something of the hawk-eye about you, too." And thus the two students of man entered into fellowship.

Hawthorne tarried at the North Adams House until the 11th of September. He bathed in the pools along Hudson's Brook, and climbed the hills at sunset. He chatted on the tavern stoop with "Uncle John" Sheldon and with Captain Carter, of whose name he was not quite certain, and which he enters in the journal as "I believe, Capt. Gavett." On rainy days he sat in the bar-room and consorted with Methodistical cattle drovers, stage agents, agents for religious and abolition newspapers, and an extraordinary variety of other people. He attended court, the menagerie, and the funeral of a child. Sometimes he took brief excursions in the neighborhood; as, for instance, to the Williams Commencement. Here he might have seen Mark Hopkins, presiding for the second time, flanked by dignitaries of the church and state; he might have listened to twenty-three orations, upon themes of which *The Influence of Deductive and Inductive Habits on the Character*, by William Bross, and *The Effect of Music on the Feelings*, by Henry M. Field, are perhaps fair examples — to say nothing of the polished periods of the Reverend Orville Dewey's address before the alumni. But, as a matter of fact, this conscienceless graduate of Bowdoin apparently spent most of his time behind the church, watching the peddlers and the negroes. The only evidence that he entered the big white meeting-house at all is his remark that there were well-dressed ladies there, "the sunburnt necks in contiguity with the delicate fabrics of the dresses showing the yeoman's daughters."

Some of the people with whom the usually taciturn Hawthorne conversed, in the course of his walks and drives, made a deep impression upon his imagination. Of an old man whose children were connected with a circus establishment, he noted, as Wordsworth might have done, "While this old man is wandering among the hills, his children are the gaze of multitudes." On the top of Hoosac Mountain he met, one day, a German Jew, traveling with a diorama. After Hawthorne had looked at it, a curious elderly dog made his appearance, which the romance-writer has described with such extreme fidelity as to give Mr. Henry James the impression of a "general vacancy in the field of Hawthorne's vision," although it will appear that Hawthorne knew what he was about. One moonlight night he ascended the mountain side, startling the lonely watcher by one of those huge lime-kilns that then, and for many years, abounded near North Adams; and, going up to the top of the kiln, the future author of *Ethan Brand* gazed down upon the red-hot marble, burning with its "bluish, lambent flame." Experiences like this were destined to reappear, more or less transformed, in his creative work; but often the incidents recorded in the journal are of the very simplest character, as, for instance, the fact that two little girls, bearing tin pails, who met him on the Notch road, "whispered one another and smiled."

North Adams is a strange place, after all, to find Oberon in — Oberon, the king of the fairies. We are not likely to understand the secret of Hawthorne's stay there unless we remember that the summer of 1838 was the most important epoch of his life.

What is first to be observed in the North Adams portion of the *American Note-Books* is the professional point of view. The writer is an artist in search of material. "Conceive something tragical to be talked about," he adds, after describing the old man whose children were in the circus, "and much might be made of this interview in a wild road among the hills." He notes elsewhere:

"A little boy named Joe, who haunts about the bar-room and the stoop, four years old, in a thin, short jacket, and full-breeched trousers, and bare feet. . . . Take this boy as the germ of a tavern-haunter, a country *roué*, to spend a wild and brutal youth, ten years of his prime in the state prison, and his old age in the poorhouse." Thus generously does the Hawthorne who himself haunts the Whig Tavern suggest to that other Hawthorne who invents stories that he might "take this boy." The suggestion was adopted, though Joe was not made to run through the melancholy course so vividly outlined for him; and readers of the *Note-Books*, who have wondered what ever became of the little fellow — whose real name was not Joe, but Edward — will doubtless be glad to learn that he grew up to be an eminently respectable citizen, and moved West! But the paragraph about Joe is a typical one.

Hawthorne was thirty-four years old that summer, and for a dozen years had devoted himself, in a solitary and more or less ineffective way, to the art of fiction. A gentleman who well remembers his sojourn at the North Adams House says that he used to walk along the street with his eyes down, and that he presented the tavern-keeper's niece with a book he had written. This book, published the year before, was *Twice-Told Tales*. In Hawthorne's well-known criticism upon these stories, written many years afterward, he accounted for their negative character — "the pale tint of flowers that blossomed in too retired a shade" — by his way of life while composing them. It had been a hermit life, a life of shadows, yet now and then of almost pathetic grasping after realities. The articles in *Twice-Told Tales* which pleased the author best were those elaborate exercises in description, valuable indeed as illustration of the accuracy of Hawthorne's self-training in detailed observation, but more valuable as evidences of his struggle to turn from his air-drawn fancies, and morbid though often extremely powerful imaginings, to the common sunshine, the trivial sweet realities of the actual world.

Now, the author of the North Adams journal is the Hawthorne of the *Toll-Gatherer's Day* and *Little Annie's Ramble*, rather than the Hawthorne of the *Prophetic Pictures* and *Fancy's Show Box*. He turns eagerly to the life about him; he notes its details with fascinated interest. Nothing comes amiss to him; the long valley of the Notch, as it sweeps up to the Bellowspipe, and a grunting drove of pigs passing the tavern at dusk, are alike entered in his note-book. Fifty years before the preface to *Pierre et Jean* was written, here was a young man in an obscure corner of Massachusetts practicing a "theory of observation" which would have satisfied De Maupassant himself. The extraordinary precision of Hawthorne's descriptions thus early in his career can be fully appreciated only by one who discovers how a mere line from the *Note-Books* will to-day serve, with the older citizens of North Adams, to identify the village characters sketched therein; or by one who will stand, with Hawthorne's words before him, by the side of Hudson's Brook, or on the desolate summit of Bald Mountain, or at that point on the Notch road where there is a view of Williamstown, "with high, mountainous swells heaving themselves up, like immense subsiding waves, far and wide around it."

There was a reason for this passion for the outer world. Solitude had done its utmost for Hawthorne, at least for the time being, and he had come to a parting of the ways.

A single sentence from a letter to an intimate friend in 1838 is like a cry from the man's inmost soul — "I want to have something to do with the material world." Wedged in between Otis Hodge and Orrin Witherell around the huge fire in the public room of the Whig Tavern, his elbows touching those stout-built, cheery-souled embodiments of pioneer virtues and vices, and casting himself into the life of the village in all its varied activities, Hawthorne found the "material world" with which he longed to come in touch. When he left North Adams, it was to enter almost at once upon the life of a weigher and gauger in the Boston Custom House, and to stand thenceforth in the ranks with his fellow-men.

But Hawthorne's new contact with actualities was something more than a mere quickening of interests, a broadening of his range, a closer focusing of his professional eye upon the object. He was a writer; he had the passion for observing, recording, recombining; he could not help it. It may well be that when such a man throws himself upon the actual, the result is simply a keener physical vision, a more perfect analysis, a more pitiless art. This fate was quite possible for Hawthorne. The fear of it haunted him, and never more so than in this very year when he made his escape from it. He wrote to Longfellow, "There is no fate in this world so horrible as to have no share in its joys and sorrows." To the mere observer as well as to the mere dreamer — and Hawthorne had been both by turns — may come that paralysis which lays hold of the very roots of life and art together; which begins in artistic detachment, and ends in the sterility of isolation. From the horror of that death in life, which has fallen in our day upon artists like Flaubert and his more brilliant nephew, Hawthorne was saved, as he believed, by the influence of the woman who afterward became his wife. In his own simple phrase, his heart was touched. "I used to think I could imagine all passions, all feelings and states of the heart and mind, but how little did I know! Indeed, we are but shadows; we are not endowed with real life; and all that seems most real about us is but the thinnest substance of a dream till the heart be touched. That touch creates us; then we begin to be; thereby we are beings of reality and inheritors of eternity."

Hawthorne had already felt that creative touch in the summer of 1838. It accounts — does it not? — for the new sense of reality so apparent in the journal. It was not simply his artistic interest, but his sympathy, that started into a quicker life. His extraordinarily sensitive mind brooded upon the risk he had run of becoming a cool observer, untaught that he had a heart; it became, in his own words, "a fearful thought" to him, and, being an artist to the finger-tips, he put his fearful thought into artistic form. In *Ethan Brand*, the story of the man who committed the Unpardonable Sin, Hawthorne embodied not only his North Adams character studies, but the very emotion that must have stirred his deepest heart during those weeks of sojourn at the Whig Tavern. He laid upon the shoulders of the lime-burner on the slope of Hoosac the awful burden whose weight he himself had almost felt.

Ethan Brand, a Chapter from an Abortive Romance, was first published in the *Dollar Magazine* under the title of *The Unpardonable Sin*, in 1851. The date of its composition is uncertain. Mr. Lathrop thinks that Hawthorne's removal to Berkshire in 1850 may have revived his interest in the old material provided by the *Note-Books;* Mr. Conway is inclined to believe that the story was written in 1848. Nor is it clear how literally the subtitle is to be taken. There are allusions in *Ethan Brand* to preceding episodes connected with the theme, of such dramatic possibilities that Hawthorne may well have sketched them in his fancy, but whether he ever seriously tried his hand upon anything more than the culminating chapter is doubtful. Two things, however, are certain: for the setting of the story, its author drew exclusively upon notes taken in North Adams; and the moral problem involved in it was Hawthorne's own problem, as a man and an artist, in the summer of 1838. Remembering how long he brooded over the *Septimius Felton* theme and the *Scarlet Letter* theme before writing a word, it will not seem improbable that the conception of *Ethan Brand* should date from the time of his first visit to Berkshire, even if the story remained unwritten for a dozen years; though, as a matter of fact, it is not at all unlikely that its composition is to be placed much earlier than the critics have surmised.

Ostensibly a fragment, and undoubtedly bearing internal evidence of some haste or dissatisfaction on the author's part, *Ethan Brand* remains one of the most powerful things that Hawthorne ever wrote. Rarely has he shown such dramatic instinct as when he marshaled his old North Adams acquaintances into the moonshine and narrow streaks of firelight that illuminated the open space before the lime-kiln on the sombre mountain side. They are all there: the stage agent, the crippled soap-boiler, the brandy-possessed doctor, the old man whose daughter had wandered away with the circus, the

German Jew with his diorama, and the curious old dog. It is little Joe who guides them into the presence of their former associate, Ethan Brand, who has committed "the one only crime for which Heaven can afford no mercy." Many notes from the journal are adopted without change. Sometimes there is a mere shifting of descriptive phrases that seem to suit Hawthorne's fancy; as when the "wild and ruined and desperate talk" attributed in the *Note-Books* to the cripple is here given to the doctor; or the sentence "Earth was so mingled with sky that it was a day-dream to look at it," originally written of Williamstown, is applied to the village of the tale. But there are more subtle adaptations of his material in two allusions to events not narrated in the story itself, however definitely Hawthorne may have outlined them in his imagination. The old man's missing daughter has become "the Esther of our tale," "whom with such cold and remorseless purpose Ethan Brand had made the subject of a psychological experiment." Reference is also made to "a professional visit of the village doctor to Ethan Brand, during the latter's supposed insanity." Hawthorne has perhaps wrought out the psychological experiment motive often enough elsewhere to indicate what would probably have been his method here; but the idea of bringing "Doctor Bob," with his huge animalism and mordant humor, "savage as a wild beast and miserable as a lost soul," to minister to the spiritual malady that preyed upon Ethan Brand, might easily have resulted in a scene unmatched in the whole range of Hawthorne's work.

If it is a pure bit of romanticism to transform the Jew of Hoosac Mountain to "the Jew of Nuremberg," the mask of the fiend himself, there is, on the other hand, in the description of the antics of the old dog an instance of the power of Hawthorne's realism. In the *Note-Books*, the trivial incident of the dog's chasing his own tail is minutely narrated, as a fact somehow worth recording. In *Ethan Brand*, the fact is nothing except as it illustrates a truth: the man who had chased the world over for something that was in his own breast, "moved by a perception of some remote analogy between his own case and that of the self-pursuing cur," broke into the awful laugh that sent the jovial party hurrying homewards through the darkening woods.

For Ethan Brand himself there is no model in the journal. None was needed. Hawthorne's own problem, in that critical year, was to keep "the counterpoise between his mind and heart." The doom he dreaded most of all was, to be "no longer a brother man, opening the chambers or the dungeons of our common nature by the key of holy sympathy, which gave him a right to share in all its secrets," but to be, like Ethan Brand, "a cold observer, looking on mankind as the subject of his experiment." The scene of the tale is the very hillside where Hawthorne wandered, brooding over the isolation that kills and the touch that makes alive. Its personages are the people that jostled against him in the tavern. But Hawthorne found Ethan Brand — or a potential Ethan Brand — in his own heart. He believed in an Unpardonable Sin; and it is by this faith in the reality of the moral life, after all is said, that he takes his rank as an artist. He chose moral problems, the truths of the human heart, and made them plastic; he created, not abstract types, but men and women, charging them with spiritual force;

and the result is that Ethan Brand, with his homely garments and heavy shoes, bending over the fiery lime-kiln on the slope of Hoosac, is a figure with all the moral passion, the tragic dignity, of Empedocles of old casting himself despairingly into the crater of Mount Etna.

It is more than fifty years since Hawthorne left the village at the foot of Greylock, never to return. Most of the companions of his sojourn there lie buried in the cone-shaped sand-hills of the crowded cemetery just beyond the Little Tunnel. The Whig Tavern changed hands shortly after his departure; and although Orrin Smith later kept another hostelry by the side of the old coaching road on the crest of Hoosac, that, too, has long since disappeared, and the site is overgrown with alders. But within ten minutes' walk of the Tunnel City may still be seen a gray lime-kiln upon which Hawthorne's eyes have rested, and the intense personal emotion of that long-past year is still vibrant in *Ethan Brand*. The romance-writers of our day have learned to stray far afield in their search for material, and they come back, too often, with such empty hands! The more's the pity, since a factory village, set in a narrow space among New England hills, was once field enough for a Hawthorne.

THE DIVINENESS OF DISCONTENT [1]

AGNES REPPLIER

WHEN a distinguished Oxford student told Americans, through the distinguished medium of Harvard College, that they were "speeding with invincible optimism down the road to destruction," they paid him the formal compliment of listening to, and commenting upon, his words. They did not go so far as to be disturbed by them, because it is the nature of men to remain unmoved by prophecies. Only the Greek chorus — or its leader — paid any heed to Cassandra; and the folly of Edgar Poe in accepting without demur the reiterated statement of his raven is apparent to all readers of a much-read poem. The world has been speeding through the centuries to destruction, and the end is still remote. Nevertheless, as it is assuredly not speeding to perfection, the word that chills our irrational content may do us some small service. It is never believed, and it is soon forgotten; but for a time it gives us food for thought.

Any one born as long ago as I was must remember that the virtue most deeply inculcated in our nurseries was content. It had no spiritual basis to lend it dignity and grace, but was of a Victorian smugness; though, indeed, it was not Victorian at all, but an inheritance from those late Georgian days which were the smuggest known to fame. It was a survival from Hannah More and Jane Taylor, ladies dissimilar in most respects, but with an

[1] From *Under Dispute*. Copyright, 1924. By permission of the publishers, Houghton Mifflin Company.

equal gift for restricting the horizon of youth. I don't remember who wrote the popular story of the "Discontented Cat" that lived in a cottage on bread and milk and mice, and that made itself unhappy because a wealthy cat of its acquaintance was given buttered crumpets for breakfast; but either Jane Taylor or her sister Ann was responsible for the "Discontented Pendulum," which grew tired of ticking in the dark, and, being reminded that it had a window to look through, retorted very sensibly that there was no use having a window, if it could not stop a second to look through it.

The nursery theory of content was built up on the presumption that you were the favoured child of fortune — or of God — while other, and no less worthy, children were objects of less kindly solicitude. Miss Taylor's "Little Ann" weeps because she sees richly clad ladies stepping into a coach while she has to walk; whereupon her mother points out to her a sick and ragged beggar child, whose

> naked feet bleed on the stones,

and with enviable hardness of heart bids her take comfort in the sight:

> This poor little beggar is hungry and cold,
>   No father nor mother has she;
> And while you can daily such objects behold,
>   You ought quite contented to be.

Hannah More amplified this theory of content to fit all classes and circumstances. She really did feel concern for her fellow creatures, for the rural poor upon whom it was not the custom of Church or State to waste sympathy or help. She refused to believe that British labourers were "predestined to be ignorant and wicked" — which was to her credit; but she did, apparently, believe that they were predestined to be wretchedly poor, and that they should be content with their poverty. She lived on the fat of the land, and left thirty thousand pounds when she died; but she held that bare existence was sufficient for a ploughman. She wrote twenty-four books, which were twenty-four too many; but she told the ever-admiring Wilberforce that she permitted "no writing for the poor." She aspired to guide the policies and the morals of England; but she was perturbed by the thought that under-paid artisans should seek to be "scholars and philosophers," though they must have stood in more need of philosophy than she did.

It was Ruskin who jolted his English readers, and some Americans, out of the selfish complacency which is degenerate content. It was he who harshly told England, then so prosperous and powerful, that prosperity and power are not virtues, that they do not indicate the sanction of the Almighty, or warrant their possessors in assuming the moral leadership of the world. It was he who assured the prim girlhood of my day that it was not the petted child of Providence, and that it had no business to be contented because it was better off than girlhood elsewhere. "Joy in nothing that separates you, as by any strange favour, from your fellow creatures, that exalts you through their degradation, exempts you from their toil, or indulges you in times of their distress."

This was a new voice falling upon the attentive ears of youth — a fresh challenge to its native and impetuous generosity. Perhaps the beggar's bare feet were not a legitimate incentive to enjoyment of our own neat shoes and stockings. Perhaps it was a sick world we lived in, and the beggar was a symptom of disease. Perhaps when Emerson (we read Emerson and Carlyle as well as Ruskin) defined discontent as an infirmity of the will, he was thinking of personal and petty discontent, as with one's breakfast or the weather; not of the discontent which we never dared to call divine, but which we dimly perceived to have in it some noble attribute of grace. That the bare existence of a moral law should so exalt a spirit that neither sin nor sorrow could subdue its gladness was a profundity which the immature mind could not be expected to grasp.

Time and circumstance lent themselves with extraordinary graciousness to Emerson's invincible optimism. It was easier to be a transcendental philosopher, and much easier to cherish a noble and a sweet content, before the laying of the Atlantic cable. Emerson was over sixty when this event took place, and, while he lived, the wires were used with commendable economy. The morning newspaper did not bring him a detailed account of the latest Turkish massacre. The morning mail did not bring him photographs of starving Russian children. His temperamental composure met with little to derange it. He abhorred slavery; but until Lincoln forced the issue, he seldom bent his mind to its consideration. He loved "potential America"; but he had a happy faculty of disregarding public affairs. Passionate partisanship, which is the basis of so much satisfaction and discontent, was alien to his soul. He loved mankind, but not men; and his avoidance of intimacies saved him much wear and tear. Mr. Brownell says that he did not care enough about his friends to discriminate between them, which was the reason he estimated Alcott so highly.

This immense power of withdrawal, this concentration upon the things of the spirit, made possible Emerson's intellectual life. He may have been, as Santayana says, "impervious to the evidence of evil"; yet there breaks from his heart an occasional sigh over the low ebb of the world's virtue, or an entirely human admission that the hopes of the morning are followed by the ennui of noon. Sustained by the supremacy of the moral law, and by a profound and majestic belief in the invincible justice, the "loaded dice" of God, he sums up in careful words his modest faith in man: "Hours of sanity and consideration are always arriving to communities as to individuals, when the truth is seen, and the martyrs are justified." Perhaps martyrs foresee the dawning of this day or ever they come to die; but to those who stand by and witness their martyrdom, the night seems dark and long.

There is a species of discontent which is more fervently optimistic than all the cheerfulness the world can boast. It is the discontent of the passionate and unpractical reformer, who believes, as Shelley believed, in the perfectibility of the human species, and who thinks, as Shelley thought, that there is a remedy for every disease of civilization. To the poet's dreaming eyes the cure was simple and sure. Destruction implied for him an automatic reconstruction, a miraculous survival and rebirth. Uncrown the king, and some noble prophet or philosopher will guide — not rule — the people. Unfrock the priest, and the erstwhile congregation will perfect itself in the practice of virtue. Take the arms from the soldier and the policeman, the cap and gown from the college president, authority from the judge, and control from the father. The nations will then be peaceful, the mobs orderly, the students studious, the criminals virtuous, the children well-behaved. An indifferent acquaintance with sociology, and a comprehensive ignorance of biology, made possible these pleasing illusions. Nor did it occur to Shelley that many men, his equals in disinterestedness and his superiors in self-restraint, would have found his reconstructed world an eminently undesirable dwelling-place.

Two counsels to content stand bravely out from the mass of contradictory admonitions with which the world's teachers have bewildered us. Saint Paul, writing to the Philippians, says simply: "I have learned, in whatsoever state I am, therewith to be content"; and Marcus Aurelius, contemplating the mighty spectacle of life and death, bids us pass serenely through our little space of time, and end our journey in content. It is the meeting-point of objective and subjective consciousness. The Apostle was having a hard time of it. The things he disciplined himself to accept with content were tangible things, of an admittedly disagreeable character — hunger and thirst, stripes and imprisonment. They were not happening to somebody else; they were happening to *him*. The Emperor, seeking refuge from action in thought, steeled himself against the nobleness of pity no less than against the weakness of complaint. John Stuart Mill, who did not suffer from enervating softness of heart, pronounced the wholesale killing of Christians in the reign of Marcus Aurelius to be one of the world's great tragedies. It was the outcome, not only of imperial policy, but of sincere conviction. Therefore historians have agreed to pass it lightly by. How can a man do better than follow the dictates of his own conscience, or of his own judgment, or of whatever directs the mighty ones of earth who make laws instead of obeying them? But the immensity of pain, the long-drawn agony involved in this protracted persecution might have disturbed even a Stoic philosopher passing serenely — though not harmlessly — through his little space of time.

This brings me to the consideration of one prolific source of discontent, the habit we have acquired — and cannot let go — of distressing ourselves over the daily progress of events. The classic world, "innocent of any essential defeat," was a pitiless world, too clear-eyed for illusions, too intelligent for sedatives. The Greeks built the structure of their lives upon an almost perfect understanding of all that it offered and denied. The Romans, running an empire and ruling a world, had much less time for thinking; yet Horace, observant and acquiescent, undeceived and undisturbed, is the friend of all the ages. It is not from him, or from any classic author, that we learn to talk about the fret and fever of living. He would have held such a phrase to be eminently ill-bred, and unworthy of man's estate.

The Middle Ages, immersed in heaving seas of trouble, and lifted Heavenward by great spiritual emotions, had scant breathing-space for the cultivation of nerves. Men endured life and enjoyed it. Their endurance and their enjoyment were unimpaired by the violence of their fellow men, or by the vision of an angry God. Cruelty, which we cannot bear to read about, and a Hell, which we will not bear to think about, failed signally to curb the zest with which they lived their days. "How high the tide of human delight rose in the Middle Ages," says Mr. Chesterton significantly, "we know only by the colossal walls they built to keep it within bounds." There is no reason to suppose that Dante, whose fervid faith compassed the redemption of mankind, disliked his dream of Hell, or that it irked him to consign to it so many eminent and agreeable people.

The Renaissance gave itself unreservedly to all the pleasures that could be extracted from the business of living, though there was no lack of troubles to damp its zeal. It is interesting and instructive to read the history of a great Italian lady, typical of her day, Isabella d'Este, Marchioness of Mantua. She was learned, adroit, able, estimable, and mistress of herself though duchies fell. She danced serenely at the ball given by the French King at Milan, after he had ousted her brother-in-law, the Duke Ludovico, and sent him to die a prisoner at Loches. When Cæsar Borgia snatched Urbino, she improved the occasion by promptly begging from him two beautiful statues which she had always coveted, and which had been the most treasured possessions of Duke Guidobaldo, her relative, and the husband of her dearest friend. A chilly heart had Isabella when others came to grief, but a stout one when disaster faced her way. If the men and women who lived through those highly coloured, harshly governed days had fretted too persistently over the misfortunes of others, or had spent their time questioning the moral intelligibility of life, the Renaissance would have failed of its fruition, and the world would be a less engaging place for us to live in now.

There is a discontent which is profoundly stimulating, and there is a discontent which is more wearisome than complacency. Both spring from a consciousness that the time is out of joint, and both have a modern back-

ground of nerves. *The Education of Henry Adams* and
the *Diaries* of Wilfrid Scawen Blunt are cases in point.
Blunt's quarrel was with his country, his world, his fellow
creatures and his God — a broad field of dissatisfaction,
which was yet too narrow to embrace himself. Nowhere
does he give any token of even a moderate self-distrust.
Britain is an "engine of evil," because his party is out
of power. "Americans" (in 1900) "are spending fifty
millions a year in slaughtering the Filipinos" — a crude
estimate of work and cost. "The Press is the most complete engine ever invented for the concealment of historic
truth." "Patriotism is the virtue of nations in decay."
"The whole white race is revelling openly in violence, as
though it had never pretended to be Christian. God's
equal curse be on them all."

"The whole white race," be it observed. For a time
Blunt dreamed fond dreams of yellow and brown and
black supremacy. Europe's civilization he esteemed a
failure. Christianity had not come up to his expecta-
tions. There remained the civilization of the East, and
Mohammedanism — an amended Mohammedanism, innocent of sensuality and averse to bloodshed. Filled
with this happy hope, the Englishman set off from Cairo
to seek religion in the desert.

Siwah gave him a rude reception. Ragged tribes,
ardent but unregenerate followers of the Prophet, pulled
down his tents, pillaged his luggage, robbed his servants,
and knocked him rudely about. Blunt's rage at this
treatment was like the rage of *Punch's* vegetarian who is
chased by a bull. "There is no hope to be found in
Islam, and I shall go no further," is his conclusion. "The
less religion in the world, perhaps the better."

Humanity and its creeds being thus disposed of, there remained only the animals to contemplate with satisfaction. "Three quarters of man's misery," says the diary, "comes from pretending to be what he is not, a separate creation, superior to that of the beasts and birds, when in reality they are wiser than we are, and infinitely happier."

This is the kind of thing Walt Whitman used now and then to say, though neither he nor Sir Wilfrid knew any more about the happiness of beasts and birds than do the rest of us. But that brave old hopeful, Whitman, would have laughed his loudest over Blunt's final analysis of the situation: "All the world would be a paradise in twenty years if man could be shut out." A paradise already imaged by Lord Holland and the poet Gray:

> Owls would have hooted in Saint Peter's choir,
> And foxes stunk and littered in Saint Paul's.

To turn from these pages of pettish and puerile complaint to the deep-seated discontent of Henry Adams is to reënter the world of the intellect. Mark Pattison confessed that he could not take a train without thinking how much better the time-table might have been planned. It was an unhappy twist of mind; but the Rector of Lincoln utilized his obtrusive critical faculties by applying them to his own labours, and scourging himself to greater effort. So did Henry Adams, though even the greater effort left him profoundly dissatisfied. He was unelated by success, and he could not reconcile himself to that degree of failure which is the common portion of mankind. His criticisms are lucid, balanced, enlightening, and occasionally prophetic, as when he comments on the Irishman's political passion for obstructing even himself, and on the perilous race-inertia of Russia. "Could inertia on such a scale be broken up, or take new scale?" he asks dismayed; and we read the answer to-day. A minority ruling with iron hand; a majority accepting what comes to them, as they accept day and night and the seasons.

If there is not an understatement in the five hundred pages of the *Education*, which thereby loses the power of persuasion, there is everywhere an appeal to man's austere equity and disciplined reason. Adams was not in love with reason. He said that the mind resorted to it for want of training, and he admitted that he had never met a perfectly trained mind. But it was the very essence of reason which made him see that friends were good to him, and the world not unkind; that the loveliness of the country about Washington gave him pleasure, even when he found "a personal grief in every tree"; and that a self-respecting man refrains from finding wordy fault with the conditions under which he lives. He did not believe, with Wordsworth, that nature is a holy and beneficent thing, or with Blake, that nature is a wicked and malevolent thing; but he knew better than to put up a quarrel with an invincible antagonist. He erred in supposing that other thoughtful men were as discontented as he was, or that disgust with the methods of Congress corroded their hours of leisure; but he expressed clearly and with moderation his unwillingness to cherish "complete and archaic deceits," or to live in a world of illusions. His summing up is the summing up of another austere and uncompromising thinker, Santayana, when confronted by the same problem: "A spirit with any honour is not willing to live except in its own way; a spirit with any wisdom is not over-eager to live at all."

As our eagerness and our reluctance are not controlling factors in the situation, it is unwise to stress them too heavily. Yet we must think, at least some of us must; and it is well to think out as clearly as we can, not the relative advantages of content and discontent — a question which briskly answers itself — but the relative rightness. Emerson believed in the essential goodness of life, in the admirable law of compensation. Santayana believes that life has evil for its condition, and is for that reason profoundly sad and equivocal. He sees in the sensuous enjoyment of the Greek, the industrial optimism of the American, only a "thin disguise for despair." Yet Emerson and Santayana reach the same general conclusion. The first says that hours of sanity and consideration come to communities as to individuals, "when the truth is seen, and the martyrs are justified"; the second that "people in all ages sometimes achieve what they have set their hearts on," and that, if our will and conduct were better disciplined, "contentment would be more frequent and more massive."

It is hard to think of these years of grace as a chosen period of sanity and consideration; and the hearts of the Turk and the Muscovite are set on things which do not make for the massive contentment of the world. The orderly processes of civilization have been so wrenched and shattered that readjustment is blocked at some point in every land, in our own no less than in others. There are those who say that the World War went beyond the bounds of human endurance; and that the peculiar horror engendered by indecent methods of attack — poison-gases, high explosives and corrosive fluids — has dimmed the faith and broken the spirit of men. But Attila managed to turn a fair proportion of the civilized world into wasteland, with only man-power as a destructive force. Europe to-day is by comparison unscathed, and there are kinsfolk dwelling upon peaceful continents to whom she may legitimately call for aid.

Legitimately, unless our content is like the content extolled by Little Ann's mother; unless our shoes and stockings are indicative of God's meaningless partiality, and unless the contemplation of our neighbour's bleeding feet enhances our pious satisfaction. "I doubt," says Mr. Wells sourly, "if it would make any very serious difference for some time in the ordinary daily life of Kansas City, if all Europe were reduced to a desert in the next five years." Why Kansas City should have been chosen as the symbol of unconcern, I do not know; but space has a deadening influence on pity as on fear. The farther we travel from the Atlantic coast, the more tepid is the sympathy for injured France. The farther we travel from the Pacific coast, the fainter is the prejudice against Japan.

It may be possible to construct a state in which men will be content with their own lot, if they be reasonable, and with their neighbour's lot, if they be generous. It is manifestly impossible to construct a world on this principle. Therefore there will always be a latent grief in the nobler part of man's soul. Therefore there will always be a content as impious as the discontent from which Pope prayed to be absolved.

The unbroken cheerfulness, no less than the personal neatness, of the British prisoners in the World War astounded the more temperamental Germans. Long, long ago it was said of England: "Even our condemned persons doe goe cheerfullie to their deths, for our nature is free, stout, hautie, prodigal of life and blood." This heroic strain, tempered to an endurance which is free from the waste of emotionalism, produces the outward semblance and the inward self-respect of a content which circumstances render impossible. It keeps the soul of man immune from whatever degradation his body may be suffering. It saves the land that bred him from the stigma of defeat. It is remotely and humanly akin to the tranquillity of the great Apostle in a Roman prison. It is wholly alien to the sin of smugness which has crept in among the domestic virtues, and rendered them more distasteful than ever to austere thinkers, and to those lonely, generous souls who starve in the midst of plenty.

There is a curious and suggestive paragraph in Mr. Chesterton's volume of loose ends, entitled *What I Saw in America*. It arrests our attention because, for once, the writer seems to be groping for a thought instead of juggling with one. He recognizes a keen and charming quality in American women, and is disturbed because he also recognizes a recoil from it in his own spirit. This is manifestly perplexing. "To complain of people for being brave and bright and kind and intelligent may not unreasonably appear unreasonable. And yet there is something in the background that can be expressed only by a symbol; something that is not shallowness, but a neglect of the subconscious, and the vaguer and slower impulses; something that can be missed amid all that laughter and light, under those starry candelabra of the ideals of the happy virtues. Sometimes it came over me in a wordless wave that I should like to see a sulky woman. How she would walk in beauty like the night, and reveal more silent spaces full of older stars! These things cannot be conveyed in their delicate proportion, even in the most large and elusive terms."

Baudelaire has conveyed them measurably in four words:

"Sois belle! Sois triste!"

Yet neither "sulky" nor "triste" is an adjective suggesting with perfect felicity the undercurrent of discontent which lends worth to courage and charm to intelligence. Back of all our lives is the sombre setting of a world ill at ease, and beset by perils. Darkening all our days is the gathering cloud of ill-will, the ugly hatred of man for man, which is the perpetual threat to progress. We Americans may not be so invincibly optimistic as our critics think us, and we may not yet be "speeding" down the road to destruction, as our critics painfully foretell; but we are part of an endangered civilization, and cannot hold up our end, unsupported by Europe. An American woman, cautiously investing her money in government bonds, said to her man of business: "These at least are perfectly secure?" "I should not say that," was the guarded reply; "but they will be the last things to go."

A few years ago there was a period that saw the workingmen and workingwomen of the United States engaged in three hundred and sixty-five strikes — one for every day of the year — and all of them on at once. Something seems lacking in the equity of our industrial life. The *Current History* of the *New York Times* is responsible for the statement that eighty-five thousand men and women met their deaths by violence in the United States during the past decade. Something seems lacking in our programme of peace.

Can it be that Mr. Wells is right when he says that the American believes in peace, but feels under no passionate urgency to organize it? Does our notable indifference to the history of the past mean that we are unconcerned about the history of the present? Two things are sure. We cannot be nobly content with our own prosperity, unless its service to the world is made manifest; grace before meat is not enough to bless the food we eat. And we cannot be nobly content with our unbroken strength, with the sublimity of size and numbers, unless there is something correspondingly sublime in our leadership of the wounded nations. Our allies, who saved us and whom we saved, face the immediate menace of poverty and assault. They face it with a slowly gathered courage which we honour to-day, and may be compelled to emulate to-morrow. "The fact that fear is rational," says Mr. Brownell, "is what makes fortitude divine."

RETROSPECT[1]

A. E.
[GEORGE W. RUSSELL]

I HAD travelled all day and was tired, but I could not
rest by the hearth in the cottage on the hill. My heart
was beating with too great an excitement. After my year
in the city I felt like a child who wickedly stays from
home through a long day, and who returns frightened
and penitent at nightfall, wondering whether it will be received with forgiveness by its mother. Would the Mother
of us all receive me again as one of her children? Would
the winds with wandering voices be as before the evan-
gelists of her love? Or would I feel like an outcast amid
the mountains, the dark valleys and the shining lakes?
I knew if benediction came how it would come. I would
sit among the rocks with shut eyes, waiting humbly as
one waits in the antechambers of the mighty, and if the
invisible ones chose me as companion they would begin
with a soft breathing of their intimacies, creeping on me
with shadowy affection like children who steal nigh to
the bowed head and suddenly whisper fondness in the
ear before it has even heard a footfall. So I stole out
of the cottage and over the dark ridges to the place of
rocks, and sat down, and let the coolness of the night chill
and still the fiery dust in the brain. I waited trembling
for the faintest touch, the shyest breathing of the Ever-

[1] From *The Candle of Vision* (1918). Reprinted by authorization of
The Macmillan Company.

lasting within my soul, the sign of reception and forgiveness. I knew it would come. I could not so desire what was not my own, and what is our own we cannot lose. Desire is hidden identity. The darkness drew me heavenward. From the hill the plains beneath slipped away grown vast and vague, remote and still. I seemed alone with immensity, and there came at last that melting of the divine darkness into the life within me for which I prayed. Yes, I still belonged, however humbly, to the heavenly household. I was not outcast. Still, though by a thread fine as that by which a spider hangs from the rafters, my being was suspended from the habitations of eternity. I longed to throw my arms about the hills, to meet with kisses the lips of the seraph wind. I felt the gaiety of childhood springing up through weariness and age, for to come into contact with that which is eternally young is to have that childhood of the spirit it must attain ere it can be moulded by the Magician of the Beautiful and enter the House of Many Mansions.

I had not always this intimacy with Nature. I never felt a light in childhood which faded in manhood into the common light of day, nor do I believe that childhood is any nearer than age to this being. If it were so what would the spirit have to hope for after youth was gone? I was not conscious in my boyhood of any heaven lying about me. I lived in the city, and the hills from which aid was to come to me were only a far flush of blue on the horizon. Yet I was drawn to them, and as years passed and legs grew longer I came nearer and nearer until at last one day I found myself on the green hillside. I came to play with other boys, but years were yet to pass before the familiar places grew strange once more and the mountains dense with fiery forms and awful as Sinai.

While the child is still in its mother's arms it is nourished by her, yet it does not know it is a mother which feeds it. It knows later in whose bosom it has lain. As the mother nourishes the body so the Mighty Mother nourishes the soul. Yet there are but few who pay reverence where reverence is due, and that is because this benign deity is like a mother who indulges the fancies of her children. With some she imparts life to their own thoughts. Others she endows with the vision of her own heart. Even of these last some love in silence, being afraid to speak of the majesty which smiled on them, and others deceived think with pride: "This vision is my own."

I was like these last for a long time. I was aged about sixteen or seventeen years, when I, the slackest and least ideal of boys, with my life already made dark by those desires of body and heart with which we so soon learn to taint our youth, became aware of a mysterious life quickening within my life. Looking back I know not of anything in friendship, anything I had read, to call this forth. It was, I thought, self-begotten. I began to be astonished with myself, for, walking along country roads, intense and passionate imaginations of another world, of an interior nature began to overpower me. They were like strangers who suddenly enter a house, who brush aside the doorkeeper, and who will not be denied. Soon I knew they were the rightful owners and heirs of the house of the body, and the doorkeeper was only one who was for a time in charge, who had neglected his duty, and who had pretended to ownership. The boy who existed before was an alien. He hid himself when the pilgrim of eternity took up his abode in the dwelling. Yet, whenever the true owner was absent, the sly creature reappeared and boasted himself as master once more.

That being from a distant country who took possession of the house began to speak in a language difficult to translate. I was tormented by limitations of understanding. Somewhere about me I knew there were comrades who were speaking to me, but I could not know what they said. As I walked in the evening down the lanes scented by the honeysuckle my senses were expectant of some unveiling about to take place, I felt that beings were looking in upon me out of the true home of man. They seemed to be saying to each other of us, "Soon they will awaken; soon they will come to us again," and for a moment I almost seemed to mix with their eternity. The tinted air glowed before me with intelligible significance like a face, a voice. The visible world became like a tapestry blown and stirred by winds behind it. If it would but raise for an instant I knew I would be in Paradise. Every form on that tapestry appeared to be the work of gods. Every flower was a word, a thought. The grass was speech; the trees were speech; the waters were speech; the winds were speech. They were the Army of the Voice marching on to conquest and dominion over the spirit; and I listened with my whole being, and then these apparitions would fade away and I would be the mean and miserable boy once more. So might one have felt who had been servant of the prophet, and had seen him go up in the fiery chariot, and the world had no more light or certitude in it with that passing. I knew these visitations for what they were and named them truly in my fantasy, for writing then in the first verses of mine which still seem to me to be poetry, I said of the earth that we and all things were her dreams:

> She is rapt in dreams divine.
> As her clouds of beauty pass
> On our glowing hearts they shine,
> Mirrored there as in a glass.
>
> Earth, whose dreams are we and they,
> With her deep heart's gladness fills
> All our human lips can say
> Or the dawn-fired singer trills.

Yet such is human nature that I still felt vanity as if this vision was mine, and I acted like one who comes across the treasure-house of a king, and spends the treasure as if it were his own. We may indeed have a personal wisdom, but spiritual vision is not to speak of as ours any more than we can say at the rising of the sun: "This glory is mine." By the sudden uprising of such vanities in the midst of vision I was often outcast, and found myself in an instant like those warriors of Irish legend, who had come upon a lordly house and feasted there and slept, and when they woke they were on the barren hillside, and the Faed Fia was drawn about that lordly house. Yet though the imagination apprehended truly that this beauty was not mine, and hailed it by its heavenly name, for some years my heart was proud, for as the beauty sank into memory it seemed to become a personal possession, and I said "I imagined this" when I should humbly have said, "The curtain was a little lifted that I might see." But the day was to come when I could not deny the Mighty Mother the reverence due, when I was indeed to know by what being I had been nourished, and to be made sweet and mad as a lover with the consciousness of her intermingling spirit.

The sages of old found that at the close of intense meditation their being was drawn into union with that which they contemplated. All desire tends to bring about unity with the object adored, and this is no less true of spiritual and elemental than of bodily desire; and I, with my imagination more and more drawn to adore an ideal nature, was tending to that vital contact in which what at first was apprehended in fantasy would become the most real of all things. When that certitude came I felt as Dante might have felt after conceiving of Beatrice close at his side and in the Happy World, if, after believing it a dream, half hoping that it might hereafter be a reality, that beloved face before his imagination grew suddenly intense, vivid and splendidly shining, and he knew beyond all doubt that her spirit was truly in that form, and had descended to dwell in it, and would be with him for evermore. So did I feel one warm summer day lying idly on the hillside, not then thinking of anything but the sunlight, and how sweet it was to drowse there, when, suddenly, I felt a fiery heart throb, and knew it was personal and intimate, and started with every sense dilated and intent, and turned inwards, and I heard first a music as of bells going away, away into that wondrous underland whither, as legend relates, the Danaan gods withdrew; and then the heart of the hills was opened to me, and I knew there was no hill for those who were there, and they were unconscious of the ponderous mountain piled above the palaces of light, and the winds were sparkling and diamond clear, yet full of colour as an opal, as they glittered through the valley, and I knew

the Golden Age was all about me, and it was we who had
been blind to it but that it had never passed away from
the world.

MR. WILLIAM MORRIS[1]

GEORGE SAINTSBURY

I THINK it probable that no long poem has for many years — indeed, since the disuse of buying such poems by tens of thousands in the days of our grandfathers — sold so well as *The Earthly Paradise;* and I believe that, though none of Mr. Morris's subsequent works has equalled this in popularity, they have none of them lacked a fair vogue. Yet it has always seemed to me that not merely the general, but even the critical public ranks him far below his proper station as a poet.

The way in which I made my own first acquaintance with him was very odd; and I have never been able fully to explain it. As a boy of certainly not more than fourteen I used, like other boys, to take in periodicals addressed *pueris* if not *virginibus*, and in one of these, the title of which I cannot remember, I can very distinctly mind me of seeing an editorial notice of a poem which had been sent in, dealing with a "tall white maid" and other things and persons. This poem was, as I afterwards found out, and as all Morrisians will recognize, *The Sailing of the Sword*, which must just have appeared, or have been just about to appear, in Mr. Morris's first volume, *The Defence of Guinevere*. This volume came out in 1858 — an *annus mirabilis*, in which some of the best wine of the century was made on the Douro, and in the Gironde, and on the Côte d'Or, and which seems to

[1] From *Corrected Impressions* (1895). Used by permission of William Heinemann, Limited, and of Dodd, Mead and Company, Inc.

have exercised a very remarkable influence on the books and persons born in it. The persons of 1858 had a singular knack of being clever or charming, or both; and the books (as biographers and bibliographers have before noticed) were unusually epoch-making.

Of these I do not myself rank *The Defence of Guinevere* least high. *The Sailing of the Sword* — the manner of the insertion of which in my *Boys' Magazine*, or whatever it was called, remains an insoluble mystery to me — is, no doubt, not one of the best. But I remember when some years afterwards I bought the little brown book — nightingale-colour — from Slatter and Rose's counter at Oxford for a price which would not buy it now, that I took it back to my rooms and read it straight through with an ecstasy of relish not surpassed by anything I have ever known of the kind. Persons of sober and classical tastes fought very shy of *Guinevere* at her first appearance; and even some of those who loved her then have fallen off now. Why should a man speak about a "choosing-cloth"? What were these strange scraps of mediæval French? Who could make sense of *The Blue Closet* or *Two Red Roses across the Moon*? Indeed, this latter very harmless and spirited ditty — of which I once offered to write a symbolic defence in any required number of pages, and which I still love wildly — had the faculty of simply infuriating the grave and precise. Oxford and Cambridge have not in my time produced better scholars, who are also humorists, or humorists who are also scholars, than the present Sir Frederick Pollock and the present Bishop of Colombo, and I believe it to be no improper revealing of secrets to say that they both at least used to abominate it. Perhaps (I hope so) they do not now. As for the incident, when the orange fell "And in came marching the ghosts of those who were slain at the war," I should like to bring up the men from the south gate and have a fleet horse ready at that postern, before setting it even now before some very respectable persons. And then it would have been more dangerous still.

For my part I loved the book at once with a love full-grown and ardent; nor do I think that that love has decreased an inch in stature or a degree in heat since. Of course there are very obvious faults and foibles. The archaic mannerism may be here and there overdone, even in the eyes of those who are well enough inclined thereto; the attention to pictorial and to musical effect may sometimes seem paid at the expense of sense. The title-poem is in parts obscure and wordy; *Sir Peter Harpdon's End,* another most important piece, would gain a great deal by cutting down; the expression sometimes lacks crispness and finish; the verse is sometimes facile and lax. But all this is redeemed and more than redeemed by the presence of the real, the true, the indefinable and unmistakable spirit of poetry. And this spirit wears, as it does at all its more remarkable appearances in the world, a distinct and novel dress. Although the so-called Romantic movement had been going on more or less for a hundred years — had been going on vigorously and decidedly for sixty or seventy — when Mr. Morris wrote, only one or two snatches of Coleridge and Keats had caught the peculiar mediæval tone which the Præ-Raphaelites in poetry, following the Præ-Raphaelites in art, were now about to sound. Even *La Belle Dame Sans Merci,* that wonderful divination in which Keats hit upon the true and very mediæval, as elsewhere upon the true and very classical spirit, is an exception, a casual inspiration rather than a full reflection. And let it be remembered that when Mr. Morris began to write, the brother poets (who afterwards a little eclipsed him, perhaps, both with the public and the critics) had published nothing (though Mr. Rossetti's sugared sonnets might be handed about among his private friends), and that the painter who is more than any one Mr. Morris's yoke-fellow, Sir Edward Burne-Jones, was hardly out of leading-strings.

The Defence of Guinevere, indeed, was not Mr. Morris's first, not even his first published, work. He contributed largely to that very remarkable and now very inaccessible miscellany, *The Oxford and Cambridge Magazine*, his chief work being, I believe, a delightful romance called *The Hollow Land*, which I read, all unknowing its authorship, at the age of sixteen, and liked, but not to loving. *The Hollow Land* was, as I remember it, after more than thirty years, a little, a very little, incoherent and apocalyptic — with painters who painted God's judgments in purple and crimson, and a heroine of the appropriate name of Swanhilda. I decline to recognize any real incoherency in *The Defence of Guinevere*. The whole book is, of course, saturated with the spirit of the Arthurian legends, of which I believe Mr. Morris was even then a great student, both in French and in English. Nor do I think that any one who does not know the originals, and has not gone through a considerable study of mediæval romance, can fully estimate the marvellous manner in which he has not merely galvanized or copied, but revivified and recreated the tone and sense of them. For — the warning has often been given, but it wants repetition still — it is quite a mistake to think that either Scott

earlier, or Lord Tennyson later, effected this revivifica-
tion, magnificent as the work of both is. Scott was an
ardent lover of the Middle Ages; but he was, after all, a
man born well within the eighteenth century. Tennyson
had read his Malory faithfully; but he was not born much
within the nineteenth. It took the work of these very
men to create the atmosphere — to get ready the stage —
in which and on which Mr. Morris and Sir Edward Burne-
Jones could appear.

That stage, that atmosphere, must always, I suppose,
find a public either enthusiastic in welcome or vehement in
refusal. It is not easy to be merely indifferent to the
works of these artists, though it is possible merely to gape
at them in uncomprehending wonder. "Pastiche" will
cry the one side; "unmeaning and overdone archaism;
sentimental maundering; indifference to the grains and the
aims of modernism; art too literary; literature too pictorial; illiberal and pusillanimous relapse on a mainly
imaginary past; deficiency in realism; reliance on trick
and *cliché*." I may be excused from setting in array
against these terms of excessive and uncritical deprecia-
tion a counter list of equally excessive appreciation and
praise. But I think myself that the school in question —
especially the poet and the painter just coupled — have
discovered, or rather rediscovered, the way to one of the
Paradises of Art, of which I shall not say much more in
this place than that to my judgment it seems a true and
genuine Paradise, and, to my taste, one delicious and re-
freshing to an extent not excelled by any other. To me
personally, no other division of literature or of art has the
qualities of a "Vale of Rest" as mediæval literature and
mediæval art have; while the renaissance of both, at the

hands of Mr. Morris and his friends, seems to me a true renaissance, not by any means a copy, possessing the qualities of its originals in a slightly altered and perhaps even more effective form.

It has a fashion of delight, standing in the most marked and interesting contrast with those fashions which may be noticed in other poets of the period. Like the Tennysonian charm, it is dreamlike; but the character of the dreams is distinct. There is more action, more story, in them; and at the same time there is a double and treble dose of the vague and the mystical in colour, form, and sound. In Tennyson there is still a sort of remnant of eighteenth-century *netteté*, of classical clearness of outline. It is only with Mr. Morris and his friends or followers that we get into the true Romantic vague. When Mr. Lang selected Mr. Morris as the chief English example of poetry which oversteps the border line between mere sound and sense, he did justly. But it is also necessary to take count in Mr. Morris of that extraordinarily decorative spirit which always makes him accompany his music with limning. He is the very embodiment of mediæval poetry as we meet it in the well known opening of the *Romance of the Rose* and a thousand other places, — a noise of musical instruments accompanying an endless procession of allegorical or purely descriptive imagery. Between William of Lorris and William Morris there are six hundred years of time, a single letter in spelling, and in spirit only a greater genius, the possession of a happier instrument of language, and a larger repertory of subject and style in the later singer.

There are certain of one's literary as of one's other

loves the progress of which is not wholly satisfactory to a person of sensibility. There may be no actual "writing out"; no positive and undeniable deterioration; but "the second temple is not like the first," later pressures do not repeat the effect of the first sprightly runnings. I at least have never felt this with Mr. William Morris. I never met him in the flesh, or exchanged letters with him, or heard very much about him personally; and *si quid id est*, I think his politics very nearly childish, and much more than very nearly mischievous. But I know no man of letters of my time who has been so thoroughly satisfactory all through to the critical lover of letters. To the critical lover, I say advisedly. And yet it must be not quite the ordinary sort of critic who shall do Mr. Morris full justice. For his faults are exactly of those which the critic who looks only at the stop-watch will least pardon; and his merits are perhaps of those which the critic who looks only at the stop-watch will least appreciate.

In the last division of this paper I have given some remarks on his work as it appeared up to and including *The Defence of Guinevere*. His next stroke was a stroke of genius, and it was, also, as strokes of genius are not always, a stroke of good luck. The hubbub about Mr. Swinburne's *Poems and Ballads* had made general and popular what had before been only partial and esoteric, — an interest in the new schools of Præ-Raphaelite art and letters which had already fixed in various ways strong holds on the Universities, especially Oxford. But "*The Life and Death of Jason*, a Poem by William Morris, London, Bell and Daldy, 1867," which lies beside me with its red buckram weathered to orange on the back, but otherwise much as I bought it at its earliest appearance, hit the bird on both wings. It gave a perfect Romantic treatment. It chose a perfect classical subject. It was not possible, as it has been since, for any one to accuse the artist of too much archaic mannerism in the mediæval and Scandinavian manner; it was not possible, on the other side, for any one not to recognize that here was an almost entirely new fashion of telling a story in verse. It was new, but it was not ancestorless; few things are. It had in its genealogy not merely Keats, but Wither and Browne. But the result, as happens sometimes in well-bred steeds, was a far more spirited and individual product than any of its forbears. Mr. Morris did to the heroic couplet what Milton and Wordsworth did to blank verse. He broke it up, changed its centres of gravity, subjected it to endless varieties of *enjambement* or overlapping. It was his main care to end a paragraph, to begin a speech, in the middle of a couplet or a line. Yet he never was harsh, and he was seldom — he was sometimes — over-fluent. The thing took by storm that portion of the public which has scholarship as well as taste. And it deserved to take it. I do not think myself that there is any one passage quite so exquisite in it as the *Nymph's Song to Hylas*, which Mr. Morris (either desirous not to let it be whelmed in a long narrative, or trying experiments on the public memory) republished twenty years after in *Songs by the Way*. But it is all more or less exquisite, and it was then all more or less novel.

It was soon to be to a certain extent antiquated by a more splendid production from the same hand. I really do not know that anything combining bulk and excellence to the same extent as *The Earthly Paradise* had appeared since Dryden's *Fables*, and the *Fables* are but small in bulk compared to the *Paradise*.

A Paradise it certainly is. It had been heralded on the fly-leaves of *Jason*, and again in its own earlier volumes, not quite in the form which it finally assumed. I have been told that all the defaulting tales exist, and I would I had them. For nothing is wrong in this enormous work. If it is sometimes voluble, it is never prosaic; the setting-pieces, intercalated prefaces, and epilogues for the several months, are as they should be, of the very best; the proem is noble; and the general contents are sublime. It is hard to seek among the two dozen for the best where all are good. For mere personal liking I should choose, I think, *The Man Born to be King* (which is worth comparing with the simplicity of the old French story), *The Doom of King Acrisius*, with the gorgeous sweep of its rendering of the Perseus legend, *The Watching of the Falcon* (a great sermon on a great text), *The Land East of the Sun and West of the Moon* (an ideal Romantic tale), its immediate forerunner, *The Death of Paris* (which will bear comparison with the early and late work of Tennyson himself), and lastly *The Ring Given to Venus* and *The Hill of Venus*, the first of which pair contains, in the procession of the dead Gods from sea to land, perhaps the very finest thing that Mr. Morris has ever done. If only Sir Edward Burne-Jones would take it for a subject!

I suppose there is no douce and reasonable Morrisian who will deny that *The Earthly Paradise* marks the apogee of its writer's talent. But it is really surprising to find how flat the trajectory of his genius is, how little he has declined from this its culmination. I have myself heard *Love is Enough* criticised in the statement that "Love isn't enough"; but this is a clear *ignoratio elenchi*. The translations, prose and verse, have perhaps attracted more unfavorable criticism than any other part of the work; and although I am not competent to decide whether Mr. Morris's sagas are or are not unfaithful to their original, I can most frankly admit that Mr. Morris's *Æneid* is not exactly Virgil, and Mr. Morris's *Odyssey* still less exactly Homer. But it really seems unnecessary to fight over again the endless battle of Translation *v.* Original. The translation is never the original, and Mr. Morris's substitutes are a great deal better than most. But *Sigurd*, at a time of life when the poetic tide often runs low in a man, showed that Mr. Morris was as good at practically original work as ever. Indeed, I hardly know another instance of a poet well advanced in years, if not old, who attempted a new and very dangerous metre with such extraordinary success. Once get the secret of this cunning mixture of anapaests and trochees, and the varying and voluble melody of it will simply amaze you.

The last collection of poems proper, *Songs by the Way*, contains chiefly gleanings of older years; and with many delightful things (especially the incomparable *Meeting in Winter*) includes a good deal of Mr. Morris's very Colonel-Newcome-like politics. But a few years ago the indefatigable poet entered on a new course. It must be admitted that the most ingeniously perverse undergraduate could not have selected anything more likely to "disgust the examiners" than the types, etc., of *The House of the Wolfings*. Whenever — which is often — I have a mind to read over the *Wood Sun's* perfectly exquisite forecast of Thiodulf's fate — the best piece of English poetry published for these ten years past except

Crossing the Bar — I have to lay my account with a pair of smarting eyes for the rest of the evening. But in this, and in *The Roots of the Mountains*, and most of all in *The Glittering Plain*, we have what before Mr. Morris even Kingsley never quite achieved, true sagas, not in the least mosaics or *pastiches* from the sagas proper, but "sets" or "cuttings" from them, instinct with genuine life, and reproducing with due variation the character of the parent stock.

In other words, we have in Mr. Morris what we have not had since Chaucer, and what no other nation has had since a time older than Chaucer's, a real *trouvère* of the first class — a person of inexhaustible fertility and power in weaving the verse and the prose of romance, and with a purely lyrical gift which even Chaucer did not often show. It is the quality of poetry — much more than the particular forms or the agreeable volume in which it manifests itself — that has always attracted me, and attracts me now as much as ever to this very remarkable writer. The quality of poetry is apt to be, if not strained, drowned when it comes to be written by the ten, the fifty, the hundred thousand verses. I have made no laboured calculation; but I really think that Mr. Morris cannot be very far off, if he has not actually reached or passed, the hundred thousand limit. He cannot be said to be quite free from the faults of such prolixity, the loose fluent phrase, the easy amble of movement, the watered and undistinguished description. And yet you shall never read many pages, seldom many lines of his, without finding side by side with these negligences the unmistakable marks which a poet, and only a poet, impresses on his work. From *The Defence of Guinevere* to the snatches in his latest prose works he has these marks, in phrase, in music, in suggestion. And still, charming as are many of the detached pieces to be culled from him, the atmosphere and the tenor of the whole seem to me to be more poetical than any of the parts. All over it is that "making the common as though it were not common" which is the best if not the only existing definition of this indefinable quality.

So, when I see in the work of certain writers whom it is unnecessary to name, and whom I do not allude to otherwise than for the sake of honour, the falling back on strained expression, on flashes of poetical epigram and conundrum, on scrambles after the grand style and fumblings after the marmoreal, I turn with relief once more to the lambent easy light, the misty lunar atmosphere shot with faint auroral colours, the low and magical music, the ever-varying panorama of poetical description and passion and thought that I have known so long, and loved so much, in the writings of the author of *The Earthly Paradise*.

SOLILOQUIES IN ENGLAND [1]

GEORGE SANTAYANA

THE BRITISH CHARACTER

WHAT is it that governs the Englishman? Certainly not intelligence; seldom passion; hardly self-interest, since what we call self-interest is nothing but some dull passion served by a brisk intelligence. The Englishman's heart is perhaps capricious or silent; it is seldom designing or mean. There are nations where people are always innocently explaining how they have been lying and cheating in small matters, to get out of some predicament, or secure some advantage; that seems to them a part of the art of living. Such is not the Englishman's way: it is easier for him to face or to break opposition than to circumvent it. If we tried to say that what governs him is convention, we should have to ask ourselves how it comes about that England is the paradise of individuality, eccentricity, heresy, anomalies, hobbies, and humours. Nowhere do we come oftener upon those two social abortions — the affected and the disaffected. Where else would a man inform you, with a sort of proud challenge, that he lived on nuts, or was in correspondence through a medium with Sir Joshua Reynolds, or had been disgustingly housed when last in prison? Where else would a young woman, in dress and manners the close copy of a man, tell you that her parents were odious, and that she desired a husband but no children, or children without a husband? It

[1] From *Soliloquies in England* (1922). By permission of Constable and Company, Limited, London, and of Charles Scribner's Sons, New York.

is true that these novelties soon become the conventions of some narrower circle, or may even have been adopted *en bloc* in emotional desperation, as when people are converted; and the oddest sects demand the strictest self-surrender. Nevertheless, when people are dissident and supercilious by temperament, they manage to wear their uniforms with a difference, turning them by some lordly adaptation into a part of their own person.

Let me come to the point boldly; what governs the Englishman is his inner atmosphere, the weather in his soul. It is nothing particularly spiritual or mysterious. When he has taken his exercise and is drinking his tea or his beer and lighting his pipe; when, in his garden or by his fire, he sprawls in an aggressively comfortable chair; when, well-washed and well-brushed, he resolutely turns in church to the east and recites the Creed (with genuflexions, if he likes genuflexions) without in the least implying that he believes one word of it; when he hears or sings the most crudely sentimental and thinnest of popular songs, unmoved but not disgusted; when he makes up his mind who is his best friend or his favorite poet; when he adopts a party or a sweetheart; when he is hunting or shooting or boating, or striding through the fields; when he is choosing his clothes or his profession — never is it a precise reason, or purpose, or outer fact that determines him; it is always the atmosphere of his inner man.

To say that this atmosphere was simply a sense of physical well-being, of coursing blood and a prosperous digestion, would be far too gross; for while psychic weather is all that, it is also a witness to some settled disposition, some ripening inclination for this or that, deeply rooted in the soul. It gives a sense of direction in life which is virtually a code of ethics, and a religion behind religion. On the other hand, to say it was the vision of any ideal or allegiance to any principle would be making it far too articulate and abstract. The inner atmosphere, when compelled to condense into words, may precipitate some curt maxim or over-simple theory as a sort of war-cry; but its puerile language does it injustice, because it broods at a much deeper level than language or even thought. It is a mass of dumb instincts and allegiances, the love of a certain quality of life, to be maintained manfully. It is pregnant with many a stubborn assertion and rejection. It fights under its trivial fluttering opinions like a smoking battleship under its flags and signals; you must consider, not what they are, but why they have been hoisted and will not be lowered. One is tempted at times to turn away in despair from the most delightful acquaintance — the picture of manliness, grace, simplicity, and honour, apparently rich in knowledge and humour — because of some enormous platitude he reverts to, some hopelessly stupid little dogma from which one knows that nothing can ever liberate him. The reformer must give him up; but why should one wish to reform a person so much better than oneself? He is like a thoroughbred horse, satisfying to the trained eye, docile to the light touch, and coursing in most wonderful unison with you through the open world. What do you care what words he uses? Are you impatient with the lark because he sings rather than talks? and if he could talk, would you be irritated by his curious opinions? Of course, if any one positively asserts what is contrary to fact, there is an error, though the error may be harmless; and most divergencies between men should interest us rather than offend us, because they are effects of perspective, or of legitimate diversity in experience and interests. Trust the man who hesitates in his speech and is quick and steady in action, but beware of long arguments and long beards. Jupiter decided the most intricate questions with a nod, and a very few words and no gestures suffice for the Englishman to make his inner mind felt most unequivocably when occasion requires.

Instinctively the Englishman is no missionary, no conqueror. He prefers the country to the town, and home to foreign parts. He is rather glad and relieved if only natives will remain natives and strangers strangers, and at a comfortable distance from himself. Yet outwardly he is most hospitable and accepts almost anybody for the time being; he travels and conquers without a settled design, because he has the instinct of exploration. His adventures are all external; they change him so little that he is not afraid of them. He carries his English weather in his heart wherever he goes, and it becomes a cool spot in the desert, and a steady and sane oracle amongst all the deliriums of mankind. Never since the heroic days of Greece has the world had such a sweet, just, boyish master. It will be a black day for the human race when scientific blackguards, conspirators, churls, and fanatics manage to supplant him.

PRIVACY

The secret of English mastery is self-mastery. The Englishman establishes a sort of satisfaction and equilibrium in his inner man, and from that citadel of rightness he easily measures the value of everything that comes within his moral horizon. In what may lie beyond he takes but a feeble interest. Enterprising enough when in a roving mood, and fond of collecting outlandish objects and ideas, he seldom allows his wanderings and discoveries to unhinge his home loyalties or ruffle his self-possession; and he remains, after all his adventures, intellectually as indolent and secure as in the beginning. As to speculative truth, he instinctively halts short of it, as it looms in the distance and threatens to cast a contemptuous and chilling shadow across his life. He would be very severe to a boy who dreaded cold water and wouldn't learn to swim; yet in the moral world he is himself subject to illusions of timidity. He does not believe, there, in the overwhelming rewards of courage. His chosen life is indeed beautiful — as the shy boy's might be — in its finitude; all the more beautiful and worth preserving because, like his country, it is an island in the sea. His domestic thermometer and barometer have sufficed to guide him to the right hygiene.

Hygiene does not require telescopes nor microscopes. It is not concerned, like medicine or psychology, with the profound hidden workings of our bodies or minds, complexities hardly less foreign to our discoursing selves than are the mysteries of the great outer world. Hygiene regards only the right regimen of man in his obvious environment, judged by his conscious well-being. If it goes afield at all, it does so in the interests of privacy. All it asks of life is that it should be comely, spontaneous, and unimpeded: all it asks of the earth is that it should be fit for sport and for habitation. Men, to be of the right hygienic sort, must love the earth, and must know how to range in it. This the Englishman knows; and just as, in spite of his insularity, he loves this whole terraqueous globe simply and genuinely, so the earth, turned into mud by the vain stampings of so many garrulous and sickly nations, would doubtless say: Let the Englishman inhabit me, and I shall be green again.

In matters of hygiene the Englishman's maxims are definite and his practice refined. He has discovered what he calls good form, and is obstinately conservative about it, not from inertia, but in the interests of pure vitality. Experience has taught him the uses to which vitality can be put, so as to preserve and refresh it. He knows the right degree of exertion normally required to do things well — to walk or to talk, for instance; he does not saunter nor scramble, he does not gesticulate nor scream. In consequence, perhaps, on extraordinary occasions he fails at first to exert himself enough; and his eloquence is not torrential nor inspired, even at those rare moments when it ought to be so. But when nothing presses, he shows abundant energy, without flurry or excess. In manners and morals, too, he has found the right mean between anarchy and servitude, and the wholesome measure of comfort. What those who dislike him call his hypocrisy is but timeliness in his instincts, and a certain modesty on their part in not intruding upon one another. Your prayers are not necessarily insincere because you pray only in church; you are not concealing a passion if for a time you forget it and slough it off. These alternations are phases of the inner man, not masks put on in turn by some insidious and calculating knave. All the Englishman's attitudes and habits — his out-of-door life, his clubs, his conventicles, his business — when they are spontaneous and truly British, are for the sake of his inner man in its privacy. Other people, unless the game calls for them, are in the way, and uninteresting. His spirit is like Wordsworth's skylark, true to the kindred points of heaven and home; and perhaps these points seem to him kindred only because they are both functions of himself. Home is the centre of his physical and moral comfort, his headquarters in the war of life, where lie his spiritual stores. Heaven is a realm of friendly inspiring breezes and setting suns, enveloping his rambles and his perplexities. The world to him is a theatre for the soliloquy of action. There is a comfortable luxuriousness in all his attitudes. He thinks the prize of life worth winning, but not worth snatching. If you snatch it, as Germans, Jews, and Americans seem inclined to do, you abdicate the sovereignty of your inner man, you miss delight, dignity, and peace; and in that case the prize of life has escaped you.

As the Englishman disdains to peer and is slow to speculate, so he resents any meddling or intrusion into his own preserves. How sedulously he plants out his garden, however tiny, from his neighbours and from the public road! If his windows look unmistakably on the street, at least he fills his window-boxes with the semblance of a hedge or a garden, and scarcely allows the dubious light to filter through his blinds and lace curtains; and the space between them, in the most dingy tenement, is blocked by an artificial plant. He is quite willing not to be able to look out, if only he can prevent other people from looking in. If they did, what would they see? Nothing shocking, surely; his attitude by his fireside is perfectly seemly. He is not throwing anything at the family; very likely they are not at home. Nor has he introduced any low-class person by the tradesman's entrance, in whose company he might blush to be spied. He is not in deshabille; if he has changed any part of his street clothes it has not been from any inclination to be slovenly in private, but on the contrary to vindicate his self-respect and domestic decorum. He does not dress to be seen of men, but of God. His elegance is an expression of comfort, and his comfort a consciousness of elegance. The eyes of men disquiet him, eminently presentable though he be, and he thinks it rude of them to stare, even in simple admiration. It takes tact and patience in strangers — perhaps at first an ostentatious indifference — to reassure him and persuade him that he would be safe in liking them. His frigid exterior is often a cuticle to protect his natural tenderness, which he forces himself not to express, lest it should seem misplaced or clumsy. There is a masculine sort of tenderness which is not fondness, but craving and premonition of things untried; and the young Englishman is full of it. His heart is quiet and full; he has not pumped it dry, like ill-bred children, in tantrums and effusive fancies. On the other hand, passions are atrophied if their expression is long suppressed, and we soon have nothing to say if we never say anything. As he grows old the Englishman may come to suspect, not without reason, that he might not reward too close a perusal. His social bristles will then protect his intellectual weakness, and he will puff himself out to disguise his vacuity.

It is intelligible that a man of deep but inarticulate character should feel more at ease in the fields and woods, at sea or in remote enterprises, than in the press of men. In the world he is obliged to maintain stiffly principles which he would prefer should be taken for granted.

Therefore when he sits in silence behind his window curtains, with his newspaper, his wife, or his dog, his monumental passivity is not a real indolence. He is busily reinforcing his character, ruffled by the day's contact with hostile or indifferent things, and he is gathering new strength for the fray. After the concessions imposed upon him by necessity or courtesy, he is recovering his natural tone. To-morrow he will issue forth fresh and confident, and exactly the same as he was yesterday. His character is like his climate, gentle and passing readily from dull to glorious, and back again; variable on the surface, yet perpetually self-restored and invincibly the same.

DISTINCTION IN ENGLISHMEN

England has been rich in poets, in novelists, in inventors, in philosophers making new beginnings, in intrepid travellers, in learned men whose researches are a hobby and almost a secret. The land was once rich in saints, and is still rich in enthusiasts. But the official leaders of the English people, the kings, prelates, professors, and politicians, have usually been secondary men; and even they have been far more distinguished in their private capacity than in their official action and mind. English genius is anti-professional; its affinities are with amateurs, and there is something of the amateur in the best English artists, actors, and generals. Delicacy of conscience, mental haze, care not to outrun the impulse of the soul, hold the Englishman back midway in his achievements; there is in him a vague respect for the unknown, a tacit diffidence in his own powers, which dissuade him from venturing on the greatest things or from carrying them

344

out in a comprehensive manner. The truth is the British do not wish to be well led. They are all individualistic and aristocratic at heart, and want no leaders in ultimate things; the inner man must be his own guide. If they had to live under the shadow of a splendid monarch, or a masterful statesman, or an authoritative religion, or a deified state they would not feel free. They wish to peck at their institutions, and tolerate only such institutions as they can peck at. A certain ineptitude thus comes to be amongst them an aptitude for office: it keeps the official from acquiring too great an ascendancy. There is a sort of ostracism by anticipation, to prevent men who are too good from coming forward and upsetting the balance of British liberties; very like the vacuum which is created in America around distinction, and which keeps the national character there so true to type, so much on one lively level. But in England distinction exists, because it escapes into privacy. It is reserved for his Grace in his library and her Ladyship at her tea-table; it fills the nursery with lisping sweetness and intrepid singleness of will; it dwells with the poets in their solitary rambles and midnight questionings; it bends with the scholar over immortal texts; it is shut off from the profane by the high barriers of school and college and hunting-field, by the sanctity and silence of clubs, by the unspoken secrets of church and home.

The greatest distinction of English people, however, is one which, whilst quite personal and private in its scope, is widely diffused and strikingly characteristic of the better part of the nation; I mean, distinction in the way of living. The Englishman does in a distinguished way the simple things that other men might slur over as unimportant or essentially gross or irremediable; he is distinguished — he is disciplined, skilful, and calm — in eating, in sport, in public gatherings, in hardship, in danger, in extremities. It is in physical and rudimentary behaviour that the Englishman is an artist; he is the ideal sailor, the ideal explorer, the ideal comrade in a tight place; he knows how to be clean without fussiness, well-dressed without show, and pleasure-loving without loudness. This is why, although he is the most disliked of men the world over (except where people need some one they can trust) he is also the most imitated. What ferocious Anglophobe, whether a white man or a black man, is not immensely flattered if you pretend to have mistaken him for an Englishman? After all, this imitation of the physical distinction of Englishmen is not absurd; here is something that *can* be imitated: it is really the easiest way of doing easy things, which only bad education and bad habits have made difficult for most people. There is nothing impossible in adopting afternoon tea, football, and boy scouts; what is impossible, and if possible very foolish, is to adopt English religion, philosophy, or political institutions. But why should any one wish to adopt them? They have their merits, of course, and their propriety at home; but they are blind compromises, and it is not in their principles that the English are distinguished, but only in their practice. Their accents are more choice than their words, and their words more choice than their ideas. This, which might sound like a gibe, is to my mind a ground for great hope and for some envy. Refinement, like charity, should begin at home. First the body ought to be made fit and decent, then speech and manners, and habits justly combining personal initiative with the power of co-operating with others; and then, as this healthy life extends, the world will begin to open out to the mind in the right perspectives: not at first, perhaps never, in its total truth and its real proportions, but with an ever-enlarging appreciation of what, for us, it can contain. The mind of the Englishman, starting in this proud and humble and profound way from the inner man, pierces very often, in single directions, to the limit of human faculty; and it seems to me to add to his humanity, without injury to his speculation, that he instinctively withdraws again into himself, as he might return home to marry and settle after tempting fortune at the antipodes. His curious knowledge and his personal opinions then become, as it were, mementoes of his distant adventures; but his sterling worth lies in himself. He is at his best when free impulse or familiar habit takes an unquestioned lead, and when the mind, not being expected to intervene, beats in easy unison with the scene and the occasion, like a rider at home in the saddle and one with his galloping horse. Then grace returns to him, so angular often in his forced acts and his express tenets; the smile comes unaffectedly, and the blithe quick words flow as they should; arm is linked spontaneously in arm, laughter points the bull's-eye of truth, the whole world and its mysteries, not being pressed, become amiable, and the soul shines happy, and beautiful, and absolute mistress in her comely house. Nothing in him then is gross; all is harmonized, all is touched with natural life. His simplicity becomes wholeness, and he no longer seems dull in any direction, but in all things sound, sensitive, tender, watchful, and brave.

THE BARBARIC NATURALISM OF THEODORE DREISER[1]

STUART P. SHERMAN

THE layman who listens reverently to the reviewers discussing the new novels and to the novelists discussing themselves can hardly escape persuasion that a great change has rather recently taken place in the spirit of the age, in the literature which reflects it, and in the criticism which judges it. The nature of the supposed revolution may be briefly summarized.

The elder generation was in love with illusions, and looked at truth through a glass darkly and timorously. The artist, tongue-tied by authority and trammeled by æsthetic and moral conventions, selected, suppressed, and rearranged the data of experience and observation. The critic, "morally subsidized," regularly professed his disdain for a work of art in which no light glimmered above "the good and the beautiful."

The present age is fearless and is freeing itself from illusions. Now, for the first time in history, men are facing unabashed the facts of life. "Death or life," we cry, "give us only reality!" Now, for the first time in the history of English literature, fiction is become a flawless mirror held up to the living world. Rejecting nothing, altering nothing, it presents to us — let us take our terms from the bright lexicon of the reviewer — a "transcript," a "cross-section," a "slice," a "photographic" or "cine-

[1] From *On Contemporary Literature* (1917), by Stuart P. Sherman. By permission of the publisher, Henry Holt and Company.

matographic" reproduction of life. The critic who keeps pace with the movement no longer asks whether the artist has created beauty or glorified goodness, but merely whether he has told the truth.

Mr. Dreiser, in his latest novel, *The Genius*, describes a canvas by a painter of this austere modern school: "Raw reds, raw greens, dirty gray paving stones — such faces! Why, this thing fairly shouted its facts. It seemed to say: 'I'm dirty, I am commonplace, I am grim, I am shabby, but I am life.' And there was no apologizing for anything in it, no glossing anything over. Bang! Smash! Crack! came the facts one after another, with a bitter, brutal insistence on their so-ness." If you do not like what is in the picture, you are to be crushed by the retort that perhaps you do not like what is in life. Perhaps you have not courage to confront reality. Perhaps you had better read the chromatic fairy-tales with the children. Men of sterner stuff exclaim, "Thank God for a realist!"

Mr. Dreiser is a novelist of the new school, for whom we have been invited off and on these fourteen years to "thank God" — a form of speech, by the way, which crept into the language before the dawn of "modern" realism. He has performed with words what his hero performed with paint. He has presented the facts of life "one after another with a bitter, brutal insistence on their so-ness," which marks him as a "man of the hour," a "portent" — the successor of Mr. Howells and Mr. James? In the case of a realist, biographical details are always relevant. Mr. Dreiser was born of German-American parents in Terre Haute, Indiana, in 1871. He was educated in the Indiana public schools and at the

State University. He was engaged in newspaper work in Chicago, St. Louis, New York, and elsewhere, from 1892 to 1910. He has published two books of travel: *A Traveller At Forty*, 1913, and a *Hoosier Holiday*, 1916, which, without the support of his fiction, would entitle him to dispute with Mr. Viereck for the title of vulgarest voice yet heard in American literature; also a collection of one-act dramas, *Plays of the Natural and Supernatural*, 1916. But he has laid reality bare for us most generously in his five novels, published as follows: *Sister Carrie*, 1901; *Jennie Gerhardt*, 1911; *The Financier*, 1912; *The Titan*, 1914; and *The Genius*, 1915. These five works constitute a singularly homogeneous mass of fiction. I do not find any moral value in them, nor any memorable beauty — of their truth I shall speak later; but I am greatly impressed by them as serious representatives of a new note in American literature, coming from that "ethnic" element of our mixed population which, we are assured by competent authorities, is to redeem us from Puritanism and insure our artistic salvation. They abundantly illustrate, furthermore, the methods and intentions of our recent courageous veracious realism. Before we thank God for it let us consider a little more closely what is offered us.

The first step toward the definition of Mr. Dreiser's special contribution is to blow away the dust with which the exponents of the new realism seek to becloud the perceptions of our "reverent layman." In their main pretensions there are large elements of conscious and unconscious sham.

It should clear the air to say that courage in facing and veracity in reporting the facts of life are no more characteristic of Theodore Dreiser than of John Bunyan. These moral traits are not the peculiar marks of the new school; they are the marks common to every great movement of literature within the memory of man. Each literary generation detaching itself from its predecessor — whether it has called its own movement Classical or Romantic or what not — has revolted in the interest of what it took to be a more adequate representation of reality. No one who is not drunken with the egotism of the hour, no one who has penetrated with sober senses into the spirit of any historical period anterior to his own, will fall into the indecency of declaring his own age pre-eminent in the desire to see and to tell the truth. The real distinction between one generation and another is in the thing which each takes for its master truth — is in the thing which each recognizes as the *essential* reality for it. The difference between Bunyan and Dreiser is in the order of facts which each reports.

It seems necessary also to declare at periodic intervals that there is no such thing as a "cross-section" or "slice" or "photograph" of life in art — least of all in the realistic novel. The use of these catch-words is but a clever hypnotizing pass of the artist, employed to win the assent of the reader to the reality of the show, and, in some cases, to evade moral responsibility for any questionable features of the exhibition. A realistic novel no more than any other kind of a novel can escape being a composition, involving preconception, imagination, and divination. Yet, hearing one of our new realists expound his doctrine, one might suppose that writing a novel was a process analogous to photographing wild animals in their habitat by trap and flashlight. He, if you will believe him, does

351

not invite his subjects, nor group them, nor compose their features, nor furnish their setting. He but exposes the sensitized plate of his mind. The pomp of life goes by, and springs the trap. The picture, of course, does not teach nor preach nor moralize. It simply re-presents. The only serious objection to this figurative explanation of the artistic process is the utter dissimilarity between the blank impartial photographic plate, commemorating everything that confronts it, and the crowded, inveterately selective mind, which, like a magnet, snatches the facts of life that are subject to its influence out of their casual order and redisposes them in a pattern of its own.

In the case of any specified novelist, the facts chosen and the pattern assumed by them are determined by his central theory or "philosophy of life"; and this is precisely criticism's justification for inquiring into the adequacy of any novelist's general ideas. In vain, the new realist throws up his hands with protestations of innocence, and cries: "Search me. I carry no concealed weapons. I run life into no preconceived mold. I have no philosophy. My business is only to observe, like a man of science, and to record what I have seen." He cannot observe without a theory, nor compose and record his observations without betraying his theory to any critical eye.

As it happens, the man of science who most profoundly influenced the development of the new realistic novel, Charles Darwin, more candid than the writers of "scientific" fiction, frankly declared that he could not observe without a theory. When he had tentatively formulated a general law, and had begun definitely to look for evidence of its operation, then first the substantiating facts leaped abundantly into his vision. His *Origin of Species* has the unity of a work of art, because the recorded observations support a thesis. The French novelists who in the last century developed the novel of contemporary life learned as much, perhaps, from Darwin's art as from his science. The technique of fiction imitated the procedure of scientific research. Balzac had emphasized the relation between man and his social milieu; the Goncourts emphasized the importance of extensive "human documents"; Zola emphasized the value of scientific hypotheses. He deliberately adopted the materialistic philosophy of the period as his guide in observation and as his unifying principle in composition. His theory of the causes of social phenomena, which was derived largely from medical and physiological treatises, operated like a powerful magnet among the chaotic facts of life, rejecting some, selecting others, and redisposing them in the pattern of the *roman naturaliste*. Judicious French critics said: "My dear man," or words to that effect, "your representations of life are inadequate. This which you are offering us with so earnest an air is not reality. It is your own private nightmare." When they had exposed his theory, they had condemned his art.

Let us, then, dismiss Mr. Dreiser's pretensions to superior courage and veracity, the photographic transcript, and unbiassed service of truth; and let us seek for his definition in his general theory of life, in the order of facts which he records, and in the pattern of his representations.

The impressive unity of effect produced by Mr. Dreiser's five novels is due to the fact that they are all illustrations of a crude and naïvely simple naturalistic philosophy, such as we find in the mouths of exponents of the new *Real-Politik*. Each book, with its bewildering mass of detail, is a ferocious argument in behalf of a few brutal generalizations. To the eye cleared of illusions it appears that the ordered life which we call civilization does not exist except on paper. In reality our so-called society is a jungle in which the struggle for existence continues, and must continue, on terms substantially unaltered by legal, moral, or social conventions. The central truth about man is that he is an animal amenable to no law but the law of his own temperament, doing as he desires, subject only to the limitations of his power. The male of the species is characterized by cupidity, pugnacity, and a simian inclination for the other sex. The female is a soft, vain, pleasure-seeking creature, devoted to personal adornment, and quite helplessly susceptible to the flattery of the male. In the struggles which arise in the jungle through the conflicting appetites of its denizens, the victory goes to the animal most physically fit and mentally ruthless, unless the weaklings, resisting absorption, combine against him and crush him by sheer force of numbers.

The idea that civilization is a sham, Mr. Dreiser sometimes sets forth explicitly, and sometimes he conveys it by the process known among journalists as "coloring the news." When Sister Carrie yields to the seductive drummer, Drouet, Mr. Dreiser judicially weighs the advantages and disadvantages attendant on the condition of being a well-kept mistress. When the institution of marriage is brushed aside by the heroine of *The Financier*, he comments "editorially" as follows: "Before Christianity was man, and after it will also be. A metaphysi-

cal idealism will always tell him that it is better to preserve a cleanly balance, and the storms of circumstance
will teach him a noble stoicism. Beyond this there is
nothing which can reasonably be imposed upon the conscience of man." A little later in the same book he says:
"Is there no law outside of the subtle will and power to
achieve? If not, it is surely high time that we knew it —
one and all. We might then agree to do as we do; but
there would be no silly illusion as to divine regulation."
His own answer to the question, his own valuation of
regulation, both divine and human, may be found in the
innumerable contemptuous epithets which fall from his
pen whenever he has occasion to mention any power set
up against the urge of instinct and the indefinite expansion of desire. Righteousness is always "legal"; conventions are always "current"; routine is always "dull";
respectability is always "unctuous"; an institution for
transforming schoolgirls into young ladies is presided
over by "owl-like conventionalists"; families in which
the parents are faithful to each other lead an "apple-pie
order of existence"; a man who yields to his impulses yet
condemns himself for yielding is a "rag-bag moralistic
ass." Jennie Gerhardt, by a facile surrender of her
chastity, shows that *she could not be readily corrupted
by the world's selfish lessons* on how to preserve oneself
from the evil to come." Surely this is "coloring the
news."

By similar devices Mr. Dreiser drives home the great
truth that man is essentially an animal, impelled by temperament, instinct, physics, chemistry — anything you
please that is irrational and uncontrollable. Sometimes
he writes an "editorial" paragraph in which the laws of

human life are explained by reference to the behavior of certain protozoa or by reference to a squid and a lobster fighting in an aquarium. His heroes and heroines have "cat-like eyes," "feline grace," "sinuous strides," eyes and jaws which vary "from those of the tiger, lynx, and bear to those of the fox, the tolerant mastiff, and the surly bulldog." One hero and his mistress are said to "have run together temperamentally like two leopards." The lady in question, admiring the large rapacity of her mate, exclaims playfully: "Oh, you big tiger! you great, big lion! Boo!" Courtship as presented in these novels is after the manner of beasts in the jungle. Mr. Dreiser's leonine men but circle once or twice about their prey, and spring, and pounce; and the struggle is over. A pure-minded serving-maid, who is suddenly held up in the hall by a "hairy, axiomatic" guest and "masterfully" kissed upon the lips, may for an instant be "horrified, stunned, *like a bird in the grasp of a cat*." But we are always assured that "through it all something tremendously vital and insistent" will be speaking to her, and in the end she will not resist the urge of the *élan vital*. I recall no one of the dozens of obliging women in these books who makes any effective resistance when summoned to capitulate. "*The psychology of the human animal*, when confronted by these tangles, these ripping tides of the heart," says the author of *The Titan*, "has little to do with so-called reason or logic." No; as he informs us elsewhere in endless iteration, it is a question of chemistry. It is the "chemistry of her being" (that of the female in question) which rouses to blazing the ordinarily dormant forces of Eugene Witla's sympathies in *The Genius*. If Stephanie Platow is disloyal to her married lover in *The*

Titan, "let no one quarrel" with her. Reason: "She was an unstable chemical compound."

Such is the Dreiserian philosophy.

By thus eliminating distinctively human motives and making animal instincts the supreme factors in human life, Mr. Dreiser reduces the problem of the novelist to the lowest possible terms. I find myself unable to go with those who admire the powerful reality of his art while deploring the puerility of his philosophy. His philosophy quite excludes him from the field in which the great realist must work. He has deliberately rejected the novelist's supreme task — understanding and presenting the development of character; he has chosen only to illustrate the unrestricted flow of temperament. He has evaded the enterprise of representing human conduct; he has confined himself to a representation of animal behavior. He demands for the demonstration of his theory a moral vacuum from which the obligations of parenthood, marriage, chivalry, and citizenship have been quite withdrawn or locked in a twilight sleep. At each critical moment in his narrative, where a realist like George Eliot or Thackeray or Trollope or Meredith would be asking how a given individual would feel, think, and act under the manifold combined stresses of organized society, Mr. Dreiser sinks supinely back upon the law of the jungle or mutters his mystical gibberish about an alteration of the chemical formula.

The possibility of making the unvarying victoriousness of jungle-motive plausible depends directly upon the suppression of the evidence of other motives. In this work of suppression Mr. Dreiser simplifies American life almost beyond recognition. Whether it is because he comes from

Indiana, or whether it is because he steadily envisages the human animal, I cannot say; I can only note that he never speaks of his men and women as "educated" or "brought up." Whatever their social status, they are invariably "raised." Raising human stock in America evidently includes feeding and clothing it, but does not include the inculcation of even the most elementary moral ideas. Hence Mr. Dreiser's field seems curiously outside American society. Yet he repeatedly informs us that his persons are typical of the American middle class, and three of the leading figures, to judge from their names — Carrie Meeber, Jennie Gerhardt, and Eugene Witla — are of our most highly "cultured" race. Frank Cowperwood, the hero of two novels, is a hawk of finance and a rake almost from the cradle; but of the powers which presided over his cradle we know nothing save that his father was a competent officer in a Philadelphia bank. What, if anything, Carrie Meeber's typical American parents taught her about the conduct of life is suppressed; for we meet the girl in a train to Chicago, on which she falls to the first drummer who accosts her. From the bosom of a typical middle-class American family, Eugene Witla emerges in his teens with a knowledge of the game called post-office, takes the train for Chicago, and without hesitation enters upon his long career of seduction. Jennie Gerhardt, of course, succumbs to the first man who puts his arm around her; but, in certain respects, her case is exceptional.

In *Jennie Gerhardt* Mr. Dreiser ventures a disastrous experiment at making the jungle-motive plausible without suppressing the evidence of other motives. He provides the girl with pious Lutheran parents, of fallen fortune, but alleged to be of sterling character, who "raise" her with utmost strictness. He even admits that the family were church-goers, and he outlines the doctrine preached by Pastor Wundt: right conduct in marriage and absolute innocence before that state as essentials of Christian living; no salvation for a daughter who failed to keep her chastity unstained, or for the parents who permitted her to fall; Hell yawning for all such; God angry with sinners every day. "Gerhardt and his wife, and also Jennie," says Mr. Dreiser, "accepted the doctrines of their church without reserve." Twenty pages later Jennie is represented as yielding her virtue in pure gratitude to a man of fifty, Senator Brander, who has let her do his laundry and in other ways has been kind to her and her family. The Senator suddenly dies; Jennie expects to become a mother; Father Gerhardt is broken-hearted; and the family moves from Columbus to Cleveland. The first episode is perhaps not altogether incredibly presented as a momentary triumph of emotional impulse over training — as an "accident." The incredible appears when Mr. Dreiser insists that an accident of this sort to a girl brought up in the conditions stated is not necessarily followed by any sense of sin or shame or regret. Upon this simple pious Lutheran he imposes his own naturalistic philosophy, and, in analyzing her psychology before the birth of her illegitimate child, pretends that she looks forward to the event "without a murmur," with "serene, unfaltering courage," "the marvel of life holding her in a trance," "with joy and satisfaction," seeing in her state "the immense possibilities of racial fulfilment." This juggling is probably expected to prepare us for her instantaneous assent, perhaps a year later, when a healthy magnetic manufacturer, who has seen her perhaps a dozen times, claps his paw upon her and says, "You belong to me," and in a perfectly cold-blooded interview, proposes the terms on which he will set her up in New York as his mistress. Jennie, who is a fond mother and a dutiful daughter, goes to her pious Lutheran mother and talks the whole matter over with her quite candidly. The mother hesitates — not on Jennie's account, gentle reader, but because she will be obliged to deceive old Gerhardt; "the difficulty of telling this lie was very great for Mrs. Gerhardt!" But she acquiesces at last. "I'll help you out with it," she concludes — "with a little sigh." The unreality of the whole transaction shrieks.

Mr. Dreiser's stubborn insistence upon the jungle-motive results in a dreary monotony in the form and substance of his novels. Interested only in the description of animal behavior, he constructs his plot in such a way as to exhibit the persistence of two or three elementary instincts through every kind of situation. He finds, for example, a subject in the career of an American captain of industry, thinly disguised under the name of Frank Cowperwood. He has just two things to tell us about Cowperwood: that he has a rapacious appetite for money; and that he has a rapacious appetite for women. In *The Financier* he "documents" these truths about Cowperwood in seventy-four chapters, in each of which he shows us how his hero made money or how he captivated women in Philadelphia. Not satisfied with the demonstration, he returns to the same thesis in *The Titan*, and shows us in sixty-two chapters how the same hero made money and captivated women in Chicago and in New York. He

promises us a third volume, in which we shall no doubt
learn in a work of sixty or seventy chapters — a sort of
huge club-sandwich composed of slices of business alter-
nating with erotic episodes — how Frank Cowperwood
made money and captivated women in London. Meanwhile Mr. Dreiser has turned aside from his great "trilogy
of desire" to give us *The Genius*, in which the hero, Witla,
alleged to be a great realistic painter, exhibits, in one
hundred chapters similarly sandwiched together, an appetite for women and money indistinguishable from that
of Cowperwood. Read one of these novels and you have
read them all. What the hero is in the first chapter, he
remains in the one hundred and first and the one hundred
and thirty-sixth. He acquires naught from his experiences but sensations. In the sum of his experience
there is nothing of the impressive mass and coherence of
activities bound together by principles and integrated in
character, for all his days have been but as isolated beads
loosely strung on the thread of his desire. And so after
the production of the hundredth document in the case of
Frank Cowperwood, one is ready to cry with fatigue:
"Hold! Enough! We believe you. Yes, it is very clear
that Frank Cowperwood had a rapacious appetite for
women and for money."

If at this point you stop and inquire why Mr. Dreiser
goes to such great lengths to establish so little, you find
yourself once more confronting the jungle-motive. Mr.
Dreiser, with a problem similar to Defoe's in *The Apparition of Mrs. Veal*, has availed himself of Defoe's
method for creating the illusion of reality. The essence of
the problem for both these authors is the certification of
the unreal by the irrelevant. If you wish to make ac-

ceptable to your reader the incredible notion that Mrs. Veal's ghost appeared to Mrs. Bargrave, divert his incredulity from the precise point at issue by telling him all sorts of detailed credible things about the poverty of Mrs. Veal's early life, the sobriety of her brother, her father's neglect, and the bad temper of Mrs. Bargrave's husband. If you wish to make acceptable to your reader the incredible notion that Aileen Butler's first breach of the seventh article in the decalogue was "a happy event," taking place "much as a marriage might have," divert his incredulity by describing with the technical accuracy of a fashion magazine not merely the gown she wore on the night of Cowperwood's reception, but also with equal detail the half-dozen other gowns that she thought she might wear, but did not. If you have been for three years editor-in-chief of the Butterick publications you can probably persuade your readers that you are a master of the subject, and having acquired credit for expert knowledge in matters of dress and millinery, you can now and then emit unchallenged a bit of philosophy such as "Life cannot be put in any one mold, and the attempt may as well be abandoned at once. . . . Besides, whether we will or not, theory or no theory, the large basic facts of chemistry and physics remain." None the less, if you expect to gain credence for the notion that your hero can have any woman in Chicago or New York that he puts his paw upon, you had probably better lead up to it by a detailed account of the street-railway system in those cities. It will necessitate the loading of your pages with a tremendous baggage of irrelevant detail. It will not sound much like the fine art of fiction. It will sound more like one of Lincoln Steffens's special articles. But it will produce an overwhelming impression of reality, which the reader will carry with him into the next chapter where you are laying bare the "chemistry" of the human animal.

It would make for clearness in our discussions of contemporary fiction if we withheld the title of "realist" from a writer like Mr. Dreiser, and called him, as Zola called himself, a "naturalist." While asserting that all great art in every period intends a representation of reality, I have tried to indicate the basis for a working distinction between the realistic novel and the naturalistic novel of the present day. Both are representations of the life of man in contemporary or nearly contemporary society, and both are presumably composed of materials within the experience and observation of the author. But the realistic novel is a representation based upon a theory of human conduct. If the theory of human conduct is adequate, the representation constitutes an addition to literature and to social history. A naturalistic novel is a representation based upon a theory of animal behavior. Since a theory of animal behavior can never be an adequate basis for a representation of the life of man in contemporary society, such a representation is an artistic blunder. When half the world attempts to assert such a theory, the other half rises in battle. And so one turns with relief from Mr. Dreiser's novels to the morning papers.

TRIVIA[1]

LOGAN PEARSALL SMITH

EMPTY SHELLS

THEY lie like empty sea-shells on the shores of Time, the old worlds which the spirit of man once built for his habitation, and then abandoned. Those little earth-centred, heaven-encrusted universes of the Greeks and Hebrews seem quaint enough to us, who have formed, thought by thought from within, the immense modern Cosmos in which we live — the great Creation of granite, planned in such immeasurable proportions, and moved by so pitiless a mechanism, that it sometimes appals even its own creators. The rush of the great rotating Sun daunts us; to think to the distance of the fixed stars cracks our brains.

But if the ephemeral Being who has imagined these eternal spheres and spaces, must dwell almost as an alien in their icy vastness, yet what a splendour lights up for him and dazzles in those great halls! Anything less limitless would be now a prison; and he even dares to think beyond their boundaries, to surmise that he may one day outgrow this vast Mausoleum, and cast from him the material Creation as an integument too narrow for his insolent Mind.

VERTIGO

No! I don't like it; I can't approve of it; I have always thought it most regrettable that serious and ethical

[1] From *Trivia* (1902; revised 1918). By permission of the author.

Thinkers like ourselves should go scuttling through space in this undignified manner. Is it seemly that I, at my age, should be hurled with my books of reference, and bed-clothes, and hot-water bottle, across the sky at the unthinkable rate of nineteen miles a second? As I say, I don't at all like it. This universe of astronomical whirligigs makes me a little giddy.

That God should spend His eternity — which might be so much better employed — in spinning countless Solar Systems, and skylarking, like a great child, with tops and teetotums — is not this a serious scandal? I wonder what all our circumgyrating Monotheists really do think of it?

THE EVIL EYE

Drawn by the unfelt wind in my little sail over the shallow estuary, I lay in my boat, lost in a dream of mere existence. The cool water glided through my trailing fingers; and leaning over, I watched the sands that slid beneath me, the weeds that languidly swayed with the boat's motion. I was the cool water, I was the gliding sand and the swaying weed, I was the sea and sky and sun, I was the whole vast Universe.

Suddenly between my eyes and the sandy bottom a mirrored face looked up at me, floating on the smooth film of water over which I glided. At one look from that too familiar, and yet how sinister and goblin a face, my immeasurable soul collapsed like a wrecked balloon; I shrank sadly back into my named personality, and sat there, shabby, hot, and very much bored with myself in my little boat.

TRIVIA

DISSATISFACTION

For one thing I hate spiders: I hate most kinds of insects. Their cold intelligence, their empty, stereotyped, unremitting industry repel me. And I am not altogether happy about the future of the human race. When I think of the earth's refrigeration, and the ultimate collapse of our Solar System, I have very grave misgivings. And all the books I have read and forgotten—the thought that my mind is really nothing but a sieve — often this, too, disconcerts me.

SELF-CONTROL

Still I am not a pessimist, nor misanthrope, nor grumbler; I bear it all, the burden of Public Affairs, the immensity of Space, the brevity of Life, and the thought of the all-swallowing Grave — all this I put up with without impatience: I accept the common lot. And if now and then for a moment it seems too much; if I get my feet wet, or have to wait too long for tea, and my soul in these wanes of the moon cries out in French, *C'est fini!* I always answer, *Pazienza!* in Italian — *abbia la santa Pazienza!*

A FANCY

More than once, too, I have pleased myself with the notion that somewhere there is good Company which will like this little Book — these Thoughts (if I may call them so) dipped up from that phantasmagoria or phosphorescence which, by some unexplained process of combustion, flickers over the large lump of soft gray matter in the bowl of my skull.

THE STARRY HEAVEN

"But what are they really? What do they say they are?" the small young lady asked me. We were looking up at the Stars, which were quivering that night in splendid hosts above the lawns and trees.

So I tried to explain some of the views that have been held about the stars. How people first of all had thought them mere candles set in the sky, to guide their own footsteps when the Sun was gone; till wise men, sitting on the Chaldean plains, and watching them with aged eyes, became impressed with the solemn view that those still and shining lights were the executioners of God's decrees, and irresistible instruments of His Wrath; and that they moved fatally among their celestial Houses to ordain and set out the fortunes and misfortunes of each race of new-born mortals. And so it was believed that every man or woman had, from the cradle, fighting for or against him or her, some great Star, Formalhaut, perhaps, Aldebaran, Altaïr: while great Heroes and Princes were more splendidly attended, and marched out to their forgotten battles with troops and armies of heavenly Constellations.

But this noble old view was not believed in now; the Stars were no longer regarded as malignant or beneficent Powers; and I explained how most serious people thought that somewhere—though just where they did not know — above the vault of Sky, was to be found the final home of earnest men and women; where, as a reward for their right views and conduct, they were to rejoice forever, wearing those diamonds of the starry night arranged in glorious crowns. This notion, however, had been disputed by Poets and Lovers: it was Love, according to these young astronomers, that moved the Sun and other

Stars; the Constellations being heavenly palaces, where people who had adored each other were to meet and live always together after Death.

Then I spoke of the modern and real immensity of the unimaginable Skies. But suddenly the vast meaning of my words rushed into my mind; I felt myself dwindling, falling through the blue. And yet, in these silent seconds, there thrilled through me in the cool sweet air and night, no chill of death or nothingness, but the taste and joy of this Earth, this orchard-plot of earth, floating unknown, far away in unfathomed space, with its Moon and meadows.

THE SPIDER

What shall I compare it to, this fantastic thing I call my Mind? To a waste-paper basket, to a sieve choked with sediment, or to a barrel full of floating froth and refuse?

No, what it is really most like is a spider's web, insecurely hung on leaves and twigs, quivering in every wind, and sprinkled with dewdrops and dead flies. And at its centre, pondering for ever the Problem of Existence, sits motionless the spider-like and uncanny Soul.

INTERROGATION[1]

SIMEON STRUNSKY

ONE day a census enumerator in the employ of the United States Government knocked at my door and left a printed list of questions for me to answer. The United States Government wished me to state how many sons and daughters I had and whether my sons were males and my daughters females. I was further required to state that not only was I of white descent and that my wife (if I had one) was of white descent, but that our children (if we had any) were also of white descent. I was also called upon to state whether any of my sons under the age of five (if I had any) had ever been in the military or naval service of the United States, and whether my grandfather (if I had one) was attending school on September 30 last. There were other questions of a like nature, but these are all I can recall at present.

Halfway through the schedule I was in a high state of irritation. The census enumerator's visit in itself I do not consider a nuisance. Like most Americans who sniff at the privileges of citizenship, I secretly delight in them. I speak cynically of boss-rule and demagogues, but I cast my vote on Election Day in a state of solemn and somewhat nervous exaltation that frequently interferes with my folding the ballot in the prescribed way. I have never been summoned for jury duty, but if I ever should be, I

[1] From *The Patient Observer* (1911). Used by permission of Dodd, Mead and Company, Inc.

shall accept with pride and in the hope that I shall not be peremptorily challenged. It needs some such official document as a census schedule to bring home the feeling that government and state exist for me and my own welfare. Filling out the answers in the list was one of the pleasant manifestations of democracy, of which paying taxes is the unpleasant side. The printed form before me embodied a solemn function. I was aware that many important problems depended upon my answering the questions properly. Only then, for instance, could the Government decide how many Congressmen should go to Washington, and what my share was of the total wealth of the country, and how I contributed to the drift from the farm to the city, and what was the average income of Methodist clergymen in cities of over one hundred thousand population.

What, then, if so many of the questions put to me by the United States Government seemed superfluous to the point of being absurd? The process may involve a certain waste of paper and ink and time, but it is the kind of waste without which the business of life would be impossible. The questions that really shape human happiness are those to which the reply is obvious. The answers that count are those the questioner knew he would get and was prepared to insist upon getting. Harrington tells me that when he was married he could not help smiling when the minister asked him whether he would take the woman by his side to be his wedded wife. "What," said Harrington, "did he think I was there for? Or did he detect any sign of wavering at the last moment?" What reply does the clergyman await when he asks the rejoicing parents whether they are willing to have their child baptized into the community of the redeemed? What is all ritual, as it has been framed to meet the needs of the human heart, but a preordained order of question and response? In birth and in burial, in joy and in sorrow, for those who have escaped shipwreck and those who have escaped the plague, the practice of the ages has laid down formulæ which the soul does not find the less adequate because they are ready-made.

Consider the multiplication-table. I don't know who first hit upon the absurd idea that questions are intended to elicit information. In so many laboratories are students putting questions to their microscope. In so many lawyers' offices are clients putting questions to their attorneys. In so many other offices are haggard men and women putting questions to their doctors. But the number of all these is quite insignificant when compared with the number of questions that are framed every day in the schoolrooms of the world. Wherefore, I say, consider the multiplication-table. A greater sum of human interest has centred about the multiplication-table than about all doctors' and lawyers' and biologists' offices since the beginning of time. Millions of schoolmasters have asked what is seven times eleven and myriads of children's brains have toiled for the answer that all the time has been reposing in the teacher's mind. What is seven times eleven? What is the capital of Dahomey? When did the Americans beat the British at Lexington? What is the meaning of the universe? We shall never escape the feeling that these questions are put only to vex us by those who know the answer.

I said that I am looking forward to be summoned for jury-duty. But I know that the solemn business of justice, like most of the world's business, is made up of the mumbled question that is seldom heard and the fixed reply that is never listened to. The clerk of the court stares at the wall and drones out the ancient formula which begins "Jusolimlyswear," and ends "Swelpyugod," and the witness on the stand blurts out "I do." The Chief Justice of the United States Supreme Court asks the President-elect whether he will be faithful to the Constitution and the laws of the United States, and the President-elect invariably says that he will. The candidate for American citizenship is asked whether he hereby renounces allegiance to foreign kings, emperors, and potentates, and fervently responds that he does. When I took my medical examination for a life-insurance policy, the physician asked me whether I suffered from asthma, bronchitis, calculus, dementia, erysipelas, and several score other afflictions, and, without waiting for an answer, he wrote "No" opposite every disease.

Whenever I think of the world and the world's opinion, I think of Mrs. Harrington in whom I see the world typified. Now Mrs. Harrington is inconceivable in a scheme where the proper reply to every question is not as thoroughly established as the rule for the proper use of forks at dinner. In the presence of an unfamiliar reply to a familiar question Mrs. Harrington is suspicious and uneasy. She scents either a joke or an insult; and we are all Mrs. Harrington. If you were to ask a stranger whom did he consider the greatest playwright of all times and, instead of Shakespeare or Molière, he were to say Racine, it would be as if one were to ask him whether he took tea or coffee for breakfast and he said arsenic. It would be as though you asked your neighbour what he thought of a beautiful sunset and he said he did not like it. It would be as if I were to say to Mrs. Harrington, "Well, I suppose I have stayed quite long enough," and she were to say, "Yes, I think you had better be going."

THE DUNES [1]

H. M. TOMLINSON

THE dunes are in another world. They are two miles across the uncertain and hazardous tide races of the estuary. The folk of the village never go over. The dunes are nothing. They are the horizon. They are only seen in idleness, or when the weather is scanned, or an incoming ship is marked. The dunes are but a pallid phantom of land so delicately golden that it is surprising to find it constant. The faint glow of that dilated shore, quavering just above the sea, the sea intensely blue and positive, might wreathe and vanish at any moment in the pour of wind from the Atlantic, whose endless strength easily bears in and over us vast involuted continents of white cloud. The dunes tremble in the broad flood of wind, light, and sea, diaphanous and fading, always on the limit of vision, the point of disappearing, but are established. They are soundless, immaterial, and far, like a pleasing and personal illusion, a luminous dream of lasting tranquillity in a better but an unapproachable place, and the thought of crossing to them never suggests anything so obvious as a boat. They look like no coast that could be reached.

It was a perverse tide on a windless day which drifted me over. The green mounds of water were flawless, with

[1] Reprinted from *Old Junk* (1918), by H. M. Tomlinson, by kind permission of and special arrangement with Alfred A. Knopf, Inc., authorized publisher in the United States. By permission of the author and of Jonathan Cape, Limited.

shadows of mysteries in their clear deeps. The boat and the tide were murmuring to each other secretly. The boat's thwarts were hot and dry in the sun. The serene immensity of the sky, the warmth and dryness of the boat's timbers, the deep and translucent waters, and the coast so low and indistinct that the silent flashing of the combers there might have been on nothing substantial, were all timeless, and could have been but a thought and a desire; they were like a memorable morning in a Floridan cay miraculously returned. The boat did not move; the shore approached, revealed itself. It was something granted on a lucky day. This country would not be on the map.

I landed on a broad margin of sand which the tide had just left. It was filmed with water. It was a mirror in which the sky was inverted. When a breath of air passed over that polished surface it was as though the earth were a shining bubble which then nearly burst. To dare that foothold might precipitate the intruder on ancient magic to cloudland floating miles beneath the feet. But I had had the propriety to go barefooted, and had lightened my mind before beginning the voyage. Here I felt I was breaking into what was still only the first day, for man had never measured this place with his countless interruptions of darkness. I don't know whether that mirror had ever been darkened till I put my foot in it. After the news I had heard on the quay that morning before starting out, news just arrived from London, the dunes were an unexpected assurance that the earth has an integrity and purity of its own, a quality which even man cannot irreparably soil; that it maintains a pristine health and bloom invulnerable to the best our heroic and intelligent activities can accomplish, and could easily survive our extinction, and even forget it once supported us.

I found an empty bottle among the dry litter and drift above the tide-mark, sole relic, as far as could be seen there, of man. No message was in the bottle. The black bottle itself was forlornly the message, but it lay there unregarded by the bright immemorial genius of that coast. Yet it settled one doubt. This was not a land which had never known man. It had merely forgotten it had known him. He had been there, but whatever difference he had made was of the same significance now as the dry bladderwrack, the mummied gull near by, and the bleached shells. The next tide probably would hide the memento for ever. At the time this did not seem an unhappy thought, though the relic had been our last witness, so enduring was the tenuous brightness of the place, the shrine of our particular star, the visible aura of earth. We rarely see it. It is something to be reminded it is not lost; that we cannot, whatever else we can do, put out a celestial light.

Above the steep beach a dry flat opened out, reached only by gales and the highest of the spring tides, a wilderness of fine sand, hot and deep, its surface studded with the opaque blue of round pebbles and mussel shells. It looked too arid to support life, but sea-rocket with fleshy emerald stems and lilac flowers was scattered about. Nothing moved in the waste but an impulsive small butterfly, blue as a fragment of sky. The silence of the desert was that of a dream, but when listening to the quiet, a murmur which had been below hearing was imagined. The dunes were quivering with the intensity of some latent energy, and it might have been that one heard, or else it was the remembrance held by that strand of a storm which had passed, or it might have been the ardent shafts of the sun. At the landward end of the waste, by the foot of the dunes, was an old beam of a ship, harsh with barnacles, its bolt-holes stopped with dust. A spinous shrub grew to one side of it. A solitary wasp, a slender creature in black and gold, quick and emotional, had made a cabin of one of the holes in the timber. For some reason that fragment of a barque was more eloquent of travel, and the work of seamen gone, than any of the craft moored at the quay I left that morning. I smoked a pipe on that timber — for all I knew, not for the first time — and did not feel at all lonely, nor that voyages for the discovery of fairer times were finished.

Now the dunes were close they appeared surprisingly high, and were formed, not like hills, but like the high Alps. They had the peaks and declivities of mountains. Their colour was of old ivory, and the long marram grass which grew on them sparsely was as fine as green hair. The hollowed slope before me was so pale, spacious, and immaculate that there was an instinctive hesitation about taking it. A dark ghost began slowly to traverse it with outspread arms, a shade so distinct on that virgin surface that not till the gull, whose shadow it was, had gone inland, following its shadow over the high yellow ridge, did I know that I had not been looking at the personality. But the surface had been darkened, and I could overcome my hesitation.

From the ridge, the country of the dunes opened inland with the enlarged likeness of a lunar landscape surveyed in a telescope. It merely appeared to be near.

The sand-hills, with their acute outlines, and their shadows flung rigidly from their peaks across the pallor of their slopes, were the apparition of inviolable seclusion. They could have been waiting upon an event secret from our knowledge, larger than the measure of our experience; so they had still the aspect of a strange world, not only infinitely remote, but superior with a greater destiny. They were old, greatly older than the ancient village across the water. Ships left the village and went by them to sea gay with the bunting of a first voyage, with a fair wind, and on a fine morning; and when such a ship came back long after as an old plank bearded with sea moss, to the dunes under which it stranded, the day was still the same, vestal and innocent; for they were on a voyage of greater length and import. They had buried many ships; but, as time moved to them, all on the same day.

Only when resting on a knoll of one of the slopes, where the shadows of a tuft of marram grass above my head lay as thin black wire on the sand, were the dunes caught in part of their secret. There was no sound. I heard the outer world from which I had come only as the whistle of a curlew. It was far away now. To this place, the news I had heard on the quay that morning would have sounded the same as Waterloo, which was yesterday, or the Armada, which was the same day — wasn't it? — or the day before, or as the whistle of a curlew. Here we were outside time. Then I thought I heard a faint whisper, but when I looked round nothing had altered. The shadows of the grass formed a fixed metallic design on the sand. But I heard the whisper again, and with a side glance caught the dune stealthily on the move.

It was alive. When you were not attentive, some of its grains would start furtively, pour in increasing mobility fanwise, and rest instantly when looked at. This hill was fluid, and circulated. It preserved an outline that was fixed through the years, a known, named, and charted locality, only to those to whom one map would serve a lifetime. But it was really unknown. It was on its way. Like the ships that were passing, it also was passing. It was only taking its own time.

Secluded within the inner ranges were little valleys, where, for a while, the dunes had ceased to travel, and were at leisure. I got into a hollow which had a floor of hoary lichen, with bronze hummocks of moss. In this moment of pause it had assumed a look of what we call antiquity. The valley was not abundant with vegetation, but enamelled and jewelled. A more concentrated, hectic, and volatile essence sent up stalks, blades, and sprays, with that direction and restraint which perfection needs. More than in a likelier and fecund spot, in this valley the ichor showed the ardour and flush of its early vitality. Even now it could shape like this, and give these dyes! Chosen by an earth astringent and tonic, the forms were few and personal. Here you should see to what influences our planet is still subject. The shapes in that valley were more than coloured; they were rare jets of light, emerald, orange, blue, and scarlet. Life burned with an original force, a steady virtue. What is "good news"? It depends on the sort of evidence for which we look.

Just showing in the drift on the seaward side of the valley were some worked stones and a little brickwork. When the sandhill paused, it had almost covered a build-

379

ing where man once worshipped. I could find nobody afterwards who remembered the church, or had even heard of it. Yet the doom of this temple, prolonged in its approach but inevitable, to those to whom the altar once had seemed as indestructible as hope, must on a day have struck the men who saw at last their temple's end was near as a hint, vague but glacial, of the transience of all their affairs.

But what were their affairs? We should have to know them before we could regret the dry sand which buried them. The valley looked very well as it was. It showed no sign of failure. Over one of the stones of the forgotten altar was a casual weed which stood like a sign of success and continuance. It was as indecipherable as the stone, but the blue of its flowers, still and deep as rapture, surprising and satisfying as an unexpected revelation of good, would have been better worth reading for a knowledge of the heart from which could be drawn the temper and intensity of that faith.

THE TWO GENTLEMEN OF VERONA [1]

A. B. WALKLEY

THERE is a subtle fascination for many of us in the more faulty work of a great artist. For one thing, it brings him, just for a moment, into line with us; we feel that he is human after all and no mere monster of perfection. We like to note the prentice hand in *Waverley*, and do not altogether dislike the symptoms of decrepitude in *Count Robert of Paris*. There is something repellent in absolute flawlessness, and we should hate the man who discovered the lost arm of the Venus in the Louvre. Nor does that feeling fully explain the fascination of the imperfect. A crude sketch often tells you more about the artist than a finished picture. And in literature there are half-failures which give you more intimate revelations of life than whole successes; *L'Éducation Sentimentale* provokes sharper thrills than *Madame Bovary*. What a comfort that Shakespeare had his weaker, that is to say, his earlier, moments! "Every schoolboy knows" the faults of *The Two Gentlemen of Verona*, and one is quite content to leave them to the schoolboys.

I had never seen the play (it has only been played in London once or twice in my time) until it was revived at the Court Theatre the other night. [2] I went with no little misgiving, and came away under so strong a charm that I almost told the cabman "To Mantua — by sea!" Was it Shakespeare that one had been enjoying or something

[1] From *Drama and Life* (1908). By permission of Brentano's.
[2] April, 1904.

from the *Théâtre Impossible* of Alfred de Musset? Who were these twain under the lady's balcony — Proteus and Thurio, or Cyrano de Bergerac and his "cadet de Gascogne?" And all this casuistry of love, was it not Marivaux — turned into archaic English? No, evidently it was Shakespeare. A leaflet, distributed with the playbill, was sufficient evidence of that ... Dr. Brandes ... Schlegel ... John Kemble ... Meres's *Palladis Tamia* ... the usual thing. I do not reproach the compiler; he did his work thoroughly. But one cannot abide a wheel, however well made, when it is used to break a butterfly. One does not want the mood created by a Shakesperian love-comedy to be disturbed by horrid matter-of-fact comments. In such a mood references to Shakespeare's borrowings from George de Montemayor are as tiresomely irrelevant as the latest Stock Exchange quotations. It is a mood of sheer hedonism. We are intent upon our pleasure, romantic, languid, voluptuous pleasure. The nights are warm in Mantua, and the ladies, though virtuous, unashamedly amorous. A rope-ladder, as Valentine knows, is an article that no gentleman's wardrobe should be without. We feel our moral standard pleasantly giving way. We can even sympathise with Proteus. He loves Julia, and no wonder, for she is as sleek and as soft and as full of mischief as a Persian kitten. The next moment, Julia being out of the way, he transfers his heart to Silvia. Why not? What could any gentleman, with eyes in his head, say to Silvia if not what Disraeli said to the Duchess who was inquisitive about Cabinet secrets — "You darling!" I observe that some writers have taken the fickle Proteus quite seriously. His conduct pains them. "Et moi qui vous croyais homme du monde!" they seem to say — as the chemist's assistant in Labiche's farce said to the man who gave him a black eye. Proteus is "no gentleman." Thus do we confound the *Pays de Tendre* with the Metropolitan Cab Radius. It is true that Shakespeare makes Proteus ashamed of himself in the end — just five bare lines of repentance. But that is "only his" — Shakespeare's — "fun." For my part, I feel sure that he had "been there." Proteus is his hint of a Don Juan "caught young" — or a Cherubino grown up. The thought gives an agreeable Mozartian blend to our pleasures. Then comes a touch of Schubert with "Who is Silvia?" I liked Mr. Holthoir's modest, breathless singing of this song better than many concert "renderings" I have heard. And he makes so handsome a Sir Thurio that you half wonder how Silvia could find it in her heart to reject him for either of the Veronese gentlemen. But I am forgetting that the play is not *A Gentleman of Mantua*. Sir Eglamour, too, is a very pretty fellow. An inconsolable widower? Fudge. All the rest (save the bandits) live "for climate and the affections." And one sits in the Court Theatre, sympathising and approving. Decidedly, this play does not make for austerity. But even the austere Pascal wrote a treatise on "Les Passions de l'Amour," and sages like Michelet and Renan — when quite elderly men, as old as the Duke of Milan or Antonio, father to Proteus — laboriously analysed these passions. Why, even this same Duke of Milan poses (falsely, but plausibly enough to deceive Valentine) as what they call on the Boulevards a *vieux marcheur* —

> There is a lady in Verona here
> Whom I affect, but she is nice and coy

And nought esteems my aged eloquence;
Now therefore would I have thee to my tutor.

Whereupon Valentine gives him "tips." Is there not, by the way, just a tinge of "decadence" in this spectacle of a youngster instructing the greybeard whom he would make his father-in-law in the tricks of abduction and the use of "ladders, quaintly made of cords"? But I do not wonder that Valentine was caught by the deception. Nothing is so flattering to a young man as to be consulted by his senior as an authority on lady-killing. These little touches in *The Two Gentlemen* ought to tell the intelligent spectator more about the secrets of Shakespeare's own life than whole volumes of facts about second-best bed-steads.

And the two ladies, Julia and Silvia, reveal to us, if we will but keep our eyes open, a good deal about the damsels of (Shakespeare's) Stratford. Their complete absorption in love, as the only thing in the world a woman ought to concern herself with, is as naïve as in Boccaccio's — or Brantôme's — women. And you observe that these women are played by our actresses to-day with perfect naturalness, without any sense of a changed point of view either on their part or the spectator's; whereas the men obviously "date." You draw your own conclusions — and, if you are wise, will keep them to yourself. The lessee of the Court Theatre has done an excellent thing in reviving this delicious comedy of love. He might, by the way, head his playbill with an appropriate remark of Dryden's (*Essay of Dramatic Poesy*): "Love is the most frequent of all the passions, and, being the private con-cernment of every person, is soothed by viewing its own image in a public entertainment."

NOTES ON AN ELIZABETHAN PLAY [1]

VIRGINIA WOOLF

THERE are, it must be admitted, some highly formidable tracts in English literature, and chief among them that jungle, forest, and wilderness which is the Elizabethan drama. For many reasons, not here to be examined, Shakespeare stands out, Shakespeare who has had the light on him from his day to ours, Shakespeare who towers highest when looked at from the level of his own contemporaries. But the plays of the lesser Elizabethans — Greene, Dekker, Peele, Chapman, Beaumont and Fletcher, — to adventure into that wilderness is for the ordinary reader an ordeal, an upsetting experience which plies him with questions, harries him with doubts, alternately delights and vexes him with pleasures and pains. For we are apt to forget, reading, as we tend to do, only the masterpieces of a bygone age how great a power the body of a literature possesses to impose itself: how it will not suffer itself to be read passively, but takes us and reads us; flouts our preconceptions; questions principles which we had got into the habit of taking for granted, and, in fact, splits us into two parts as we read, making us, even as we enjoy, yield our ground or stick to our guns.

At the outset in reading an Elizabethan play we are overcome by the extraordinary discrepancy between the Elizabethan view of reality and our own. The reality to which we have grown accustomed, is, speaking roughly,

[1] From *The Common Reader*, by Virginia Woolf; copyright, 1925, by Harcourt, Brace and Company, Inc. By permission.

based upon the life and death of some knight called Smith, who succeeded his father in the family business of pitwood importers, timber merchants and coal exporters, was well known in political, temperance, and church circles, did much for the poor of Liverpool, and died last Wednesday of pneumonia while on a visit to his son at Muswell Hill. That is the world we know. That is the reality which our poets and novelists have to expound and illuminate. Then we open the first Elizabethan play that comes to hand and read how

> I once did see
> In my young travels through Armenia
> An angry unicorn in his full career
> Charge with too swift a foot a jeweller
> That watch'd him for the treasure of his brow
> And ere he could get shelter of a tree
> Nail him with his rich antlers to the earth.

Where is Smith, we ask, where is Liverpool? And the groves of Elizabethan drama echo "Where?" Exquisite is the delight, sublime the relief of being set free to wander in the land of the unicorn and the jeweller among dukes and grandees, Gonzaloes and Bellimperias, who spend their lives in murder and intrigue, dress up as men if they are women, as women if they are men, see ghosts, run mad, and die in the greatest profusion on the slightest provocation, uttering as they fall imprecations of superb vigour or elegies of the wildest despair. But soon the low, the relentless voice, which if we wish to identify it we must suppose typical of a reader fed on modern English literature, and French and Russian, asks why, then, with all this to stimulate and enchant, these old plays are for long stretches of time so intolerably dull? Is it not that literature, if it is to keep us on the alert through five acts or thirty-two chapters must somehow be based on Smith, have one toe touching Liverpool, take off into whatever heights it pleases from reality? We are not so purblind as to suppose that a man because his name is Smith and he lives at Liverpool is therefore "real." We know indeed that this reality is a chameleon quality, the fantastic becoming as we grow used to it often the closest to the truth, the sober the farthest from it, and nothing proving a writer's greatness more than his capacity to consolidate his scene by the use of what, until he touched them, seemed wisps of cloud and threads of gossamer. Our contention merely is that there is a station, somewhere in mid-air, whence Smith and Liverpool can be seen to the best advantage; that the great artist is the man who knows where to place himself above the shifting scenery; that while he never loses sight of Liverpool he never sees it in the wrong perspective. The Elizabethans bore us, then, because their Smiths are all changed to dukes, their Liverpools to fabulous islands and palaces in Genoa. Instead of keeping a proper poise above life they soar miles into the empyrean, where nothing is visible for long hours at a time but clouds at their revelry, and a cloud landscape is not ultimately satisfactory to human eyes. The Elizabethans bore us because they suffocate our imaginations rather than set them to work.

Still, though potent enough, the boredom of an Elizabethan play is of a different quality altogether from the boredom which a nineteenth-century play, a Tennyson or a Henry Taylor play, inflicts. The riot of images, the violent volubility of language, all that cloys and satiates in the Elizabethans yet appears to be drawn up with a roar as a feeble fire is sucked up by a newspaper. There is, even in the worst, an intermittent bawling vigour which gives us the sense in our quiet arm-chairs of ostlers and orange-girls catching up the lines, flinging them back, hissing or stamping applause. But the deliberate drama of the Victorian age is evidently written in a study. It has for audience ticking clocks and rows of classics bound in half morocco. There is no stamping, no applause. It does not, as, with all its faults, the Elizabethan audience did, leaven the mass with fire. Rhetorical and bombastic, the lines are flung and hurried into existence and reach the same impromptu felicities, have the same lip-moulded profusion and unexpectedness, which speech sometimes achieves, but seldom in our day the deliberate, solitary pen. Indeed half the work of the dramatists one feels was done in the Elizabethan age by the public.

Against that, however, is to be set the fact that the influence of the public was in many respects detestable. To its door we must lay the greatest infliction that Elizabethan drama puts upon us — the plot; the incessant, improbable, almost unintelligible convolutions which presumably gratified the spirit of an excitable and unlettered public actually in the play-house, but only confuse and fatigue a reader with the book before him. Undoubtedly something must happen; undoubtedly a play where nothing happens is an impossibility. But we have a right to demand (since the Greeks have proved that it is perfectly possible) that what happens shall have an end in view. It shall agitate great emotions; bring into existence memorable scenes; stir the actors to say what could not be said without this stimulus. Nobody can fail to remember the plot of the *Antigone*, because what happens is so closely bound up with the emotions of the actors that we remember the people and the plot at one and the same time. But who can tell us what happens in the *White Devil*, or the *Maid's Tragedy*, except by remembering the story apart from the emotions which it has aroused? As for the lesser Elizabethans, like Greene and Kyd, the complexities of their plots are so great, and the violence which those plots demand so terrific, that the actors themselves are obliterated and emotions which, according to our convention at least, deserve the most careful investigation, the most delicate analysis, are clean sponged off the slate. And the result is inevitable. Outside Shakespeare and perhaps Ben Jonson, there are no characters in Elizabethan drama, only violences whom we know so little that we can scarcely care what becomes of them. Take any hero or heroine in those early plays — Bellimperia in the *Spanish Tragedy* will serve as well as another — and can we honestly say that we care a jot for the unfortunate lady who runs the whole gamut of human misery to kill herself in the end? No more than for an animated broomstick, we must reply, and in a work dealing with men and women the prevalence of broomsticks is a drawback. But the *Spanish Tragedy* is admittedly a crude forerunner, chiefly valuable because such primitive efforts lay bare the formidable framework which greater dramatists could modify, but had to use. Ford, it is claimed, is of the school of Stendhal and of Flaubert; Ford is a psychologist. Ford is an analyst. "This man," says Mr. Havelock Ellis, "writes of women not as a dramatist nor as a lover, but as one who has searched intimately and felt with instinctive sympathy the fibres of their hearts."

NOTES ON AN ELIZABETHAN PLAY

The play — *'Tis Pity She's a Whore* — upon which this judgement is chiefly based shows us the whole nature of Annabella spun from pole to pole in a series of tremendous vicissitudes. First, her brother tells her that he loves her; next she confesses her love for him; next finds herself with child by him; next forces herself to marry Soranzo; next is discovered; next repents; finally is killed, and it is her lover and brother who kills her. To trace the trail of feelings which such crises and calamities might be expected to breed in a woman of ordinary sensibility might have filled volumes. A dramatist of course has no volumes to fill. He is forced to contract. Even so, he can illumine; he can reveal enough for us to guess the rest. But what is it that we know without using microscopes and splitting hairs about the character of Annabella? Gropingly we make out that she is a spirited girl, with her defiance of her husband when he abuses her, her snatches of Italian song, her ready wit, her simple glad love-making. But of character as we understand the word there is no trace. We do not know how she reaches her conclusions, only that she has reached them. Nobody describes her. She is always at the height of her passion, never at its approach. Compare her with Anna Karenina. The Russian woman is flesh and blood, nerves and temperament, has heart, brain, body and mind where the English girl is flat and crude as a face painted on a playing card; she is without depth, without range, without intricacy. But as we say this we know that we have missed something. We have let the meaning of the play slip through our hands. We have ignored the emotion which has been accumulating because it has accumulated in places where we have not expected to find it. We have been comparing the play with prose, and the play, after all, is poetry.

The play is poetry we say, and the novel prose. Let us attempt to obliterate detail, and place the two before us side by side, feeling, so far as we can, the angles and edges of each, recalling each, so far as we are able, as a whole. Then, at once, the prime differences emerge; the long leisurely accumulated novel; the little contracted play; the emotion all split up, dissipated and then woven together, slowly and gradually massed into a whole, in the novel; the emotion concentrated, generalised, heightened in the play. What moments of intensity, what phrases of astonishing beauty the play shot at us!

> O, my lords,
> I but deceived your eyes with antic gesture,
> When one news straight came huddling on another
> Of death! and death! and death! still I danced forward.

or

> You have oft for these two lips
> Neglected cassia or the natural sweets
> Of the spring-violet: they are not yet much wither'd.

With all her reality, Anna Karenina could never say

> "You have oft, for these two lips
> Neglected cassia."

Some of the most profound of human emotions are therefore beyond her reach. The extremes of passion are not for the novelist; the perfect marriages of sense and sound are not for him; he must tame his swiftness to sluggardry; keep his eyes on the ground, not on the sky: suggest by description, not reveal by illumination. Instead of singing

> Lay a garland on my hearse
>   Of the dismal yew;
> Maidens, willow branches bear;
>   Say I died true,

he must enumerate the chrysanthemums fading on the grave and the undertakers' men snuffling past in their four-wheelers. How then can we compare this lumbering and lagging art with poetry? Granted all the little dexterities by which the novelist makes us know the individual and recognise the real, the dramatist goes beyond the single and the separate, shows us not Annabella in love, but love itself; not Anna Karenina throwing herself under the train, but ruin and death and the

> ... soul, like a ship in a black storm,
> ... driven, I know not whither.

So with pardonable impatience we might exclaim as we shut our Elizabethan play. But what then is the exclamation with which we close *War and Peace*? Not one of disappointment; we are not left lamenting the superficiality, upbraiding the triviality of the novelist's art. Rather we are made more than ever aware of the inexhaustible richness of human sensibility. Here, in the play, we recognise the general; here, in the novel, the particular. Here we gather all our energies into a bunch and spring. Here we extend and expand and let come slowly in from all quarters deliberate impressions, accumulated messages. The mind is so saturated with sensibility, language so inadequate to its experience, that far from ruling off one form of literature or decreeing its inferiority to others we complain that they are still unable to keep pace with the wealth of material, and wait impatiently the creation of what may yet be devised to liberate us of the enormous burden of the unexpressed.

Thus, in spite of dullness, bombast, rhetoric, and confusion we still read the lesser Elizabethans, still find ourselves adventuring in the land of the jeweller and the unicorn. The familiar factories of Liverpool fade into thin air and we scarcely recognise any likeness between the knight who imported timber and died of pneumonia at Muswell Hill and the Armenian Duke who fell like a Roman on his sword while the owl shrieked in the ivy and the Duchess gave birth to a still-born babe 'mongst women howling. To join those territories and recognise the same man in different disguises we have to adjust and revise. But make the necessary alterations in perspective, draw in those filaments of sensibility which the moderns have so marvellously developed, use instead the ear and the eye which the moderns have so basely starved, hear words as they are laughed and shouted, not as they are printed in black letters on the page, see before your eyes the changing faces and living bodies of men and women, put yourself, in short, into a different, but not more elementary stage of your reading development and then the true merits of Elizabethan drama will assert themselves. The power of the whole is undeniable. Theirs, too, is the word-coining genius, as if thought plunged into a sea of words and came up dripping. Theirs is that broad humour based upon the nakedness of the body, which, however arduously the public spirited may try, is impossible, since the body is draped. Then at the back of this, imposing not unity but some sort of stability, is what we may briefly call a sense of the presence of the Gods. He would be a bold critic who should attempt to impose any creed

upon the swarm and variety of the Elizabethan dramatists, and yet it implies some timidity if we take it for
granted that a whole literature with common characteristics is a mere evaporation of high spirits, a money-
making enterprise, a fluke of the mind which, owing to
favourable circumstances, came off successfully. Even
in the jungle and the wilderness the compass still points.

> "Lord, Lord, that I were dead!"

they are for ever crying.

> O thou soft natural death that art joint-twin
> To sweetest slumber —

The pageant of the world is marvellous, but the pageant
of the world is vanity.

> Glories
> Of human greatness are but pleasing dreams
> And shadows soon decaying: on the stage
> Of my mortality my youth hath acted
> Some scenes of vanity —

To die and be quit of it all is their desire; the bell that
tolls throughout the drama is death and disenchantment.

> All life is but a wandering to find home,
> When we're gone, we're there.

Ruin, weariness, death, perpetually death, stand grimly
to confront the other presence of Elizabethan drama
which is life: life compact of frigates, fir trees and ivory,
of dolphins and the juice of July flowers, of the milk of
unicorns and panthers' breath, of ropes of pearl, brains
of peacocks and Cretan wine. To this, life at its most
reckless and abundant, they reply

> Man is a tree that hath no top in cares,
> No root in comforts; all his power to live
> Is given to no end but t' have power to grieve.

It is this echo flung back and back from the other side of the play which, if it has not the name, still has the effect of the presence of the Gods.

So we ramble through the jungle, forest, and wilderness of Elizabethan drama. So we consort with Emperors and clowns, jewellers and unicorns, and laugh and exult and marvel at the splendour and humour and fantasy of it all. A noble rage consumes us when the curtain falls; we are bored too, and nauseated by the wearisome old tricks and florid bombast. A dozen deaths of full-grown men and women move us less than the suffering of one of Tolstoy's flies. Wandering in the maze of the impossible and tedious story suddenly some passionate intensity seizes us; some sublimity exalts, or some melodious snatch of song enchants. It is a world full of tedium and delight; pleasure and curiosity, of extravagant laughter, poetry, and splendour. But gradually it comes over us, what then are we being denied? What is it that we are coming to want so persistently that unless we get it instantly we must seek elsewhere? It is solitude. There is no privacy here. Always the door opens and some one comes in. All is shared, made visible, audible, dramatic. Meanwhile, as if tired with company, the mind steals off to muse in solitude; to think, not to act; to comment, not to share; to explore its own darkness, not the bright-lit-up surfaces of others. It turns to Donne, to Montaigne, to Sir Thomas Browne — the keepers of the keys of solitude.

APPENDIX

BIOGRAPHICAL AND BIBLIOGRAPHICAL NOTES

THE supplementary information regarding the lives and works of the authors represented in this volume has been obtained from *Who's Who*, *Who's Who in America*, *The New International Cyclopædia*, and the catalogue of the Library of Congress, supplemented by special books or articles on a few authors, and by the notes in Manly and Rickert's *Contemporary British Literature* and *Contemporary American Literature*. The biographical information is at best scanty, except in the case of two or three major figures, and the bibliographical is sometimes confusing or contradictory. In spite of careful comparison and collation, therefore, it is not to be expected that errors of omission and commission have been escaped; yet the data presented here, some part of which has not been made generally available before, should be of considerable helpfulness.

It should be noted that the notes avoid criticism altogether. The lists of works of the various authors, though reasonably full, are seldom complete and are sometimes severely selective; they aim to be representative only.

The editor is indebted to various friends and colleagues for suggestions, particularly to Professor Benjamin C. Clough, whose special knowledge of the field has been generously made available, and to Mr. B. K. Hart, of the *Providence Journal*.

I

LIVES AND WORKS OF THE AUTHORS

Beerbohm, Max (1872–   )

Born in London, August 24, 1872, son of Julius E. Beerbohm and Eliza Draper, and half-brother of Sir Herbert Beerbohm Tree. Educated at Charterhouse and at Merton College, Oxford, where he matriculated in 1890; visited America in 1895 with his half-brother. Began his literary career by contributing to *The Yellow Book;* became a contributor to London periodicals. Married, 1910, Florence Kahn of Memphis, Tennessee. Has lived in Rapallo, Italy, since 1911. Essayist and caricaturist.

Essays: *The Works of Max Beerbohm*, 1896; *More*, 1899; *Yet Again*, 1909; *And Even Now*, 1920.

Parodies: *The Christmas Garland*, 1912.

Narratives: *The Happy Hypocrite*, 1897; *Zuleika Dobson*, 1911; *Seven Men*, 1919.

Belloc, Joseph Hilaire Pierre (1870–   )

Born July 27, 1870, near Paris, of French and Irish stock. Educated in England at Edgbaston Oratory School and Balliol College, Oxford, where he held a scholarship and won a First Class in the Honor Schools in History in 1895. Served in the French army. Married, 1896, Elodie Agnes Hogan of Napa, California. Naturalized British subject in 1903. Represented, as a Liberal, the South Salford district in Parliament, 1906–10.

Essays: *The Old Road*, 1904; *On Nothing*, 1908; *On Everything*, 1909; *On Anything*, 1910; *On Something*, 1910; *First and Last*, 1911; *This and That*, 1912; *On*, 1923.

Books of Travel: *The Path to Rome*, 1902; *Esto Perpetua*, 1906; *The Hills and the Sea*, 1906; *The Historic Thames*, 1907.

Historical works: *Danton*, 1899 (revised, 1911); *Robespierre*, 1901; *The Eye Witness*, 1908; *Marie Antoinette*, 1912.

Novels: *Emmanuel Burden*, 1904; *Mr. Clutterbuck's Election*, 1908; *Pongo and the Bull*, 1910; *The Green Overcoat*, 1912; *Mr. Petre*, 1925.

Poems: *Verses and Sonnets*, 1895; *The Bad Child's Book of Beasts*, 1896; *Verses*, 1910.

Benson, Arthur Christopher (1862–1925)

Born April 24, 1862, son of E. W. Benson, Archbishop of Canterbury; brother of E. F. Benson, and R. H. Benson. Educated at Eton and at King's College, Cambridge, where he won a First Class in Classics in 1884. Master at Eton, 1885–1903; Fellow of Magdalene College, Cambridge, 1904–15; Master of Magdalene, 1915–25. LL.D., Cambridge, 1915; Fellow, Royal Historical Society; Vice-President, Royal Society of Literature Died June 17, 1925.

Essays: *The House of Quiet*, 1903; *The Upton Letters*, 1905;

APPENDIX

The Thread of Gold, 1906; *From a College Window*, 1906; *At Large*, 1908; *Along the Road*, 1913; *Escape, and other Essays*, 1915.

Biographical studies: *Memoirs of Arthur Hamilton*, 1886; *Archbishop Laud*, 1887; *Life of Archbishop Benson*, 1899; *Tennyson*, 1903; *Rossetti*, 1904, *Edward Fitzgerald*, 1905, and *Walter Pater*, 1906, in English Men of Letters Series; *Ruskin*, 1911; *Hugh: Memoirs of a Brother*, 1915.

Narratives: *Beside Still Waters*, 1907; *The Altar Fire*, 1907.

Poems: *Poems*, 1893; *Lyrics*, 1895; *The Professor and other Poems*, 1900; *Poems* (collected), 1909.

Bourne, Randolph Silliman (1886–1918)

Born May 30, 1886, in Bloomfield, New Jersey. A.B., Columbia, 1913; in Europe on the Gilder Fellowship, 1913–14; member of contributing staffs of *The New Republic*, *The Seven Arts*, and *The Dial*. Died December 22, 1918.

Works: *Youth and Life*, 1913; *The Early Schools*, 1916; *Education and Living*, 1917; *Untimely Papers*, 1919; *The History of a Literary Radical and other Essays*, 1920.

Brooks, Van Wyck (1886–   )

Born February 16, 1886, at Plainfield, New Jersey. A.B., Harvard, 1907; married Eleanor Kenyon Stimson, 1911. With Doubleday, Page and Company, 1908–09, and The Century Company, 1915–18; instructor in English, Leland Stanford University, 1911–13; associate editor of *The Freeman*, 1920–24.

Works: *The Wine of the Puritans*, 1909; *The Malady of the Ideal*, 1913; *John Addington Symonds — a Biographical Study*, 1914; *The World of H. G. Wells*, 1915; *America's Coming-of-Age*, 1915; *Letters and Leadership*, 1918; *The Ordeal of Mark Twain*, 1920; *The Pilgrimage of Henry James*, 1925; *Emerson and Others*, 1927.

Broun, Heywood Campbell (1888–   )

Born December 7, 1888, at Brooklyn, New York. At Harvard, 1906–10; married Ruth Hale, 1917. With the *Morning Telegraph*, New York, 1908–09, 1910–12; *New York Tribune*, 1912–21; *New York World*, 1921–27. Contributing editor, *The Nation*, 1927–   . War correspondent with the A.E.F., 1917; lecturer at Columbia University, 1920; at Rand School, 1921.

APPENDIX

Works: *A.E.F. — With General Pershing and the American Forces*, 1918; *Seeing Things at Night*, 1921; *Pieces of Hate*, 1922; *The Boy Grew Older*, 1922; *The Sun Field*, 1923; *Sitting on the World*, 1924; *Gandle Follows his Nose*, 1926; *Anthony Comstock, Roundsman of the Lord* (in collaboration), 1927.

Canby, Henry Seidel (1878–   )

Born September 6, 1878, at Wilmington, Delaware; Ph.B., Yale, 1899; Ph.D., 1905; married Marion Ponsonby Gause, 1907. Assistant, instructor, and assistant Professor of English, Yale, 1900–16; adviser and lecturer, Yale, since 1916.   Assistant editor of the *Yale Review*, 1911–20; editor of the *Literary Review*, 1920–24, and of the *Saturday Review of Literature* since 1924.

Essays: Three studies of the Short Story, 1902, 1909, 1913; *College Sons and College Fathers*, 1915; *Education by Violence*, 1919; *Everyday Americans*, 1920; *Definitions*, two series, 1922, 1924.

Chesterton, Gilbert Keith (1874–   )

Born in London in 1874.   Educated at St. Paul's School and at the Slade School of Art; married Frances Blogg, 1901.   Began literary career as reviewer of books on art for *The Bookman* and *The Speaker;* has been contributor to the *London Daily News*, the *Pall Mall Magazine*, the *Bystander*, the *Fortnightly*, and the *Independent Review*, the *Illustrated London News*, etc.

Critical Biographies: *Robert Browning* (English Men of Letters), 1903; *G. F. Watts*, 1904; *George Bernard Shaw*, 1909; *William Cobbett*, 1926.

Critical Essays: *Twelve Types* (American edition, *Varied Types*), 1903; *Dickens*, 1906; *The Victorian Age in Literature*, 1913.

Miscellaneous Works: *Heretics*, 1905; *Orthodoxy*, 1908; *Alarms and Discursions*, 1911; *The Crimes of England*, 1915; *A Short History of England*, 1917; *The Uses of Diversity*, 1921; *The Outline of Sanity*, 1926.

Fiction: *The Napoleon of Notting Hill*, 1904; *The Club of Queer Trades*, 1905; *The Man who was Thursday*, 1908; *The Ball and the Cross*, 1910; *The Innocence of Father Brown*, 1911; *Manalive*, 1912; *The Flying Inn*, 1914; *The Wisdom of Father Brown*, 1914;

APPENDIX

The Man who Knew too Much, 1922; *Tales of the Long Bow*, 1925; *The Incredulity of Father Brown*, 1926.

Poems: *The Ballad of the White Horse*, 1911; *Poems*, 1915; *The Ballad of St. Barbara*, 1923.

Conrad, Joseph (1857–1924) [Teodor Josef Konrad Korzeniowski]

Born December 6, 1857, in the Ukraine, southern Poland, of a family belonging to the landed gentry; in 1862 his father, banished for revolutionary activity, was accompanied by wife and child to Vologda; mother died in 1865, father in 1870; Conrad educated at Cracow, 1869–74. To sea from Marseilles in 1874, his aim to become master of an English merchantman; to England in 1878; rose from seaman to master by 1884; naturalized, 1884; voyages to Australia, East Indies, Africa. Resigned, 1894, from ill health; first novel, *Almayer's Folly*, written on sea and ashore from 1889 on, accepted for publication. Married, 1896, an Englishwoman; resided in Essex and Kent; visited America in 1923; died August 3, 1924.

Essays and Sketches: *The Mirror of the Sea*, 1906; *Some Reminiscences* (American ed., *A Personal Record*), 1912; *Notes on Life and Letters*, 1921; *Last Essays*, 1926.

Novels: *Almayer's Folly*, 1895; *An Outcast of the Islands*, 1896; *The Nigger of the "Narcissus,"* 1897; *Lord Jim*, 1900; *The Inheritors*, 1901, in collaboration with F. M. Ford; *Romance*, 1903, in collaboration with F. M. Ford; *Nostromo*, 1904; *The Secret Agent*, 1907; *Under Western Eyes*, 1911; *Chance*, 1913; *Victory*, 1915; *The Shadow-Line*, 1917; *The Arrow of Gold*, 1919; *The Rescue*, 1920; *The Rover*, 1923; *Suspense* (unfinished), 1925.

Short Stories: *Tales of Unrest*, 1898; *Typhoon and Other Stories*, 1902–03; *Youth*, etc., 1902; *A Set of Six*, 1908; *'Twixt Land and Sea*, 1912; *Within the Tides*, 1915.

Crothers, Samuel McChord (1857–1927)

Born June 7, 1857, at Oswego, Illinois; graduated Wittenberg College, 1873, Princeton, 1874; student at Union Theological Seminary, 1874–77, and at Harvard Divinity School, 1881–82; D.D., Harvard, Litt.D., St. Lawrence, Princeton, Western Reserve. Married Louise M. Bronson, September 9, 1882. Presbyterian minister, 1877–81, with pastorates in Nevada and California. Became a Unitarian minister, 1882; pastorates in Brattleboro, Vermont, St. Paul, Minnesota, and from 1894 at the First Church, Cambridge, Massachusetts. Died November 9, 1927.

Juveniles: *Miss Muffett's Christmas Party*, 1901; *The Children of Dickens*, 1925.

Religious Essays: *Members of One Body*, 1894; *The Understanding Heart*, 1903; *The Endless Life:* Ingersoll Lecture, 1905; *Three Lords of Destiny:* Raymond F. West Lectures, 1913.

Criticism: *Oliver Wendell Holmes: The Autocrat and his Fellow Boarders*, 1909; *How to know Emerson*, 1920.

Miscellaneous Essays: *The Gentle Reader*, 1903; *The Pardoner's Wallet*, 1905; *By the Christmas Fire*, 1908; *Among Friends*, 1910; *Humanly Speaking*, 1912; *Meditations on Votes for Women*, 1914; *The Pleasures of an Absentee Landlord*, 1916; *The Dame School of Experience*, 1919; *The Cheerful Giver*, 1923.

Dickinson, Goldsworthy Lowes (1862–   )

Born in 1862; son of Lowes Dickinson (1819–1908), a well-known portrait painter. Educated at the Charterhouse School and at King's College, Cambridge. Fellow of King's College, Cambridge; lecturer at the London School of Economics and Political Science.

Works: *The Greek View of Life*, 1890; *From King to King: The Tragedy of the Puritan* (17th Century England) *Revolution*, 1891; *Revolution and Reaction in Modern France*, 1892; *The Development of Parliament During the Nineteenth Century*, 1895; *Letters from John Chinaman*, 1901 (American ed., *Letters of a Chinese Official*, 1903. See reply by W. J. Bryan: *Letters to a Chinese Official*, 1906); *Religion: a Criticism and a Forecast*, 1905; *A Modern Symposium*, 1905; *Justice and Liberty*, 1908; *Is Immortality Desirable?* 1909; *Religion and Immortality*, 1911; *Appearances: Notes of Travel, East and West*, 1914; *An Essay on the Civilization of India, China, and Japan*, 1914; *After the War*, 1915; *The European Anarchy*, 1916; *The Choice Before Us*, 1917; *The Magic Flute: A Fantasia*, 1920; *War: Its Nature, Cause and Cure*, 1923; *The International Anarchy*, 1904–14, 1926.

Eastman, Max (1883–   )

Born January 4, 1883, at Canandaigua, New York. A.B., Williams College, 1905; graduate student, Columbia University,

APPENDIX

1907–10; assistant in philosophy, 1907–10, associate, 1911. Columbia University. Writer and lecturer. Editor of *The Masses*, 1913–17; founder and editor of *The Liberator*, 1917–22. Went to Russia in 1922 to study the "Soviet" civilization.

Poems: *The Child of the Amazons and Other Poems*, 1913; *Colors of Life*, 1918.

Fiction: *Venture*, 1927.

Criticism: *The Enjoyment of Poetry*, 1913; *The Sense of Humor*, 1921.

Miscellaneous Works: *Journalism versus Art*, 1916; *Understanding Germany*, 1916; *Leon Trotsky: the Portrait of a Youth*, 1925; *Marx and Lenin: The Science of Revolution*, 1926.

Eaton, Walter Prichard (1878–   )

Born August 24, 1878, at Malden, Massachusetts; A.B., Harvard, 1900; married Elise Morris Underhill of New York, June 30, 1910. Dramatic critic, *New York Tribune*, 1902–07, *New York Sun*, 1907–08, *American Magazine*, 1909–18. Lecturer on the drama; member National Institute of Arts and Letters.

Dramatic Criticism and Essays: *The American Stage of Today*, 1908; *At the New Theatre and Others*, 1910; *Plays and Players*, 1916; *The Actor's Heritage*, 1924.

Books about Nature: *Barn Doors and Byways*, 1913; *Green Trails and Upland Pastures*, 1917; *In Berkshire Fields*, 1919; *On the Edge of the Wilderness*, 1920; *Skyline Camps*, 1922.

Poems: *Echoes and Realities*, 1918.

Plays: *Queen Victoria* (with David Carb), 1923.

Novels: *The Runaway Place* (with Elise Underhill), 1909; *The Idyl of Twin Fires*, 1915; *The Bird House Man*, 1916.

Juveniles: *Boy Scouts of Berkshire*, 1912; *Boy Scouts in the Dismal Swamp*, 1913; etc.

Eliot, Thomas Stearns (1888–   )

Born in 1888, at St. Louis, Missouri; studied at Harvard (A.B., 1909, A.M., 1910), at the Sorbonne, at the Harvard Graduate School, and at Merton College, Oxford. Married Vivien Haigh-Wood. Resident in London since 1913; became headmaster of Highgate School, and lecturer under both the Oxford and the University of London extension systems, about 1914; assistant editor, *The Egoist*, 1917–19; founder and editor of *The New Criterion*, a quarterly.

APPENDIX

Poems: *Poems*, 1909, 1919; *Prufrock and Other Observations*, 1917; *The Waste Land*, 1922.

Criticism: *The Sacred Wood: Essays on Poetry and Criticism*, 1920; *Homage to John Dryden*, 1924.

Ellis, Henry Havelock (1859–   )

Born February 2, 1859, at Croydon, Surrey; educated in private schools, and, for the practice of medicine, at St. Thomas's Hospital, London; married, 1891, Edith M. O. Lees, author of novels and plays, who died in 1916. Taught in New South Wales, 1875–79; practised medicine a short time in England; then devoted his life to literary and scientific work. Editor, Mermaid Series of the Old Dramatists, 1887–89; Contemporary Science Series, 1889–1914.

Scientific Works: *The Criminal*, 1890; *Man and Woman*, 1894; *Studies in the Psychology of Sex*, six series, 1897–1910; *A Study of British Genius*, 1904.

Miscellaneous Works: *The New Spirit* (essays on Diderot, Heine, Whitman, Ibsen, and Tolstoi), 3d ed., 1892; *Affirmations*, 1897; *The Nineteenth Century: A Dialogue in Utopia*, 1900; *The Soul of Spain*, 1908; *The World of Dreams*, 1911; *Impressions and Comments*, three series, 1914, 1921, 1924; *Essays in War-Time*, 1916; *The Philosophy of Conflict and Other Essays*, 1919; *Little Essays of Love and Virtue*, 1922; *The Dance of Life*, 1923.

Galsworthy, John (1867–   )

Born August 14, 1867, at Coombe, Surrey; educated at Harrow, 1881–86, and at New College, Oxford, 1886–89; admitted to the bar, Lincoln's Inn, in 1890; traveled for about two years; engaged in literary work since 1897.

Essays and Sketches: *A Commentary*, 1908; *A Motley*, 1910; *The Inn of Tranquillity*, 1912; *A Sheaf*, 1916; *Another Sheaf*, 1919.

Novels: *Jocelyn*, 1898; *Villa Rubein*, 1900 (new edition with other stories, 1909); *A Man of Devon*, 1901; *The Island Pharisees*, 1904 (revised, 1908); *The Man of Property*, 1906; *The Patrician*, 1911; *The Dark Flower*, 1913; *The Freelands*, 1915; *Saints' Progress*, 1919; *In Chancery*, 1920; *To Let*, 1921; *The Forsyte Saga*, 1922 (including, *The Man of Property*, *In Chancery*, *To Let*); *The White Monkey*, 1924; *The Silver Spoon*, 1926.

APPENDIX

Short Stories: *The Little Man and Other Satires*, 1915; *Caravan*, 1925.

Plays: *The Silver Box*, 1906; *Strife*, 1909; *Justice*, 1910; *The Pigeon*, 1912; *Loyalties*, 1922; etc., etc.

Gosse, Sir Edmund William (1849–   )

Born September 21, 1849, at London; educated privately in Devonshire; married Ellen Epps. Honorary degrees from Cambridge University, St. Andrews University, Strassburg, Gothenburg, Paris (Sorbonne); Knight of Norwegian, Swedish, and Danish orders; knighted 1925. Assistant Librarian, British Museum, 1867–75; Clark Lecturer in English Literature, Trinity College, Cambridge, 1884–90; Librarian, House of Lords, 1904–14; Chairman of the board of Scandinavian Studies, University College, London, 1917; President of the English Association, 1921.

Criticism: *Northern Studies*, 1879; *Seventeenth Century Studies*, 1883; *History of Eighteenth Century Literature*, 1889; *Questions at Issue*, 1893; *Jacobean Poets*, 1894; *Critical Kit-Kats*, 1896; *French Profiles*, 1905; *Portraits and Studies*, 1912; *Three French Moralists*, 1918; *Books on the Table*, 1921; *Aspects and Impressions*, 1922; *Silhouettes*, 1925.

Critical Biography: *Gray*, 1882; *Congreve*, 1888; *Dr. John Donne*, 1899; *Jeremy Taylor*, 1904; *Father and Son* (autobiographical), 1907; *Algernon Charles Swinburne*, 1917.

Poems: *On Viol and Flute*, 1873; *New Poems*, 1879; *Collected Poems*, 1911.

Guedalla, Philip (1889–   )

Born March 12, 1889; educated at Rugby and at Balliol College, Oxford, where he won First Class Honor Moderations (1910) and a final First Class in Modern History (1912). Barrister of the Inner Temple, 1913–23; Liberal candidate for Parliament in 1922, 1923, 1924.

Political, historical, and literary essays: *The Partition of Europe, 1715–1815*, 1914; *Supers and Supermen*, 1920; *The Industrial Future*, 1921; *The Second Empire*, 1922; *Masters and Men*, 1923; *A Gallery*, 1924; *A Council of Industry*, 1925; *Independence Day* (American ed., *Fathers of the Revolution*), 1926; *Palmerston*, 1927.

APPENDIX

Gwynn, Stephen Lucius (1864–   )

Born February 13, 1864, in Ireland, son of the Reverend John Gwynn, D.D.; educated at St. Columba's College, Rathfarnham, and at Brasenose College, Oxford, where he won First Class Honor Moderations (1884) and Literæ Humaniores (1886). Teacher of the Classics, 1887–96; married in December, 1889; journalist in London, 1896–1904, when he returned to Ireland to live. Irish (Nationalist) member of Parliament, 1906–18. Enlisted as a private in the Great War, January, 1915, rose to captaincy, and won decoration of Legion of Honor; member of Irish Convention, 1917–18.

Essays: *The Decay of Sensibility*, 1900; *Fishing Holidays*, 1903; *For Second Reading*, 1918; *Garden Wisdom*, 1921; *Duffer's Luck*, 1924.

Books about Ireland: *Highways and Byeways in Donegal and Antrim*, 1899; *Today and Tomorrow in Ireland*, 1902; *The Fair Hills of Ireland*, 1906; *A Holiday in Connemara*, 1909; *The Famous Cities of Ireland*, 1916; *Irish Books and Irish People*, 1919; *The Irish Situation*, 1921; *The History of Ireland*, 1923.

Biography and Criticism: *Tennyson*, 1899; *Thomas Moore* (English Men of Letters), 1904; *John Redmond's Last Years*, 1919; *Experiences of a Literary Man*, 1926.

Fiction: *The Old Knowledge*, 1901; *John Maxwell's Marriage*, 1903; *The Glade in the Forest*, 1907; *Robert Emmet: a Historical Romance*, 1909.

Poems: *The Queen's Chronicler*, 1901; *A Lay of Ossian and Patrick*, 1903; *Collected Poems*, 1923.

Harris, Frank (1855–   )

Born February 14, 1855, in Galway, Ireland; came to the United States in 1870; a naturalized citizen. Student at University of Kansas and at Paris, Heidelberg, Strassburg, Göttingen, Berlin, Vienna, and Athens; married Helen O'Hara of Dublin, Ireland. Admitted to the Kansas bar, 1875; returned to Europe; became editor, successively, of *Evening News* (London), *Fortnightly Review*, *Saturday Review*, *Candid Friend*, *Vanity Fair*. Member Royal Geographic Society. Lived in the United States for some years, recently, but now resident in France.

Biographical-Critical Studies: *The Man Shakespeare*, 1909; *The Women of Shakespeare*, 1911; *Contemporary Portraits*, four series, 1914, 1919, 1921, 1923; *Oscar Wilde: His Life and Confessions*, 2v., 1916; *My Life*, 1925.

Novels and Stories: *Elder Conklin*, 1892; *Montes the Matador*, 1900, 1910; *The Bomb*, 1908; *Unpath'd Waters*, 1913; *Veils of Isis and Other Stories*, 1914; *Great Days*, 1914; *Love in Youth*, 1914; *Undream'd of Shores*, 1924.

Plays: *Mr. and Mrs. Daventry*, 1900; *Shakespeare and his Love*, 1910.

Hewlett, Maurice Henry (1861–1923)

Born January 22, 1861, at Weybridge, Surrey; student in private schools and at London International College, Spring Grove, Isleworth, to 1878; married Hilda Beatrice Herbert, 1888; admitted to the bar, 1891. Lecturer on medieval thought and art at South Kensington University College. Keeper of Land Revenue Records and Enrolments, 1896–1900; member of Academic Committee, Royal Society of Literature, 1910; Justice of the Peace, and County Alderman, Wiltshire. Contributed to *London Times, Manchester Guardian, Fortnightly Review, Nineteenth Century and After, Cornhill Magazine*, etc. Died June 15, 1923.

Essays: *Earthwork out of Tuscany*, 1895; *In a Green Shade*, 1920; *Wiltshire Essays*, 1921; *Extemporary Essays*, 1922; *Last Essays*, 1924.

Poems: *Songs and Meditations*, 1896; *Artemision: Idylls and Songs*, 1909; *Helen Redeemed and Other Poems*, 1913; *Gai Saber: Tales and Songs*, 1916; *Flowers in the Grass*, 1920.

Poetical Drama: *The Masque of Dead Florentines*, 1895; *Pan and the Young Shepherd*, 1899; *The Agonists: A Trilogy of God and Man*, 1911 (composed 1895–97).

Novels and Tales: *The Forest Lovers*, 1898; *Little Novels of Italy*, 1899; *Richard Yea-and-Nay*, 1900; *New Canterbury Tales*, 1901; *The Queen's Quair*, 1904; *Half-way House*, 1908; *Open Country*, 1909; *Rest Harrow*, 1910; *Brazenhead the Great*, 1911; etc.

Holliday, Robert Cortes (1880–   )

Born July 18, 1880, at Indianapolis, Indiana; student at the Art Students' League, New York, 1899–1902, and at the University of Kansas, 1903–04; married Estelle Alice Hickman on

July 12, 1913. Magazine illustrator, 1904–05; bookseller, 1906–11; librarian, 1912–13. Editorial work with *New York Tribune, Fishing Gazette*, Doubleday, Page and Company, George H. Doran Company, 1913–17. Associate editor, *The Bookman*, 1918; editor, 1919–20; contributing editor, 1921– . Staff writer, *Leslie's Weekly*, 1921– ; writer of special articles for Central Press Association.

Works: *Booth Tarkington*, 1918; *The Walking-Stick Papers*, 1918; *Joyce Kilmer, A Memoir*, 1918; *Peeps at People*, 1919; *Broome Street Straws*, 1919; *Men and Books and Cities*, 1920; *Turns about Town*, 1921; *Literary Lanes and Other Byways*, 1925.

Huxley, Aldous Leonard (1894–)

Born July 26, 1894, son of Leonard Huxley, editor of the *Cornhill Magazine*, and grandson of Thomas Henry Huxley; educated at Eton and at Balliol College, Oxford; married Maria Nys in 1919. Editorial staff, *The Atheneum*, 1919–20; dramatic critic, *Westminster Gazette*, 1920–21.

Essays: *On the Margin*, 1923; *Along the Road*, 1925; *Jesting Pilate*, 1926.

Stories: *Limbo*, 1920; *Crome Yellow*, 1921; *Mortal Coils*, 1922; *Antic Hay*, 1923; *Little Mexican* (American ed., *Young Archimedes*), 1924; *Those Barren Leaves*, 1925; *Two or Three Graces*, 1926.

Poems: *The Burning Wheel*, 1916; *The Defeat of Youth*, 1918; *Leda*, 1920.

Lucas, Edward Verrall (1868–)

Born June 12, 1868. Educated at University College, London. On the staff of the *London Globe*, 1893–1900; of *The Academy*, 1896–1901; of *Punch* from about 1898. Chairman of Methuen and Company.

Essays: *Fireside and Sunshine*, 1906; *Character and Comedy*, 1907; *One Day and Another*, 1909; *Loiterer's Harvest*, 1913; *Cloud and Silver*, 1916; *Encounters and Diversions*, 1924; etc.

Novels: *Listener's Lure*, 1906; *Over Bemerton's*, 1908; *Mr. Ingleside*, 1910; *London Lavender*, 1912; etc.

Travel Books: *A Wanderer in Holland*, 1905; *A Wanderer in London*, 1906; etc.

Biography: *Life of Charles Lamb*, 2v., 1905; *Life and Work of E. A. Abbey*, 1921; etc.

Children's Books: *A Book of Verses for Children*, 1897; *Forgotten Tales of Long Ago*, 1906; *The Slowcoach*, 1910; etc.

Marquis, Donald Robert Perry (1878–)

Born July 29, 1878, at Walnut, Illinois; student at Knox School and at School of Arts, Washington; reporter on the *Washington Times;* married, June 8, 1909, Reina Melcher of Atlanta, Georgia, who died December 2, 1923. Conductor of "The Sun Dial" of the *New York Evening Sun* until 1924.

Essays and Sketches: *Hermione and her Little Group of Serious Thinkers*, 1916; *Prefaces*, 1919; *The Old Soak*, 1921; *The Old Soak's History of the World*, 1924; *The Almost Perfect State*, 1927.

Poems: *Dreams and Dust*, 1915; *Hail and Farewell* (published with *The Old Soak*), 1921; *Poems and Portraits*, 1922; *Sonnets to a Red Haired Lady*, 1922; *The Awakening and Other Poems*, 1924.

Plays: *The Old Soak*, 1922; *The Dark Hours*, 1924; *Out of the Sea*, 1927.

Novels and Stories: *Danny's Own Story*, 1912; *The Cruise of the Jasper B.*, 1916; *Carter and Other People*, 1921; *The Revolt of the Oyster*, 1922.

Mencken, Henry Louis (1880–)

Born September 12, 1880, at Baltimore, Maryland; educated in private schools and at the Baltimore Polytechnic Institute. On the staff of the Baltimore *Morning Herald* and *Evening Herald*, 1899, 1903–06; *Baltimore Sun* and *Evening Sun*, 1906– ; war correspondent with the German army, 1916–17. Literary critic, *The Smart Set*, 1908–23, and co-editor, 1914–23; editor, *The American Mercury*, 1924– ; contributing editor, *The Nation*, 1921– .

Works: *Ventures into Verse*, 1903; *George Bernard Shaw — His Plays*, 1905; *The Philosophy of Friedrich Nietzsche*, 1908; *The Artist* (play), 1912; *A Book of Burlesques*, 1916; *A Little Book in C Major*, 1916; *A Book of Prefaces*, 1917; *In Defense of Women*, 1917; *Damn! a Book of Calumny*, 1917; *Prejudices*, five series, 1919, 1920, 1922, 1924, 1926; *The American Credo* (with G. J. Nathan), 1920.

APPENDIX

Meynell, Alice Christina (Thompson) (1850–1922)

Born in 1850; privately educated by her father, **T. J.** Thompson; lived a good deal in Italy in youth; married Wilfrid Meynell in 1877; mother of Everard Meynell, journalist, and of Viola Meynell, the novelist. Died November 27, 1922.

Essays: *The Rhythm of Life*, 1893; *The Colour of Life*, 1896; *The Children*, 1896; *The Spirit of Peace*, 1898; *Ceres' Runaway*, 1910; *Selected Essays*, 1914; *The Second Person Singular and Other Essays*, 1921.

Poems: *Preludes* (republished, as *Poems*, 1893); *Later Poems*, 1901; *Collected Poems*, 1913; *A Father of Women and Other Poems*, 1917; *Poems*, complete edition, 1923.

Montague, Charles Edward (1867–   )

Born January 1, 1867; educated at City of London School and Balliol College, Oxford; married, 1898, Madeline Scott, daughter of C. P. Scott, editor of the *Manchester Guardian*. On the *Guardian* since 1890; enlisted in the War as a private, and served 1915–19.

Essays: *Dramatic Values*, 1911; *Disenchantment*, 1922; *The Right Place: a Book of Pleasures*, 1924.

Novels and Stories: *A Hind Let Loose*, 1910; *The Morning's War*, 1913; *Fiery Particles*, 1923; *Rough Justice*, 1926; *Right off the Map*, 1927.

More, Paul Elmer (1864–   )

Born December 12, 1864, at St. Louis, Missouri; studied at Washington University, St. Louis (A.B., 1887, A.M., 1892), and at Harvard University (A.M., 1893); married Henrietta Beck of St. Louis on June 12, 1900. Honorary degree of LL.D. from Washington University, 1913, and of Litt.D. from Columbia, Dartmouth, and Princeton. Taught Sanskrit at Harvard, 1894–95, and Sanskrit and Classics at Bryn Mawr, 1895–97. Literary editor, *The Independent*, 1901–03; *New York Evening Post*, 1903–09; editor, *The Nation*, 1909–14.

Works: *Shelburne Essays*, 11 vols, 1904–   ; *Life of Benjamin Franklin*, 1900; *Platonism*, 1917; *The Religion of Plato*, 1921; *Hellenistic Philosophies*, 1923; *The Christ of the New Testament*, 1924.

Translations: *A Century of Indian Epigrams*, 1898; etc.

APPENDIX

Morley, Christopher Darlington (1890–   )

Born May 5, 1890, at Haverford, Pennsylvania; educated at Haverford College (A.B., 1910), and as Rhodes Scholar at New College, Oxford, 1910–13; married Helen Booth Fairchild of New York, June 3, 1914. With Doubleday, Page and Company, 1913–17; *The Ladies' Home Journal*, 1917–18; *Philadelphia Evening Public Ledger*, 1918–20; *New York Evening Post*, 1920–24; contributing editor, *Saturday Review of Literature*.

Essays and Sketches: *Shandygaff*, 1918; *Mince Pie*, 1919; *Travels in Philadelphia*, 1920; *Pipefuls*, 1920; *Plum Pudding*, 1921; *The Powder of Sympathy*, 1923; *Inward Ho!* 1923; *The Romany Stain*, 1926; *Pleased to Meet You*, 1927.

Novels and Stories: *Parnassus on Wheels*, 1917; *The Haunted Bookshop*, 1919; *Kathleen*, 1920; *Tales from a Rolltop Desk*, 1921; *Where the Blue Begins*, 1922; *Thunder on the Left*, 1925.

Poems: *Songs for a Little House*, 1917; *Hide and Seek*, 1920; *Parson's Pleasure*, 1923.

Plays: *One Act Plays*, 1924.

Perry, Bliss (1860–   )

Born November 25, 1860, at Williamstown, Massachusetts; studied at Williams College (A.B., 1881, A.M., 1883), and at Berlin and Strassburg; married Annie L. Bliss of New Haven, Connecticut, in 1888; honorary degrees, L.H.D., Litt.D., LL.D. Professor of English, Williams College, 1886–93; Princeton, 1893–1900; editor, *Atlantic Monthly*, 1899–1909; Professor of English literature, Harvard, 1907–   . Harvard lecturer at the University of Paris, 1909–10.

Essays: *The Amateur Spirit*, 1904; *Park Street Papers*, 1909; *The American Mind*, 1912; *The Praise of Folly*, 1923; *Pools and Ripples*, 1927.

Criticism: *A Study of Prose Fiction*, 1902; *Walt Whitman*, 1906; *Whittier*, 1907; *Carlyle*, 1915; *The American Spirit in Literature*, 1918; *A Study of Poetry*, 1920.

Novels and Stories: *The Broughton House*, 1890; *Salem Kittredge*, 1894; *The Plated City*, 1895; *The Powers at Play*, 1899.

Repplier, Agnes (1858–   )

Born April 1, 1858, at Philadelphia; of French parentage; educated at the Sacred Heart Convent, Torresdale, Pennsylvania;

honorary degree of Litt.D., from University of Pennsylvania, 1902, and Yale, 1925. In recent years spent much time in Europe.

Works: *Books and Men*, 1888; *Points of View*, 1891; *Essays in Miniature*, 1892; *Essays in Idleness*, 1893; *In the Dozy Hours*, 1894; *Varia*, 1897; *The Fireside Sphinx*, 1901; *Compromises*, 1904; *In Our Convent Days*, 1905; *A Happy Half-Century*, 1908; *Americans and Others*, 1912; *Counter Currents*, 1915; *Points of Friction*, 1920; *Under Dispute*, 1924.

Russell, George William ["A.E."] (1867–   )

Born April 10, 1867, at Lurgan, Armagh County, Ireland; educated at a school in Rathmines; at Dublin School of Art, 1883–85; cashier in a draper's shop; organizer of rural banks, 1897–1905. Has been painter, poet, essayist, and a leader (with Douglas Hyde, Lady Gregory, and W. B. Yeats) in the Celtic Renaissance; a mystic.

Essays and Miscellaneous Prose: *Literary Ideals in Ireland* (in collaboration), 1899; *The Nuts of Knowledge*, 1903; *Irish Essays*, 1906; *Imaginations and Reveries*, 1915; *The Candle of Vision*, 1919.

Poems: *Homeward, Songs by the Way*, 1894; *The Earth Breath*, 1897; *The Divine Vision*, 1904; *Voices of the Stones*, 1925. *Collected Poems*, 1913 (with additions, 1919; second edition, 1926).

Narratives: *The Mask of Apollo* (short stories: "my first effort to write"); *The Interpreters* ("a symposium between scattered portions of one nature dramatically sundered as the soul is in dream"), 1922.

Saintsbury, George Edward Bateman (1845–   )

Born October 23, 1845, at Southampton; educated at King's College School, London, and at Merton College, Oxford, of which he became Honorary Fellow in 1909; married Emily Fenn in 1868. Honorary degrees of LL.D., Aberdeen and Edinburgh, and D.Litt., Durham and Oxford; Fellow of the British Academy, 1911. Teaching, 1868–76; journalist in London, 1876–95; Professor of Rhetoric and English Literature, Edinburgh University, 1895–1915.

Essays: *Essays in English Literature*, 2 series, 1890, 1895;

Essays on French Novelists, 1891; *Corrected Impressions*, 1895; *The Peace of the Augustans*, 1915; *Notes on a Cellar Book*, 1920.

Miscellaneous Works of Criticism include: *A Short History of English Literature*, 1898; *A History of Criticism*, 3v., 1900–04; *A History of English Prosody*, 3v., 1906–10.

Santayana, George (1863–   )

Born December 16, 1863, at Madrid, Spain; came to the United States in 1872; studied at Harvard (A.B., 1886, A.M., Ph.D., 1889), at Berlin (1886–88), and at King's College, Cambridge (1896–97). Taught philosophy at Harvard, 1889–1911; Hyde Lecturer at the Sorbonne, 1905–06; Spencer Lecturer at Oxford, 1923. Resident abroad since 1912.

Prose Works: *The Sense of Beauty*, 1896; *Interpretations of Poetry and Religion*, 1900; *Three Philosophical Poets: Lucretius, Dante and Goethe*, 1910; *Little Essays*, 1920; *Character and Opinion in the United States*, 1920; *Soliloquies in England and Later Soliloquies*, 1922; *Dialogues in Limbo*, 1925.

Poems: *Sonnets and Other Verses*, 1894; *Lucifer, a Theological Tragedy*, 1898; *The Hermit of Carmel and Other Poems*, 1901; *Poems* (selected and revised), 1923.

Sherman, Stuart Pratt (1881–1926)

Born October 1, 1881, at Anita, Iowa; educated at Williams College (A.B., 1903) and at Harvard (A.M., 1904, Ph.D., 1906); married Ruth Bartlett Mears of Williamstown, Massachusetts, on December 25, 1906; honorary degree, L.H.D., Williams, 1922. Instructor in English, Northwestern University, 1906–07; in Department of English, University of Illinois, 1907–24 (professor, 1911–24); associate editor, *Cambridge History of American Literature*, 1917; literary editor, *New York Herald-Tribune*, 1924–26. Member American Academy of Arts and Letters, 1923. Died, August 21, 1926.

Works: *Matthew Arnold*, 1917; *On Contemporary Literature*, 1917; *Americans*, 1922; *The Genius of America*, 1923; *Men of Letters of the British Isles* (in collaboration), 1924; *My dear Cornelia*, 1924; *Points of View*, 1924; *Critical Woodcuts*, 1926; *The Main Stream*, 1927.

Edited: *Treasure Island*, 1911; *Essays and Poems of Emerson*,

1921; *Leaves of Grass*, 1922; *Poetical Works of Joaquin Miller*, 1923; etc.

Smith, Logan Pearsall (1865–   )

Born October 18, 1865, at Millville, New Jersey, son of Robert Pearsall Smith. Studied at Haverford College, 1881–84, Harvard, 1884–85, Berlin, 1885–86, and Oxford, 1888–92; B.A., Oxon., 1892. After a year in business, has devoted himself to literary work; resides in England.

Works: *The Youth of Parnassus and Other Stories*, 1895; *Trivia*, 1902 (revised, 1918); *More Trivia*, 1921; etc.

Strunsky, Simeon (1879–   )

Born July 23, 1879, at Vitebsk, Russia; educated at Horace Mann High School, New York, and at Columbia (A.B., 1900); married Manya Gordon of New York, September 11, 1910. Department editor, *New International Encyclopœdia*, 1900–06; editorial writer (1906–20) and editor (1920–24), *New York Evening Post;* editorial staff, *New York Times*, 1924–   .

Works: *The Patient Observer*, 1911; *Post-Impressions*, 1914; *Belshazzer Court*, 1914; *Professor Latimer's Progress*, 1918; *Little Journeys to Paris*, 1918; *Sinbad and his Friends*, 1921.

Tomlinson, H. M. (1873–   )

Born in 1873; he was "an office boy and a clerk among London's ships," he reports (Morley: *Modern Essays*, p. 210), "in the last days of the clippers." Editorial writer, *Morning Leader* and *Daily News*, from 1904; war correspondent, 1914–15; at headquarters, 1915–17. Literary editor, *The Nation and Atheneum*, 1917–23.

Works: *The Sea and the Jungle*, 1912; *Old Junk*, 1918; *London River*, 1921; *Waiting for Daylight*, 1922; *Tidemarks*, 1924; *Under the Red Ensign*, 1926; *Gifts of Fortune*, 1926.

Walkley, Arthur Bingham (1855–   )

Born December 17, 1855, at Bristol, England; educated at Warminster and at Balliol and Corpus Christi Colleges, Oxford; married Frances Eldridge; in the Secretary's office, General Post Office, from 1877; assistant Secretary, 1911–19; secretary and delegate to various international postal congresses; Fellow of the

Royal Society of Literature, 1907. Dramatic critic of the London *Times*, 1902–   ; formerly dramatic critic of the *Star* and the *Speaker*, and on literary staff of the *Daily Chronicle*.

Works: *Playhouse Impressions*, 1892; *Frames of Mind*, 1899; *Dramatic Criticism*, 1903; *Drama and Life*, 1907; *Pastiche and Prejudice*, 1921; *More Prejudice*, 1923; *Still More Prejudice*, 1925.

Woolf, Adeline Virginia (Stephen) (1882–   )

Daughter of Sir Leslie Stephen (third child by his second wife), born in 1882. Married Leonard Sidney Woolf.

Essays: *Mr. Bennett and Mrs. Brown*, 1924; *The Common Reader*, 1925.

Novels: *The Voyage Out*, 1915; *Night and Day*, 1919; *Monday or Tuesday*, 1921; *Jacob's Room*, 1922; *Mrs. Dalloway*, 1925; *To the Lighthouse*, 1927.

II

The volumes in the list which follows will be found useful in the study of the present literary generation, or of the essay form, or of individual essayists. Following certain titles the names of authors discussed are given in brackets. In addition to these volumes the reader should consult the critical works listed in the preceding bibliography, particularly the essays of Brooks, Canby, Gosse, Harris, Mencken, Repplier, and Sherman.

Adams, E. L.: *Joseph Conrad, the Man*, 1925.

Beer, T.: *The Mauve Decade*, 1926.

Bennett, A.: *Books and Persons*, 1917. (Benson, Chesterton, Galsworthy, Lucas, Montague.)

Binyon, L., ed.: *Letters of Maurice Hewlett* (with introductory memoir by Edward Hewlett), 1926.

Boyd, E.: *Appreciations and Depreciations*, 1917. (Russell.)

Boyd, E.: *H. L. Mencken*, 1925.

Boyd, E.: *Ireland's Literary Renaissance*, 1916. (Russell.)

Boynton, P. H.: *Some Contemporary Americans*, 1924.

Bronner, M.: *Maurice Hewlett: a Critical Review of his Prose and Poetry*, 1910.

Brooks, Van W.: *Emerson and Others*, 1927.

Chesterton: *Heretics*, 1905. ("Paganism and Mr. Lowes Dickinson.")

APPENDIX

Conrad, Mrs. Jessie: *Joseph Conrad as I Knew Him*, 1926.

Conway, A. M.: *The Essay in American Literature*, 1914.

Cooper, F. T.: *Some English Story Tellers*, 1912. (Conrad, Galsworthy, Hewlett.)

Crothers, S. M.: *The Modern Essay*, 1926. (Vol. 24, in *Reading with a Purpose*, American Library Association.)

Cunliffe, J. W.: *English Literature during the Last Half Century*, 1919. (Conrad, Galsworthy.)

Curle, R.: *Joseph Conrad*, 1914.

Ervine, St. J. G.: *Some Impressions of my Elders*, 1922. (Chesterton, Galsworthy, Russell.)

Figgis, D.: *AE*. 1916.

Follett, H. T. and W.: *Some Modern Novelists*, 1918. (Conrad, Galsworthy.)

Ford, F. M.: *Joseph Conrad: a Personal Remembrance*, 1924.

Goldberg, I.: *Havelock Ellis: a Biographical and Critical Survey*, 1926.

Gosse, E.: *Books on the Table*, 1921. (Hewlett, Lucas, Saintsbury.)

Gwynn, S.: *Experiences of a Literary Man*, 1926. (Beerbohm, Chesterton, Hewlett, Lucas, Russell.)

Halsey, F. W.: *Women Authors of the Day in their Homes*, 1903. (Repplier.)

Jackson, H.: *The Eighteen Nineties*, 1913.

Jackson, H.: *All Manner of Folk*, 1912. (Beerbohm.)

Lynch, J. G. B.: *Max Beerbohm in Perspective*, 1921.

Mais, S. P. B.: *Books and Their Writers*, 1920. (Meynell.)

Moore, G.: *Hail and Farewell: Ave*, 1911. (Russell.)

More, P. E.: *Shelburne Essays*, Seventh Series, 1910. ("The Socialism of G. Lowes Dickinson.")

Overton, G.: *When Winter Comes to Main Street*, 1922. (Holliday, Huxley.)

Overton, G.: *Arabian Nights Entertainments*, 1923. (Conrad, Galsworthy, Morley.)

Overton, G.: *Cargoes for Crusoes*, 1924. (Huxley, Lucas.)

Pattee, F. L.: *A History of American Literature since 1870*, 1915. (Crothers, More, Repplier.)

Pattee, F. L.: *Side-Lights on American Literature*, 1922. (Mencken.)

Payne, W. M.: *Leading American Essayists*, 1910.

Perry, B.: *The American Spirit in Literature*, 1918.

APPENDIX

Phelps, W. L.: *The Advance of the English Novel*, 1916.   (Conrad, Galsworthy.)

Scott, D.: *Men of Letters*, 1916.   (Beerbohm, Chesterton, Meynell, Montague.)

Scott, W. T.: *Chesterton and Other Essays*, 1912.

Stearns, H. E., ed.: *Civilization in the United States*, 1922.

Tuell, A. K.: *Mrs. Meynell and her Literary Generation*, 1925.

Tynan, K.: *Twenty-five Years*, 1913.   (Russell.)

Waugh, A.: *Tradition and Change*, 1919.   (Conrad, Galsworthy, Lucas.)

Wells, H. G.: *Social Forces in England and America*, 1914. ("About Chesterton and Belloc.")

West, J.: *G. K. Chesterton: A Critical Study*, 1916.

Williams, H.: *Modern English Writers*, 1918.   (Chesterton.)